Not What the Doctor Ordered

Third Edition

Not What the Doctor Ordered

Liberating Caregivers and Empowering Consumers for Successful Health Reform

Third Edition

Jeffrey C. Bauer

CRC Press
Taylor & Francis Group
Boca Raton London New York

CRC Press is an imprint of the
Taylor & Francis Group, an **informa** business

A PRODUCTIVITY PRESS BOOK

Third edition published in 2020
by Routledge/Productivity Press
52 Vanderbilt Avenue, 11th Floor New York, NY 10017

2 Park Square, Milton Park, Abingdon, Oxon OX14 4RN, UK

© 2020 by Taylor & Francis Group, LLC
Routledge/Productivity Press is an imprint of Taylor & Francis Group, an informa business

No claim to original US government works

Printed on acid-free paper

International Standard Book Number-13: 978-1-138-05080-8 (hardback)
International Standard Book Number-13: 978-1-315-16864-7 (eBook)

Library of Congress Cataloging-in-Publication Data

Names: Bauer, Jeffrey C., author.
Title: Not what the doctor ordered : liberating caregivers and empowering consumers for successful health reform / Jeffrey C. Bauer.
Description: 3rd [edition], 25th Anniversary edition. | Boca Raton : Taylor & Francis, 2020. | "A Routledge title, part of the Taylor & Francis imprint, a member of the Taylor & Francis Group, the academic division of T&F Informa plc." | Includes bibliographical references and index.
Identifiers: LCCN 2019010656 (print) | LCCN 2019012918 (ebook) | ISBN 9781315168647 (e-Book) | ISBN 9781138050808 (hardback : alk. paper)
Subjects: LCSH: Medical care--United States. | Medical economics--United States. | Managed care plans (Medical care)--United States.
Classification: LCC RA395.A3 (ebook) | LCC RA395.A3 B295 2020 (print) | DDC 338.4/736210973--dc23
LC record available at https://lccn.loc.gov/2019010656

Visit the Taylor & Francis Web site at
http://www.taylorandfrancis.com

This edition is dedicated to Dr. Loretta C. (Lee) Ford

Contents

About the Author

Dr. Bauer is an internationally recognized health futurist and medical economist. As an independent industry thought leader, he forecasts the evolution of health care and develops practical approaches to improving the medical sector of the American economy. He is widely known for his specific proposals to create efficient, effective health care through multi-stakeholder partnerships and other initiatives focused in the private sector.

Dr. Bauer has more than 275 publications on health care delivery. His most recent books, prior to this edition of *Not What the Doctor Ordered,* are *Paradox and Imperatives in Health Care: Redirecting Reform for Efficiency and Effectiveness* (2015) and *Upgrading Leadership's Crystal Ball: Five Reasons Why Forecasting Must Replace Predicting and How to Make the Strategic Change in Business and Public Policy* (2014). Previous books include *Statistical Analysis for Health Care Decision-Makers* (CRC Press, 2009), and *Telemedicine and the Reinvention of Health Care: The Seventh Revolution in Medicine* (McGraw-Hill, 1999).

As a consultant, he has assisted hundreds of provider, purchaser, and payer organizations with strategic planning and performance improvement initiatives. He served as Vice President for Health Care Forecasting and Strategy for ACS, a Xerox Company, from 1999 to 2010. His own consulting firm, The Bauer Group, specialized in consumer-focused strategic planning and clinical affiliation agreements for multi-hospital networks from 1984 to 1992.

In addition, Dr. Bauer was a full-time teacher and administrator at the University of Colorado Health Sciences Center in Denver from 1973 to 1984, where he held appointments as Associate Professor and Assistant Chancellor for Planning and Program Development. He also served for four years as Health Policy Adviser to Colorado Governor Richard D. Lamm. From 1992 to 1999, Dr. Bauer was a visiting professor in Administrative Medicine at the Medical School of the University of Wisconsin-Madison.

He received his PhD in economics from the University of Colorado-Boulder. He graduated from Colorado College in Colorado Springs with a BA in economics and completed a certificate in political studies at the University of Paris (France). During his academic career, he was a Boettcher Scholar, a Ford Foundation

Independent Scholar, a Fulbright Scholar (Switzerland), and a Kellogg Foundation National Fellow. He is an Honorary Fellow in the American Association of Nurse Practitioners. Dr. Bauer lives in Madison, Wisconsin, where he spends his spare time painting (conceptual art in acrylics), playing the viola da gamba (precursor to the cello), and actively serving on the board of directors of the Madison Symphony Orchestra.

Acknowledgments

I am extremely grateful to dozens of individuals who supported this book in a variety of ways. The book is much better for all their contributions. If I had used all the great information and material they shared with me, the book would be several times longer. (Deciding what material to exclude was a difficult task; important points have undoubtedly been lost in the process.) Friends and acquaintances who provided valuable input are listed here in alphabetical order (of last names), with apologies for any omissions:

Cynthia Ackerman, Jean Aertker, Amy Anderson, William Bailey, Suzanne Bailey, Tom Bauer, Herman Baumann, David Benton, Tina Bettin, Dawn Birkland, William Boissonault, Laura Borgelt, Jon Bowser, Jeff Brady, Jason Brown, Jesse Casten, Ben Chaska, Betty Chewning, Brittany Crabb, Abbie Cunningham, Muhammad Dahleh, Christine Dawson, Tina DeGroot, Karen Delvecchio, Bill Demarco, Melissa De Santis, Toni Dichiacchio, Jennifer Disabato, Bob Donaldson, Greg Downing, Eduardo Duquez, Michelle Edwards, David Elton, Bill Felkey, Gail Finley, Doug Flow, Brent Fox, Dennis Freeman, Roger Fogg, Ann Froese-Fretz, Mary Jo Goolsby, Amy Gotvaslee, David Greathouse, MaryLou Hagan, Ted Harms, Ben Harnke, LuAnne Hicks, Joel Hornberger, Molly Jagla, Michaelene Jansen, Peggy Jenkins, Richelle Johnson, Jan Jones-Schenk, Alan Kalker, Jesse Kasten, Tay Kapanos, Louise Kaplan, Nikki Kelly, Gopal Khanna, Parinda Khatri, Cassie King, Darrell Kirch, Marilyn Krajicek, Aaron Lech, Elizabeth Lewan, Jim Lifton, Richard Lindrooth, Ricki Loar, Edi Matsumoto, Brittany McAllister, Cathy McCann, John McDonough, Nina McHale, Julie McLaughlin, Meredith Mealer, Gaylene Miller, Ben Miller, Jonathan Morgan, Max Morton, Gina Moore, Amy Nacht, Gerard Nussbaum, Timothy Olson, Wendy Paracka, Kim Paxton, Mona Pearl, Gregg Perry, Charon Pierson, Debra Plass, Leigh Pomeroy, George Quinn, Dan Rahn, Randolph Rasch, Lynn Reede, John Reilly, Jr., Richard Ricciardi, Dale Richardson, Jennifer Riffel, Marc Ringel, Laura Rosenthal, Barbara Safriet, Kip Schick, Diane Seibert, Freddy Sennhauser, Tim Size, Audra Smith, Marvin Smoot, Marissa Sotiriou, Andrew Steinhauer, Bill Tanner, Kristin Thomas, Jeff Thompson, Sarah Thompson, Jan Towers, Jack Westfall, Erin Youngblood, George Zangaro, and Ann Zenk.

Of course, as all authors should duly note, I alone am responsible for final content. Last, but not least, I give very special thanks to my wife, Beth, who put up with me for the year I was in "book mode," and to my editor at Taylor & Francis, Kris Mednansky, who managed the process of getting my nine latest books into print. I could not have done this one without both of them.

Chapter 1

Introduction and Background: 25 Years Later

This book updates two earlier works that explained why Americans must be allowed to purchase health care directly from caregivers who provide an expanding array of medical services at least as well as physicians—at lower cost. It shows why giving consumers the right to choose advanced practitioners is the top priority for improving our overpriced, underperforming medical care delivery system. Health reform's traditional focus on expanding insurance coverage is doomed to ongoing failure until state governments eliminate antiquated laws that allow doctors to control other comparably qualified health professionals.

Our nation's medical monopoly, created early in the twentieth century, was justifiable back then in the name of consumer protection. University-trained medical doctors (MDs) methodically studied human health and treatment of disease. Physicians' competitors did not; they were charlatans with no science to validate or improve their practices. This book shows how much the situation has improved in recent decades, providing ample evidence that today's advanced practitioners (APs) now rival physicians in scientific knowledge and caregiving skills within well-defined scopes of practice. Therefore, a very large number of Americans suffer physically and fiscally from licensure laws and reimbursement policies that give physicians unfair competitive advantage in the medical marketplace.

My proposal to end the medical monopoly was a revolutionary challenge to conventional wisdom when *Not What the Doctor Ordered* first appeared in 1993. One of the nation's best-known radio reporters terminated a studio interview with me at the time, declaring that further discussion of the new book would hurt her journalistic credibility because "no American would *ever* trust a nurse to diagnose a disease or a pharmacist to change a medication." Well, there's been a lot of progress since then. Tens of thousands of Americans disprove the reporter's mistaken view every day in choosing to be treated by advanced practitioners in hospitals, clinics, workplaces, and drug stores all across the country. Data not only show that these consumers are happy with the savings and convenience of direct access, but that they are satisfied with the quality of care provided by highly trained health professionals who are not traditional doctors.

In spite of improvement in consumer choice since the 1993 edition, a relatively small group of change-resistant doctors still fights to prevent competition from qualified non-physicians—competition proven to improve efficiency and effectiveness in the medical marketplace. I am therefore updating *Not What the Doctor Ordered* because there's still much progress to be made and more reform needed to give all Americans a choice they deserve, especially as they are being asked to pay more for health care out of pocket. This third edition is a guide for Americans who want to get a better deal in the medical marketplace by ending outdated restrictions on competition among qualified health professionals. It is full of information and ideas to educate not only consumers and their employers, but also elected officials and policy-makers who are still under the influence of doctors fighting to preserve an outdated monopoly. It is written to promote informed public discussion of the imperative for change, sooner rather than later.

Key Issue: Regulation vs. Competition in Health Reform

A contentious national debate over health reform was at its peak when the first edition appeared about 25 years ago. The book directly challenged the Democrats' push to expand government control over how health care was reimbursed when the real problem was how it was provided. Contrary to the widely prevalent view in 1993–1994 that the Clinton health reform was inevitable—a question of when, not whether—I predicted early on that Hillary and the hundreds of experts on her task force (including several personal friends and professional acquaintances) would fail to cap medical spending by reinventing health insurance. Fail they did, but my alternative focus on competition between providers and changing how they deliver care did not prevail, either.

The good news is that the first edition sold well in spite of its contrarian views on the Clintons' paternalistic approach to reform, euphemistically called *managed competition*. The bad news is that few political leaders were interested in pursuing other changes once Hillary's grand scheme collapsed. A Republican landslide in the 1994 mid-term elections diverted attention from any significant health reform efforts for another decade; the party's leaders argued that American medical care was the best in the world and did not need fixing. Sensing reform fatigue at the national level, I refocused on teaching statistics and research at a medical school and studying how information technology and telemedicine could improve the delivery of medical services.

Government intervention to manage competition by restructuring reimbursement clearly fell "off the radar." In its place, a new concept rooted in the private insurance sector, *managed care*, was widely expected to solve the health care crisis all by itself. With Republicans in control of the House and the Senate, the government's role was to get out of the way and let private enterprise develop its own mechanisms to reduce demand. Even if its publisher (Probus) had stayed in business, the first edition (1993) of *Not What the Doctor Ordered* probably would have been the last one, too, because it did not explicitly address managed care. McGraw-Hill picked up the rights and asked me to publish a second edition (1998) in collaboration with the Healthcare Financial Management Association (HFMA) on the condition that I update it to encompass this new trend. The subtitle was changed to *How to End the Medical Monopoly in Pursuit of Managed Care.*

Managed care ultimately turned out not to be a panacea. It did not make medical services less expensive or more accessible, and it certainly did not produce any savings for consumers. As shown in Chapter 2, the only people who benefited monetarily from managed care were financial managers and venture capitalists who restructured the capitalization of health systems and health plans—without improving the overall performance of either in the process. Consumers (patients) and purchasers (governments and employers) did not get a better deal, just a different deal where "gatekeepers" restricted patient access to traditional services and health spending continued to increase at a disturbing rate.

Americans continued to be disenchanted with the deficiencies of their health care system. They remembered the astronomical costs and other scary features of the Clinton plan, especially the bureaucracy and taxes it would have created, but they did not clamor for Congress to try reform again any time soon. They wanted competition and choice, but not at the expense of quality and access. Consumer choice in competitive markets was addressed in depth in both previous editions of *Not What the Doctor Ordered*, but it did not yet have the transformative power of "an idea whose time had come" (in the celebrated words of Victor Hugo) because medical societies were fulminating about long waits for textbook care, no choice of doctors, rationing, and other alleged horrors of socialized medicine. Hopefully, this third edition is the good luck charm that finally defuses sensationalists' scare tactics and creates public access to an efficient, effective, fair, and competitive health care delivery system.

The Making of a Contrarian Health Economist

Having proudly earned a reputation as the health industry's constructive contrarian, I digress here to explain the origins of my unconventional perspective. Readers who are eager to get to economic analysis and policy recommendations can skip this section's summary of 50 years of experience in the medical marketplace, but it explains why I unabashedly "think different" about American health care. It's fine with me if you proceed directly to the next section (page 7), but please come back to read this one if you subsequently find yourself asking how I could possibly reach the conclusions embodied in this book. There *are* good reasons.

Unlike many conservative economists who oppose all government intervention in principle, I believe governments should protect public health, regulate safety of goods and services, and promote fair competition. I have never seen any evidence that the so-called "free market" accomplishes these goals in our medical market-place. And, unlike liberal economists who want public entities to finance and even deliver medical services (e.g. Medicare for All, or other single-payer insurance, or public hospitals), I strongly believe that American health care is best when delivered in truly competitive markets by private sector organizations, both for-profit and not-for-profit.

I am extremely grateful to several very special people who helped me avoid the dogmatic views of either political extreme. They taught me new ways to look at things, giving me courage to buck conventional wisdom and be creative. My fundamental self-image—being a teacher—was shaped at an early age by my father and grandfather. Both were university engineering professors. They purposefully stressed the art of problem-solving when teaching me how to fish, repair a car, play baseball, or build a bookshelf. They also involved me in their academic work; as a kid, I spent many hours helping them in their university offices and research laboratories. I was raised to be a professor. The only major career dilemma I ever remember facing was *what* I would teach, not *whether* I would teach. Even thoughts about going into politics were based on the assumption I would be doing it on leave from an academic position.

My father and grandfather exposed me to many careers, but not the one I ulti-mately pursued. The thought of becoming a medical economist hadn't even crossed my mind when I began college, planning to major in physics. Four years and four majors later, I found myself graduating from Colorado College with a bachelor's degree in economics and a Fulbright Scholarship to study economic development planning in Switzerland. I had also been accepted to graduate programs in inter-national economics and atmospheric physics. (OK, I was unfocused, but it was the sixties ... and I did inhale.)

If the Selective Service had not sent me a draft notice the same month I gradu-ated from college, I might today be one of the world's leading authorities on some arcane subject like economic development planning in Pakistan (the topic of my master's thesis) or the formation of hailstones in cumulonimbus clouds (the topic of my first scientific paper, published by the *Journal of Atmospheric Physics* in 1967). But because I am a pacifist, my draft board denied a request to travel to Switzerland for the Fulbright on the grounds that I might not return to the United States after-ward. Instead, I was drafted and assigned to perform two years of alternative service at Penrose Hospital in Colorado Springs as a medical records clerk on the "grave-yard" shift.

The punitive drudgery of working nights quickly ended when the hospital's Director of Medical Laboratories recognized me as a freelance photographer whose pictures had appeared in the local newspapers when I was a local college student. I already had the advanced camera and darkroom skills he was seeking in someone to run a division of medical photography, and the salary dictated by my draft board was a fraction of the going wage for a clinical photographer. Thus, for almost two years, I worked alongside practicing physicians and medical residents who asked me as many questions about photography as I asked them about medical science and health care delivery.

One physician in particular, Dr. Morgan Berthrong, taught me an incredible amount about the theory and practice of medicine and strongly urged me to become a physician. Doctor Berthrong, also a professor at the University of Colorado School of Medicine, took pride in giving me many clinical experiences taught in the third and fourth years of medical school. However, I did not have the basic sciences of the first and second years. The thought of learning this material and cramming for the dreaded Medical College Admission Test (MCAT) deterred me, so I applied for graduate programs in meteorology and economic development instead.

Becoming a medical economist still was not part of my plan. That path was set unexpectedly by Sister Myra James Bradley, Penrose Hospital's CEO. She was extremely kind to me from the day I began working there, occasionally inviting me to her office for chats about weather forecasting and economics (my final major at Colorado College). The curious reason for her interest in economics was not clear until the day she summoned me to attend a meeting with her and Dr. Berthrong. The topic was a new piece of diagnostic equipment installed in the medical laboratory that morning. Tests had already been run on the machine, but the fees had not been determined.

I prepared a mini-lecture on price theory to help Sister Myra James and Dr. Berthrong decide how much to charge for the tests, but she never gave me the opportunity to deliver it. Rather, she reported that the very same diagnostic device was already in use at two other Catholic hospitals in Colorado, with a $10 charge 40 miles to the south in Pueblo and a $15 charge 60 miles to the north in Denver. She proposed charging $12 at Penrose because Colorado Springs was between Pueblo and Denver, but closer to Pueblo. Dr. Berthrong quickly agreed, and the meeting was over.

I was chagrined by the lost opportunity to explain economic factors that should have been used to set the price, but Sister Myra James casually told me as we walked out the door, "Health care really needs medical economists. I want you to become one." Like Jake and Elwood in *The Blues Brothers*, I felt life's calling at that very moment—I'm not even Catholic, much less religious—and began contacting the graduate schools that had accepted me in their economic development programs to see if I could specialize in medical economics instead. (For the record, I dedicated the first edition of this book to Sister Myra James.)

A private university back East denied the requested change on grounds that medical economics was not a recognized field of study in its economics department—which was generally the case across the country back in 1971. A state university in the upper Midwest was receptive because a professor there had begun to apply economic analysis to the allocation of health resources, but the admissions office said my financial aid was tied to studying economic development. (Ironically, I subsequently spent seven years as a part-time professor at the university's medical school, where I wrote a textbook used to teach physicians how to do research and evaluate data.)

Fortunately, financial aid at my home state university was not tied to the course of study, so I entered the PhD program in economics at the University of Colorado at Boulder after completing the Fulbright Scholarship in Switzerland at the University of Geneva. The lack of a medical economics track at the University of Colorado was disappointing at first, but it turned out to be a blessing in disguise. Four professors deserve special recognition for customizing my development as a medical economist. Their intellectual guidance gave me the courage to become an innovator in the new specialty. (If sequential numbers were issued to PhD graduates who specialized in medical economics, my number would be somewhere in the teens or low twenties. I am probably the first PhD health economist who also had prior experience with health care and medical practice.)

My academic advisor throughout the PhD program, Dr. Larry Singell, convinced me to become a good general economist before focusing on medical economics. At his urging, I initially studied microeconomic theory with more dedication than I might have otherwise devoted to it. I also served for two years as his teaching associate, absorbing his superb skills in making economics understandable to non-economists. If this book presents economic theory clearly and meaningfully, Dr. Singell deserves much credit for teaching me how to do it.

Dr. Wes Yordon, supervisor of my PhD research on doctors' fee-setting behavior, convinced me not to treat doctors as a "special case." (*Special case* is the way economists justify government regulation when normal market forces presumably do not work in a particular market. It is behind most economists' unsuccessful approaches to health reform. More on this later.) Following Dr. Yordon's advice, I successfully defended my dissertation before a committee of outside professors, including two from the medical school, who were initially bothered that I was studying health care with the same conceptual tools used to explain pricing in competitive industries. Fortunately, my analysis using conventional microeconomic tools made sense to the dubious doctors; they approved the thesis.

Kenneth Boulding, one of our country's most prominent and iconoclastic economists at the time, became my main mentor throughout graduate school. (He and I played together in a recorder concert. I played a significant role in his decision to come to Colorado a few years earlier, but that's another story.) Kenneth, famous for developing the concepts of systems thinking and creative tension, did more than any other economist to prepare my mind for the perspectives embodied in all three editions of this book. He argued, for example, that a hospital was like an automobile repair shop, only cleaner. Were it not for Sister Myra James Bradley, I would not be a medical economist. Were it not for Kenneth Boulding, I might have become an irrelevant economist who believed health care was a "special case."

My appreciation also goes to a Nobel Prize-winning Harvard economist, Wassily Leontief, who was a frequent guest lecturer at the University of Colorado when I was a graduate student there. After one of his presentations, I asked him to define the role of an economist. He said a good economist was like a chef who identified the ingredients in the pantry, then determined all the dishes that could be made from them and the costs involved. Ever since, I have approached the medical marketplace as a Leontief-inspired chef—looking at the available resources and determining the different things that could be done with them and the related costs, translating items in the health care "pantry" into a menu from which consumers can make choices. (Another famous economist's idea, *creative destruction,** and a French saying, "To make an omelet, you must break eggs," have also emboldened me throughout my career to propose new menu items for the medical marketplace. I have used restaurant menus many times as a teaching device.)

Doctors and Substitution in Consumption

The economist-as-chef image illustrates an important concept of conventional economic theory: *substitution in consumption*. Although a consumer might want to purchase a specific good or service, s/he is often willing to accept a close substitute if qualitative differences between competing items are less important than the differences in their prices. For example, many people who would like to purchase a Cadillac Escalade are instead willing to buy a Ford Explorer when they see that the vehicles meet many of the same needs, but at very different price points. Having the freedom to make this choice is as American as apple pie; brand prestige is not worth a higher price to many people. Hence, consumers should not be forced to pay a doctor's fee for care when they can purchase an acceptable substitute directly from an advanced practitioner (i.e., a comparably qualified non-physician) for less money. The twentieth-century laws that allow doctors to prevent informed patients from buying comparable services directly from advanced practitioners are like giving Cadillac dealers the right to control who can buy a Ford.

---

* The classic definition of this Marxist concept is presented by Joseph Schumpeter in *Capitalism, Socialism, and Democracy* (London: Routledge, 1942): "the process of industrial mutation that incessantly revolutionizes the economic structure from within, incessantly destroying the old one, incessantly creating a new one." It led to understanding of the business cycle.

Designating advanced practitioners as acceptable substitutes for medical doctors absolutely does not suggest that physicians have declined as a rational consumer choice. It's the opposite: advanced practitioners have risen. In fact, I believe the overall quality of our nation's physicians has improved since I started working with them 50 years ago. It's simply time to end doctors' monopoly because other caregivers have become at least as good within professionally defined scopes of practice. Some readers will believe I am being too kind to the medical profession because there are incompetent and/or dishonest doctors. This is sadly true, but there are also bad advanced practitioners, quite possibly in equal proportions.

As proposed in Chapter 4, the appropriate way to solve the "bad apple" problem is to ensure that measurable standards of competence are consistently, accountably, and transparently enforced in all health professions. In economic terms of opportunity costs, the time and money that medicine's die-hard traditionalists spend on marginalizing advanced practitioners would be much better spent improving the skills of marginal physicians. Organized medicine should be ensuring that physicians are doing the right things—"Physician, heal thyself," as a famous philosopher has said—and expecting leaders in other health professions to exert equal oversight over their peers. Advanced practitioners could then devote their efforts to self-improvement rather than self-defense against unsubstantiated attacks from organized medicine.

Unfortunately, self-serving doctors take any opportunity to argue that there's no substitute for a physician at the top of the health care hierarchy. I have experienced this mindset many times, such as when an article I wrote on CPOE.* My piece spelled out the acronym as Computerized *Practitioner* Order Entry, recognizing that advanced practitioners are authorized to enter data into electronic health records in many states. Several physicians complained to the publication's editor on the grounds that the P in CPOE meant *Physician* and asked him to publish a correction in the journal. The editor refused, to my relief, but other doctors complained to my employer's medical director, who then formally asked me to use the P only for Physician in the future (which I refused). Monopolists work hard to suppress substitution.

Medical doctors should be the only choice when there are no acceptable substitutes, but they should not be protected against competition from advanced practitioners who are equally capable of meeting a patient's specific needs. As we will see from several perspectives, including case studies at the end of the book, most doctors agree with this perspective. Many of my best friends are physicians who have spent hours sharing their honest assessments of the strengths and weaknesses of American health care. They are caring, open-minded professionals committed to efficiency and effectiveness across the health care delivery system. They understand the need for radical economic transformation of our medical marketplace, even if

---

* JC Bauer, "Why CPOE must become SOP," *Journal of Healthcare Information Management*, 18(1): 9–10, 2006.

the existence of acceptable substitutes makes some of them uncomfortable. They all encouraged me to update this book, which would not have been the case if they were monopolistically inclined.

Differences 25 Years Have Made

The French have an insightful saying, "The more things change, the more they stay the same." I've struggled with this paradoxical thought while updating *Not What the Doctor Ordered* for the twenty-first century. On the one hand, qualified non-physician practitioners have gained considerable acceptance since the first two editions were published—more progress than most people would have thought possible. Remember that a nationally prominent health reporter told me in 1993 this acceptance would *never* happen. Well, it has. People in approximately two dozen states now have direct access to advanced practitioners who can treat them without a physician's consent or oversight. As shown by extensive evidence presented throughout this book, Americans in these competitive medical markets are demonstrably better off than those who are not.

On the other hand, the good fight for fair competition is *far* from over. People in slightly more than half of all states must still get a referral from a physician to be seen by an advanced practitioner, if they can see one at all. Even in markets where independent practice by qualified non-physicians is legal, the medical establishment can exert indirect control to prevent competition (e.g., by pressuring insurance companies not to reimburse non-physicians and preventing hospitals from granting them practice privileges). No available data define how many Americans are denied direct access to advanced practitioners, but I'll bet it's still at least half the US population.

Another change since the two previous editions—one for which the overall medical community deserves kudos—is a perceptible increase in the number of physicians who support direct consumer access to qualified non-physicians or, at least, do not actively get in its way. Most industry insiders agreed with me back in the 1990s that physicians were split 50–50 for and against allowing direct consumer access to competitors. I informally polled a lot of physicians and other health professionals while preparing this edition in 2018, yielding a consensus that the split is now at least 70% in favor of or neutral toward direct consumer access to advanced practitioners, with fewer than 30% opposed.*

However, even if the number of obstructionists is declining, their power in many states is not. Physicians who defend medical monopoly continue to make large political contributions. They continue to make anecdote-driven, "Trust me,

---

* For consistent evidence, see E Kraus and JM DuBois, "Knowing your limits: A qualitative study of physician and nurse practitioner perspectives on NP independence in primary care," *Journal of General Internal Medicine*, 2017; 32(3): 284–290.

I'm a doctor" statements about the need for physician control—even though they do not have any published scientific studies to support their assertions. They had none 25 years ago, and they have none now. In the meantime, as shown throughout this book, hundreds of research studies supporting advanced practitioners have been published in peer-reviewed publications, including respected medical journals. The situation reminds me of an in-joke about the disproportional power of dissenting doctors: "Question: What do you call a 99–1 vote in a group of doctors? Answer: A tie." The future of medicine is not decided by majority rule. One doctor can prevent change favored by the vast majority of a medical school faculty or hospital medical staff. I've personally seen it happen, a lot.

Finally, the earlier editions' hypothetical scenarios are replaced with real case studies in this one. Nurse practitioners and midwives in their own private offices, pharmacists in charge of medication management for entire clinical services, and independent physical therapists and clinical psychologists were so uncommon 25 years ago that I had to invent believable examples to show what was possible in a marketplace no longer constrained by doctors' orders. This latest edition concludes with seven in-depth case studies demonstrating great things that actually happened when advanced practitioners were allowed to exercise their full scopes of practice. Dozens of similar success stories were called to my attention over the past year; I wish I could have included all of them in this edition.

And the Winner Is … Advanced Practitioners

In the absence of a commonly accepted term 25 years ago, I had to invent a designation for doctors' worthy competitors. I called them qualified non-physician practitioners (QNPPs). This generic title has not come into common use in the meantime. I never really liked it, truth be told, but I couldn't come up with a better term that accurately described the professionals it encompassed. Neither could anyone else at the time. A few synonyms for QNPP now appear with some regularity, including the redundant *advanced practice practitioners* (APPs) and *advanced practice caregivers* or *advanced practice clinicians* (APCs). In the interests of brevity, I am using a third, increasingly common designation, *advanced practitioners* (APs), throughout this book. I hope even more writers and editors will also adopt AP as the term for all the health professionals who qualify to compete directly with physicians.

Two important semantic nuances must be addressed before we delve into the problems of medical monopoly and how to solve them.

■ *Alternative* is sometimes used as a synonym for *advanced*, a substitution that is not appropriate even though both words begin with the letter *a*. AP should not be used interchangeably as an acronym for advanced practitioners and alternative practitioners. *Alternative* signifies health care practices with a long-standing tradition, but outside the medical mainstream and without a comparable scientific base. It already has a commonly accepted name, complementary and alternative medicine (CAM). Key examples of CAM are herbalism, acupuncture, phrenology, reflexology, lay midwifery, massage therapy, and shamanism. CAM caregivers are not trained in the academic health sciences centers that educate advanced practitioners, nor are they subject to advanced practitioners' professional standards of licensure and liability. Some alternative health practices may meet the standards of advanced practice in the future, but they do not at present.

■ The advanced practitioners covered in this book should *never* be called "mid-level" practitioners. The term may have had some validity when the advanced practices were in early stages of development back in the 1970s and 1980s, but it is totally inappropriate now. There's absolutely nothing intermediate about today's advanced practitioners. They meet the *top-level* standards of their respective professions—qualifying for independent practice authority under the same scientific and legal standards that physicians have used for over a century to justify their power as "captain of the ship," as shown in depth in Chapter 4.

What This Book Is Not

This title's negation of a common phrase, "just what the doctor ordered," foretells its contrarian and competitive approach to solving our persistent problems of cost, quality, and access. It refers directly to ending doctor-established control of the medical marketplace—purposefully taking an innovative path to reform outside the traditional realm of policy options. Hence, it's appropriate to conclude the introduction with a few comments about what this book is not.

First, this book is not full of data and statistics. Health reform debates over the past five decades have unleashed a plethora of facts and figures on how bad things are under the status quo, or how good they would be after implementing a proposed reform. Opponents and proponents draw diametrically opposed conclusions from their respective analyses, but both have relied predominantly on statistic to make their points—how many Americans have health insurance, how much health costs have risen, how serious the doctor shortage has become, etc. The statistics usually are not meaningful measures of the underlying issues, and many of the numbers are distorted measures of reality, if not outright fabrications.* If the numbers can't be trusted, why bother with them?

---

* I've written extensively on how "experts" lie with statistics in publications about health care. For many examples of problems with the validity and reliability of data, see JC Bauer, *Statistical Analysis for Decision-Makers in Health Care: Understanding and Evaluating Critical Information in Changing Times*, second edition (Boca Raton: CRC Press, 2009).

Regardless of data quality, confrontations over reform are so full of scary statistics that reasoned thinking is often hard to find beneath all the numbers. Dubious data surely help explain why people don't want to start yet another health reform debate immediately after the previous one has ended. One battle every ten years seems to be what Americans have been willing and able to tolerate since Medicare and Medicaid—the first major health reforms—were created in 1965. Given that the Affordable Care Act was passed in 2010, we might normally expect health reform to become a major issue in the presidential election in 2020. However, given today's dysfunctional politics, we shouldn't expect anything to happen in the future as it did in the past, nor should we suddenly expect good data to illuminate the debate. Discrediting an opponent with inaccurate and/or misleading information has become more important than presenting a viable solution, and it happens all the time.

If statistics alone could show us the way to create a better health care system, this book would be unnecessary because no other country in the world has generated so many statistics about the medical marketplace. The United States is indisputably the world's #1 producer of health data—which may help explain why it is #1 in per capita expenditures on health care. Data collection, processing, analysis, and reporting aren't cheap. Ironically, our country is consistently at or near the bottom of international lists that rank nations' health. Every other modern industrialized nation spends considerably less on health care and has a healthier population—all without relying so extensively on data and statistical analysis.

Besides getting in the way of clear thinking, data and statistics present other dangers. Data dependency paves the way for highly complex, numbers-driven schemes to regulate health care delivery, creating the need for ever larger bureaucracies to sort through all the measurements. And, because most data are at least a year or two old by the time they are converted into usable information, we will never have current measures of the problems reforms are intended to solve. In addition, policy-makers generally know next to nothing about how health care's numbers are collected and analyzed. They seem unaware of the universal relevance of the well-known expression about data and computers, "Garbage in, garbage out."

My cynicism toward data-driven health reform is not based on fear or loathing of numbers. I am a "numbers guy" with considerable expertise in data collection and quantitative analysis. I've written several books and dozens of articles on data-oriented topics, taught research and statistics in medical and graduate schools for 20+ years, and served as an expert statistical witness in two dozen court cases. I am simply practicing in this book what I have preached in all these endeavors: thinking comes first, then the numbers can follow. This book is a success if it gives policy-makers something to think about first, to be followed by appropriate collection and analysis of good data to explore the menu of possibilities. Unfortunately, that's not the common approach to health reform.

Second, this book is not targeted at health professionals, academicians, and policy wonks.* The vocabulary and thought processes of these "insiders" are not readily comprehensible to the general public—the people who ought to be deciding what they want from their health care providers, especially because patients are now expected to be actively involved in their own health care. Professional literature (e.g., articles in *JAMA, New England Journal of Medicine, Health Affairs, Medical Care*, etc.) generally doesn't help consumers understand competitive options that ought to be available to them. The experts tend to present theoretical, complex, and untested proposals in professional language that is unintelligible to the people whose health care is being "reformed." (Health reform proposals are often unintelligible to me, and I speak the professional language.) Well over 300 peer-reviewed publications are referenced in the following pages for anyone who wants to delve into the supportive professional literature—proof that I did my homework—but they are unobtrusively presented in footnotes throughout the book and in an "Additional Reading" section at the end (pages 137–149).

This book would be full of professional jargon, data, charts, diagrams, and academic concepts if health policy professionals were the intended audience. But consumers want understandable information about different ways to meet their health care needs—not different ways to pay for a health system managed in the economic interest of doctors. It is therefore written in straightforward terms to explain the harms of medical monopoly and the benefits of bringing appropriate competition to the medical marketplace. The target audience is consumers, business executives, community leaders, journalists, and others who are paying more and getting less than they should when they spend their increasingly scarce resources on health care. I am writing for non-professionals who will hopefully join me in telling experts they are missing the real meaning of health reform—rebuilding the product from the customer's point of view, in the eloquent words of Peter Drucker.†

Third, this book does not propose a partisan plan for national health reform. There's no refinement *or* replacement for the Affordable Care Act in these pages. Given the complete political dysfunction in Washington, where the two parties are hell bent on defeating each other rather than solving Americans' problems, I would be wasting everyone's time if my goal here were to launch the next Congressional battle over health reform. (No wonder it's said that the opposite of *pro*gress is *Con*gress.) Instead, I am writing to promote state-level action for a solution not tied to any political faction, lobbying organization, or other special interest group.

I am an "equal opportunity" gadfly, critical of both political parties for their dogmatic approaches to health reform. The core concept in this book should appeal to Democrats *and* Republicans, as long as they are ready to work for the benefit of

---

* *Policy wonk* (syn: policy junkie) is a term for people who present themselves as experts in providing advice on public policy. It's significant that *wonk* is *know* spelled backward.
† Drucker, Peter Management: Tasks, Responsibilities, Practices (New York: Harper and Row, 1973), p.63.

consumers rather than medical associations. I find considerable encouragement in the fact that the Obama* and Trump† administrations both issued similar position papers in defense of competition between qualified caregivers as a key to health reform. These remarkably parallel statements of White House policy do not mirror the two parties' confrontational positions in Congress, but they provide strong support for key points made in this book.

Given my desire to be politically unbiased—decidedly not the same as politically correct—this edition does not include a foreword by a recognizable public figure. There are several national experts whose endorsement I would love to have at the beginning of the book, but I couldn't think of anyone who wouldn't offend one or more of the factions that need to be brought together. The proposal in this book clashes with traditional Republican and Democratic approaches to health reform, which hopefully makes it acceptable to both parties because neither can assume that I am an undercover agent for the other side.

My goal is to motivate state lawmakers and regulators to update laws and policies that unnecessarily restrict consumer choice. States, not the federal government, have ultimate power to decide who provides health care within their borders. Ending the medical monopoly therefore requires concerted action in state capitals, led by strong coalitions of consumer advocates (e.g., AARP, League of Women Voters), employers, chambers of commerce, business groups on health, farmers' organizations, social networks, service clubs, neighborhood associations, and other organizations that will benefit from competition among all qualified health professionals. Experience generally suggests that success is more likely when the fight for competition is led by consumers and their allies on the demand side of the marketplace.

To avoid appearing self-serving, advanced practitioners and their allies on the supply side should generally stay on the sidelines. Their most productive work will be behind the scenes—educating and empowering consumer advocacy groups to engineer the necessary changes in state laws and regulations. Doctors who defend medical monopoly are usually skilled at diverting attention from the real issues at hand through intimidation of the subordinates they have historically ordered around—and the subordinates are conditioned to acquiesce. Fortunately, the arguments in favor of giving full practice authority to advanced practitioners are now incontrovertible, but best made by the people who will benefit from having choices in the medical marketplace—the consumers.

---

* The White House: Department of the Treasury Office of Economic Policy, Council of Economic Advisers, Department of Labor, "Occupational licensing: A framework for policymakers," 2015; https://obamawhitehouse.archives.gov/sites/default/files/docs/licensing_report_final_nonembargo.pdf.

† US Department of Health and Human Services, Department of the Treasury, Department of Labor, "Reforming America's healthcare system through choice and competition," 2018; https://www.hhs.gov/sites/default/files/Reforming-Americas-Healthcare-System-Through-Choice-and-Competition.pdf.

Fourth, this book is not a comparative survey of different national health systems. While much can be learned from studying medical services in other countries, copying the models of foreign nations is not a productive way to improve our medical marketplace and the health of the American population. Political and cultural differences make just about every country (including ours, for sure) a special case. From Canada to Great Britain, Japan to Germany, or France to Sweden, each country has unique concepts of social welfare, education, political power, and economic organization—hence the major differences between health systems and the minimal relevance of theirs to ours.

These other countries designed their current health systems in the years immediately following World War II, pursuing social goals and political philosophies formally rejected in the United States at the time. (I am not joking when I talk about medical school colleagues who truly believed in the 1970s that Medicare and health maintenance organizations were part of a Communist plot to destroy the United States.) Doctors in Europe and Great Britain had very little to do with putting medical marketplaces in order; their governments did it. The United States is the only Western country that has allowed physicians to control the way the delivery system is organized and how care is reimbursed. (I must note that these other countries also built their unique health systems with little or no input from medical economists—and all of their medical marketplaces work more efficiently than ours.*)

Because studying medical care in other countries won't produce much of value for American health reform, this book is based firmly on the premise that the United States needs to develop its own solutions to its own problems. I'm still a believer in the great potential of American exceptionalism. Our country is unique in many ways, including health care. Besides, most other countries with "model" health systems are now experiencing their own serious problems with cost, quality, and access—albeit from different historical and political baselines.

Ironically, the competition described in this book likely offers a reform solution for other countries. Winston Churchill was perceptive when he declared, "In the long run, you can always count on Americans to do the right thing … after they have exhausted all the other possibilities." Providing medical doctors with competition from advanced practitioners is a major step in the right direction. Although we are far behind where we ought to be in giving all consumers direct access to APs, we are far ahead of most other countries in training and using them. Our challenge is to eliminate barriers that prevent an existing supply of advanced practitioners from

---

* There's a remarkable irony in this observation. Although the national health systems in other countries produce a better return for money spent on health care, the world's most respected individual health care delivery systems (e.g., Mayo, Geisinger, Kaiser-Permanente, Virginia Mason, Intermountain) are located in the United States. But that's another story, described in another book: JC Bauer, *Paradox and Imperatives in Health Care: Redirecting Reform for Efficiency and Effectiveness* (New York: CRC Press, 2015).

meeting demand for their services. Other countries still need to create the supply. They could learn how to do it from us.

Finally, this book is not an exercise in "doctor bashing." In spite of its negative title, *Not What the Doctor Ordered* advances a generally positive view of the medical profession. I unabashedly present medicine as a benchmark for other health professions in many ways. The problem addressed in this book is not physicians as caregivers. It is their profession's power to prevent consumers from directly accessing other practitioners who are at least as qualified to see patients without a doctor's order or supervision, according to the same criteria that doctors have used to justify authority over other health professions for more than 100 years.

Whether doctors fear losing control or losing income—or both—many feel most threatened by the suggestion that they are no longer more knowledgeable than health professionals who did not graduate from medical school. (I've often heard physicians say, "If the nurse wanted to practice medicine, she should have gone to medical school.") However, as we shall see, other professional schools impart equally valid knowledge and skills within their own state-approved clinical models. They now provide a viable alternative to doctor-controlled health care, an alternative that consumers everywhere should be free to choose. Let's begin our analysis of the new order by exploring the economic concepts of monopoly, how the medical monopoly came into existence, and the now-outdated principles that physicians have used to justify control of the medical marketplace.

Chapter 2

Medical Monopoly: What the Doctor Ordered

Monopoly A market structure with only one seller of a commodity. In pure monopoly, the single seller exercises absolute control over market price at which he sells, since there is no competitive supply of goods in the market. He can choose the most profitable price and does so by raising his price and restricting his output below that which would be achieved under competition. Monopoly thus leads to a higher selling price, a lower output, and excess profits.

The McGraw-Hill Dictionary of Modern Economics

A **monopoly** exists when a specific person or enterprise is the only supplier of a particular commodity. Monopolies are thus characterized by a lack of economic competition to produce the good or service, a lack of viable substitute goods, and the possibility of a high monopoly price well above the seller's marginal cost that leads to a high monopoly profit. Although monopolies may be big businesses, size is not a characteristic of a monopoly. A small business may still have the power to raise prices in a small industry (or market).

Wikipedia

Monopoly market is the situation where one producer (or a group of producers acting in concert) controls supply of a good or service, and where the entry of new producers is prevented or highly restricted. Monopolist firms (in their attempt to maximize profits) keep the price high and restrict the output, and show little or no responsiveness to the needs of their customers.

businessdictionary.com

This book raises questions about a monopoly that has exerted great influence over our lives—and deaths—for the past century. Its defenders tell us that the monopoly is necessary because its goods and services are the best in the world, that quality would be degraded by anyone else offering the same products outside the guild's control. We have rewarded the monopolists with high incomes, given them special titles, built factories according to their specifications, and generally gone out of our way to keep them happy. The monopolists in question are highly skilled, hard-working professionals whose leaders would have us believe that their potential competitors are not qualified to work without supervision. We have been conditioned to meet the monopolists' expectations without question. We are expected to trust them because they are, after all, doctors.

Few of us realize that the medical monopoly is a relatively recent invention and a uniquely American phenomenon. Before receiving protected economic status in the early 1900s, as explained in the next chapter, medical doctors were only one of many different groups ministering to the sick. The proverbial snake-oil salesmen and other purveyors of unproven remedies were among a wide variety of "experts" who treated Americans' illnesses and injuries. Just about anyone could hang out a shingle and claim to be a doctor back then, consistent with the classic image of the country doctor in many Western movies.

University-trained physicians (allopathic medical doctors (MDs) and doctors of osteopathic medicine (DOs)) clearly offered the best alternative a century ago—arguably, the only acceptable alternative—but competition from many other types of self-proclaimed doctors kept physicians' incomes very low. By taking actions to remove charlatans and other dubious practitioners from the medical marketplace, medical doctors were doing a public service, and they were able to rise economically from lower-class to upper-class in just a few decades.

Doctors have worked hard ever since to maintain this market power by declaring that anyone with lesser or different training should only be allowed to provide health care services under doctors' orders, if allowed to provide any services at all. This justification for preventing competition was defensible throughout most of the twentieth century. No other health professions had developed anything that was comparable to the art and science that doctors learn in medical school, nor did any others have as many years of university education in human health. The competitors a century ago were mostly *quacks*—ignorant, misinformed, or dishonest practitioners of medicine.*

From an economic perspective, physicians were not in the habit of charging exorbitant prices, nor were they restricting the supply of their services, when they

---

* *Merriam-Webster Dictionary* (online).

initially took control of the medical marketplace. Anyone who can remember the 1950s (as I can) knows that fees were based on ability to pay. Doctors billed different amounts for the same service, based on assessment of a family's financial status as low-income, middle-income, or high-income. Physicians took the Hippocratic Oath upon graduating from medical school, agreeing that money would not be a consideration in giving people the care they needed. Doctors often engaged in barter, accepting services like yard work or house painting from patients who did not have enough money to pay the fee. (Although from a middle-class family, I remember that the Wyoming doctor who delivered my brother in 1957 was paid with a case of whiskey, which I personally delivered to the doctor's house in a wheelbarrow.) Individual physicians were not behaving like monopolists, and they enjoyed excellent reputations.

Early signs of monopoly at the professional level were nevertheless beginning to appear. Health insurance grew from uncommon in the 1930s to widespread by the 1950s as wartime price controls forced employers to provide workers with more benefits rather than better pay. In the process, private health insurance evolved from indemnity plans that paid patients fixed sums for specific illnesses or injuries to fee-for-service plans that assigned payments directly to doctors for each service they provided. (My grandmother's health insurance policy directly paid her a set amount each time she was hospitalized for back pain in the 1950s. This fixed payment had no relationship to the fee her doctor charged or the care he provided, and it was sent directly to my grandmother. She could do whatever she wanted with the money from the insurance company ... but I'm sure she paid her doctor.) Physicians soon began sending itemized bills for all the specific medical services they provided, not a global bill for the condition they treated, and made sure the insurance payments were sent directly to them, not to the patient. They also used this power to prevent direct insurance payments to any other health professionals who worked under their supervision—a reimbursement policy that doctors' professional organizations have diligently defended even as the others have gained the right to independent practice.

Medicare and Medicaid immediately started boosting demand for health care when the programs were created in 1965, but the supply of doctors was fixed in the short run. (The minimum time from deciding to open a medical school to graduating its first class of residency-trained physicians would have been around a dozen years then.) Exactly as predicted by economic theory, excess demand led to large and rapid increases in the cost of medical services. In response, President Richard Nixon froze doctors' fees in 1971. A nationwide doctor shortage was officially declared, leading to the creation of several dozen new medical schools over the next two decades. When the price freeze was lifted in 1973, rapid fee increases and an unmet demand for services led directly to "skyrocketing" increases in the cost of private health insurance—and the first Medicare-era health reform laws in 1973 and 1974. In less than ten years, federal spending on health care was more than twice what it was predicted to be when Medicare and Medicaid were passed.

Major health reform campaigns have occurred every decade since then, but none of the efforts has directly addressed—much less solved—the problem of rising prices that increases total spending on medical care. Exercising their economic power, leaders of the medical community have kept the public and politicians focused on the price of health insurance—purposefully and successfully diverting attention from the prices that health insurance subsequently pays to doctors. (Organized medicine spends a lot to protect its economic interests in this way. The American Medical Association is perennially among the top ten lobbyists in Washington.) For decades, medical economists and health policy experts have obediently concocted a succession of new ways for insurance to reimburse doctors, but they have consistently bypassed the question of whether doctors' fees are fair and economically defensible. Doctors argue that price competition would be dangerous because, in effect, "you get what you pay for." They allege that non-physicians would undercut their fees by providing inferior services. This argument had merit in the past, but, as we will see in subsequent chapters, it is no longer true.

Now that employers and governments have reached the limits of what they are willing and able to spend on health insurance for their beneficiaries, patients are expected to pay a higher portion of total insurance costs (i.e., annual premiums, coinsurance rates, deductibles, and other out-of-pocket payments). Policy-makers on both sides of the political divide have assumed that a patient "with skin in the game" will become a price-conscious buyer, but they haven't developed any policy proposals to create meaningful price competition. A lot has been said and written over the past decade on why and how patients should pay an increasing portion of total expenditures on health care … and almost nothing has been said or written about how to reduce the price component of total expenditures.

Medical Monopoly and Prices for Health Care

Public policy's monopoly-manipulated focus on the price of health insurance rather than the consumer's ultimate concern with the price of health services exposes another serious limitation of "special case" economics. The price of services should have been a major consideration all along because it is a key variable in one of the fundamental concepts of microeconomics: total spending equals quantity consumed multiplied by prices paid (usually simplified as an equation, $\sum\$ = P \times Q$). The price of goods and services sold is a central focus of economic analysis and public policy in every industry—except health care.

Historically, most medical economists have believed that price doesn't explain medical spending because consumers don't pay the price of health care. Insurance does, from this theoretical perspective. Sadly, it overlooks the fact that governments and employers are consumers. They pay the price when they buy health insurance coverage for their beneficiaries, who then pay the rest of the price after reaching the plans' limits. Health insurance companies, after all, are just third-party intermediaries; they make a profit—usually a very nice profit—by converting premiums paid by employers into fees paid to doctors and other providers. However, employers-cum-consumers are beginning to care a lot about the prices they pay for care delivered to their employees—as shown by accelerating activities of regional business groups on health and national innovations like the joint venture of Amazon, Berkshire-Hathaway, and Chase/JPMorgan.

Health economists' "special case" myopia also helps explain why several recent studies have found little or no evidence that insured patients take price into account when purchasing health services. Consumers have been given lots of information about price-based shopping for health insurance, but that's not at all the same thing as price-based shopping for health services (with or without insurance). Prices for specific medical goods and services—a poor proxy for a consumer's total out-of-pocket cost when all costs for an episode of illness or injury are taken into account—do vary within geographic markets, but the lowest price is still not a fair price if it is higher than the price would be in a competitive market. Consumers have very good reason to be cynical under such circumstances. Expecting consumers to buy care based on price differences simply doesn't solve the problem of monopoly pricing. Therefore, creating competition by giving consumers direct access to all qualified health professionals—the main point of this book—is an absolutely essential step toward the bipartisan goal of price-based shopping. Medical monopoly prevents consumers from making choices based on the lower costs of advanced practitioners.

Ever since doing my doctoral research on how doctors set fees, I've been one of the few medical economists consistently studying how to lower prices of medical services rather than how to make insurance "affordable." Reducing the price of insurance—which in reality means reducing the relative increase in annual premiums, not lowering the absolute premium—isn't a long-term solution to market failure if it simply subsidizes more people to buy medical goods and services at monopoly prices. Fortunately, after decades of misguided efforts to reform the way we Americans pay for health care, rather than the way our doctors provide it,* the policy world is beginning to address the high price we pay, literally and figuratively. The conclusion of a *JAMA* article in 2018 has suddenly focused attention on the significance and magnitude of the problem:

> The United States spent approximately twice as much as other high-income countries on medical care, yet utilization rates in the United States were largely similar to those in other nations. Prices of labor [physicians' incomes—author's note] and goods, including pharmaceuticals, and administrative costs appeared to be the major drivers of the difference in overall cost between the United States and other high-income countries. As patients, physicians, policy makers, and

---

* For a detailed review of how regulatory mechanisms have failed to solve the price problem, see TL Greaney, "Coping with concentration," *Health Affairs*, 2017; 36(9): 1564–1571.

legislators actively debate the future of the US health system, data such as these are needed to inform policy decisions.*

The same conclusion was reinforced in early 2019 in a *Health Affairs* update of a well-known article that highlighted the need to refocus health policy on prices of US medical services:

> A 2003 article titled "It's the Prices, Stupid," and coauthored by the three of us and the recently deceased Uwe Reinhardt found that the sizable differences in health spending between the US and other countries were explained mainly by health care prices. As a tribute to him, we used Organization for Economic Cooperation and Development (OECD) Health Statistics to update these analyses and review critiques of the original article. The conclusion that prices are the primary reason why the US spends more on health care than any other country remains valid, despite health policy reforms and health systems restructuring that have occurred in the US and other industrialized countries since the 2003 article's publication. On key measures of health care resources per capita (hospital beds, physicians, and nurses), the US still provides significantly fewer resources compared to the OECD median country. Since the US is not consuming greater resources than other countries, the most logical factor is the higher prices paid in the US. Because the differential between what the public and private sectors pay for medical services has grown significantly in the past fifteen years, US policy makers should focus on prices in the private sector.[†]

Anyone who has paid for medical care in another country has personally experienced the price difference created by our medical monopoly. American tourists who incur health care bills abroad are almost always amazed how little they are charged by foreign doctors, even though the care seems to be comparable with services they receive at home. Well, there's a reason: doctors in other countries have never enjoyed monopoly power. They have always faced competition from other practitioners, and they have never exercised control over legislators and regulators. This is the lesson we need to learn from other countries if we really want to get a better deal on health care. True health reform in the United States will not come from replicating Britain's National Health Service, France's insurance mutuals, or some other country's single-payer system. It will come instead from reforms like eliminating

---

* I Papanicolas, LR Woskie; AK Jha, "Health care spending in the United States and other high-income countries," *JAMA*, 2018; 319(10): 1024–1039.

† GF Anderson, P Hussey, and V Petrosyan "It's still the prices, stupid: Why the US spends so much on health care, and a tribute to Uwe Reinhardt," *Health Affairs*, January 2019; 38(1); https://www-healthaffairs-org.proxy.hsl.ucdenver.edu/doi/10.1377/hlthaff.2018.05144.

state laws that allow doctors to charge high fees by controlling consumer access to comparably qualified competitors.

The embarrassingly high prices of American health care can also be attributed to other anti-competitive policies, including certificate-of-need laws that protect market positions of existing provider organizations and rules that prohibit the federal government from negotiating drug prices—important topics for another book by another author. Of course, public policy's major concern of late has been the increasing concentration of providers in specific geographic markets. Costs of health care have tended to rise in areas where the number of providers is reduced as one provider becomes dominant through mergers and acquisitions, all other things being equal. Larger organizations created in the process argue that they are more efficient due to economies of scale, but evidence in support of this claim is mixed at best.*

I am leaving to other experts the in-depth analysis of providers' obvious ability to raise prices through consolidation that is moving us away from the "many buyers, many sellers" market, where prices are kept in check by competition. It is important, but it diverts us from confronting another dimension of monopoly that can be addressed more effectively and more expeditiously: the significant economic harms created by sellers who control inputs to production. Yes, consumers usually pay higher prices as fewer and bigger sellers take over a market, but even a small seller in a big market can increase prices and profits by controlling the labor, capital, land, or technology that the other sellers need.

That's the aspect of monopoly that I am not leaving to other experts. Doctors' use of market power to restrict access to alternative approaches to production (i.e., advanced practitioners) is a central focus of this book. I am disappointed that so few economists have chosen to explore this glaring manifestation of monopoly in the medical marketplace. Anyone with a graduate degree in economics studied it in advanced courses on market performance, and it has figured prominently in antitrust actions over the past century, except in health care. Perhaps market concentration among health systems and medical groups gets all the attention for the same reason that the price of health insurance, not the price of care, is the focus of health reform. Monopolists love to divert our attention with red herrings. I don't.

With labor costs comprising the largest portion of the total costs of producing goods and services in the medical marketplace, it makes the most sense to concentrate on lowering them first. Besides, today's dysfunctional political system is lucky if it can tackle even one economic problem at a time. Trying to solve all the problems of American health care in one fell swoop would almost certainly result in none being solved at all. We should follow the wise counsel of Sutton's law and go where the money is—labor costs that are unnecessarily high due to physicians'

---

* Evidence is also beginning to suggest that hospital industry concentration is lowering the quality of care. For a summary of relevant information, see A Frakt, "Hospital Mergers Improve Health? Evidence Shows the Opposite" *The New York Times*, February 11, 2019, p. B7; https://www.nytimes.com/2019/02/11/upshot/hospital-mergers-hurt-health-care-quality.html.

control over other health professionals who provide comparable services at lower cost. In the following chapters, we'll see how improvements in advanced practitioners' training, knowledge, and experience have eliminated historical justification for allowing physicians to control them. First, let's look at how eliminating the medical monopoly moves us toward another key goal of health reform, lowering the prices of American health care.

Advanced Practitioners and the Costs of Care

A comparative list of prices charged by physicians and advanced practitioners would seem like a good way to start illustrating how much money consumers could save through interprofessional competition, but it would be meaningless. Providers' published fees for health services are almost never the same as the amount they actually expect to be paid, and the amount actually paid for any given service at any given time varies substantially by payer. It's a major reason why health care enterprises advertise quality, convenience, or other subjective features of the way they do business. It's also a major reason why studies show that patients "with skin in the game" are not shopping for care on the basis of price.

Back in the 1970s, I did extensive research on how doctors priced their services. My study identified several different *ad hoc* approaches to setting fees—all art, no science. The situation has changed little since then, but it really doesn't matter because most practitioners now work for a salary that has little or no relationship to the prices charged for their services. It's become very difficult for a doctor to increase income by lowering fees to sell more services, and mounting pressure to eliminate unnecessary care adds an ethical roadblock to "making it up on volume" by manipulating the prices of individual services. Besides, a consumer's concern is the total out-of-pocket cost of treatment for a particular medical problem, not the prices of individual services billed to health insurance. That's why reimbursement policy is moving away from itemized bills to bundled payment.

It's also why health care delivery organizations are starting to get serious about reinventing the way they deliver care. Using the tools of performance improvement (Lean, Six Sigma, etc.) is now a management imperative. If medical practice managers were given the choice between spending their limited time on improving performance or setting prices, all would choose performance improvement because cutting waste out of daily operations is essential for long-run survival. Setting prices is not. Performance improvement requires finding the least-expensive way to produce a good or service of specified quality, not computing some "right price" to charge. To this end, substituting advanced practitioners for physicians whenever possible is a no-brainer. Anyone who runs the business end of a health care delivery organization needs to be free to make this substitution whenever a task traditionally performed by a physician can be performed at least as well by an advanced practitioner. Why? Because APs cost less—usually a lot less.

For example, the median annual wage of family practice physicians is around $219,000. The comparable cost of an advanced practice nurse performing the same or similar tasks is $106,000. The average salary for a clinical pharmacist is $125,000 per year, a real saving when the PharmD handles drug management tasks of physicians who are paid an average annual salary of $299,000. (This substitution liberates physicians to perform higher-value services for which they are uniquely qualified, which increases organizational revenue.) Anesthesiologists earn on average between $266,000 and $386,000, while certified registered nurse anesthetists who provide the same services make between $169,000 and $182,000. MD psychiatrists earn $273,000 on average each year, compared to PsyD clinical psychologists, who treat many of the same mental health problems and earn $121,000. At an average salary of $87,000 per annum, a doctorally trained physical therapist can obviously help an organization cut costs by treating many conditions that otherwise would have been handled by an orthopedic surgeon who is paid between $497,000 and $579,000 a year.*

You don't need a PhD in medical economics to get the point here: physicians have the market power to make *very* good incomes in comparison with advanced practitioners. Of course, medical doctors deserve higher income for the 30% of services that only they are qualified to provide. To protect higher incomes across the board, however, medical monopoly makes it difficult for health systems and other provider organizations to achieve efficiencies in production through input substitution. Even in states where advanced practitioners have full practice authority, protectionist physicians still work to deny hospital staff privileges to APs or to control the conditions of their employment and compensation. These actions are serious signs of monopoly power, every bit as much as rising costs associated with mergers and acquisitions. Hence, to help provider organizations with lower costs of delivering care, states must prevent physicians from restricting the work of APs within hospitals and health systems.

It does help to have a PhD in medical economics to estimate economic gains that could be produced by labor substitution in competitive markets. My model to determine potential savings begins with the conservative assumption that APs cost 50% less than physicians for services that can be provided by either group (derived from the salary data cited above). Using the standard rule-of-thumb that labor costs are 65% of total costs in health care, the model's cost of producing a $100 service with physician labor would be $65 for the doctor and $35 for non-labor inputs. In comparison, the same service provided by an AP would cost only $68, the sum of

---

* More detailed information about the annual earnings of the health professions can be found at the sites where I gathered this information: United States Department of Labor, Bureau of Labor Statistics. National Occupational Employment and Wage Estimates, United States, May 2017; https://www.bls.gov/oes/current/oes_nat.htm#29-0000; Medscape Physician Compensation Report, 2018; https://www.medscape.com/slideshow/2018-compensation-overview-6009667; and Medscape APRN Compensation Report, 2017; https://www.medscape.com/slideshow/2017-aprn-compensation-report-6009192.

the $35 for non-labor inputs and $33 for the AP (one-half the $65 cost of a physician, rounded up to be on the conservative side). The input substitution reduces the cost of producing the service from $100 to $68, or by 32%.

Then, applying the commonly reported estimate that APs can perform 70% of the services provided by their physician counterparts, as discussed in the following chapters, the total cost of services that could be performed by either physicians or advanced practitioners is 70% of $695 billion paid to physicians in 2017, or $473 billion. (In other words, 30% of services costing $695 billion cannot be produced as well and less expensively by advanced practitioners.) *The bottom line: substituting APs for physicians could reduce the total cost of health care by 32%, producing annual savings of $155 billion—approximately 4.5% of total spending on all health services in the US.*

No other approach to health reform even comes close to yielding this potential for real savings. In fact, no other approach really saves any money at all. So-called savings from health insurance reforms are only relative reductions in expected increases in premiums, not absolute reductions in medical spending. So let's take the next step in economic analysis by looking at the opportunity costs of preserving the medical monopoly. What else could we do with $155,000,000,000? I vote for keeping the money in the medical marketplace and expanding access to disease management services that actually reduce long-run spending on health care.

However, many economists and politicians would rather reduce medical expenditure by the same amount. What to do with the potential savings is a very important question, but it is not the purpose of this book.* However, the very existence of opportunity costs raises other questions that must enter the health reform debate sooner rather than later. How can lawmakers and regulators perpetuate physicians' control over advanced practitioners who could ably meet consumers' needs at a lower cost? How can our elected representatives protect a monopoly that costs $155 billion more than a competitive marketplace? How can they possibly expect consumers (patients, employers, and governments) to pay this unjustifiable price?

As shown in depth in Chapter 4, today's advanced practitioners qualify for the full scope of practice authority—the right to offer their services directly to consumers without supervision—according to the same criteria that physicians used to establish control over the medical marketplace early in the twentieth century. Advanced practitioners are ready, willing, and able to provide care that will appreciably reduce the costs of care[†] and make billions of dollars available for other uses (such as making more health services available). Government officials in the majority of the states must therefore update professional licensure laws and health industry regulations to make this competition possible—sooner rather than later because health care's economic problems are not going to be solved anytime soon at the national level.

---

* It is among the key policy recommendations in Chapter 6 of JC Bauer *Paradox and Imperatives in Health Care: Redirecting Reform for Efficiency and Effectiveness* (New York: CRC Press, 2015).

† YT Yang and MR Meiners, "Care coordination and the expansion of nursing scopes of practice." *Journal of Law, Medicine & Ethics*, 2014; 42(1): 93–103.

However, I must make one essential point before moving on to an overview of monopoly and discussion of responsive public policy. Advanced practitioners who receive independent practice authority must understand that it is not a license to start enjoying the economic spoils of monopoly power. Back in the 1990s, some leaders within the AP community understandably raised the argument of equal pay for equal work when health insurance began to reimburse advanced practice nurses directly under some circumstances, such as providing primary care in underserved rural and urban areas. However, the insurance payment to advanced practice nurses was usually around 70% of the amount paid to a doctor for doing the same thing. Although the differential never got a lot of attention, it was based on early studies that showed the costs of the non-physician care were proportionally less.

The relative cost data were correct, but the proposed payment policy was misguided. Ever the constructive contrarian, I recommended reimbursing physicians the lower fee (i.e., the APs' competitive price) rather than paying advanced practitioners the higher fee (i.e., the doctors' monopoly price) for the areas where both provided the same service. The physician should be absolutely free to charge the higher price, in my opinion, but insurance should only reimburse the lower price. Patients who insist on seeing a physician rather than an advanced practitioner should be free to pay the price difference, but insurance should not subsidize the monopoly differential. The earlier versions of this book included a proposal for least-cost qualified practitioner (LCQP) reimbursement by health insurance companies, but I'm intentionally not resurrecting it here. It is a red herring as reimbursement moves from fee-for-service toward fixed, bundled payments for treating disease entities and episodes of care.

The takeaway for consumers is that overall costs of care are lower when less-expensive workers can be substituted for more-expensive workers without sacrificing quality of service in competitive markets. The takeaway for advanced practitioners is that they should proudly proclaim their commitment to being those less-expensive, equally qualified workers. They should *not* expect that the right to compete with physicians means the right to charge like physicians (i.e., monopolists). For physicians, the takeaway is to prepare for competition by improving the efficiency of medical practice, not by battling to control comparably qualified competitors. The takeaway for elected and appointed officials in all states is to eliminate the medical monopoly by granting full practice authority to advanced practitioners. It's time for competition in the medical marketplace—updating state laws and regulations so that consumers are free to choose between physicians and advanced practitioners who are fully qualified to provide care according to state standards of professional practice.

Background: What's Wrong with Monopoly?

Medical monopoly needs to be considered in a bigger context; it does not merit a "special case" exemption from conventional economic analysis. The rise and fall of monopolies is a central theme of American history. Indeed, the United States was created as a reaction to the British monopoly over colonial trade. Under cries of "freedom" and "liberty," American revolutionaries launched their struggle against British control in order to establish not only a nation where "all men are created equal," but also a nation whose citizens were free to buy what they wanted from whomever they wished. If our ancestors had been more receptive to the monopolies imposed by King George III, we might be getting our medical care from the British National Health Service—a prospect not generally well received throughout our postwar history of health reform. Even today's single-payer movement is something very different from Britain's single-provider system.

New ideas, new technologies, and new industries quickly generated tremendous economic growth in the New World. Not surprisingly, monopolies arose just as quickly as predictable outgrowths of unregulated, laissez-faire capitalism. Given governments' roles in our lives today, we can easily forget that federal intervention in economic affairs was anathema when our country was new. Production and consumption were to be controlled by the "invisible hand" of the marketplace, so wondrously described in the year of our nation's independence by Adam Smith in *The Wealth of Nations* (1776). The Constitutional Convention effectively rejected government regulation of the economy. Caveat emptor (buyer beware) and the laws of supply and demand shaped commercial enterprise.

Well, we needed almost one hundred years to learn that completely unregulated markets do not produce desirable economic outcomes for the population at large. Leaving the economy totally under the direction of the "invisible hand" led to the creation of single entities in most major marketplaces. Sellers ruled; buyers obeyed. Over time, monopolies took control in iron and steel, railroads, agriculture, oil and gas, and other leading sectors of the nineteenth-century American economy. After driving out competitors with various strong-arm business tactics, monopolists took over in the markets they controlled. They could get away with charging high prices because consumers had no choice. Either buy from the monopolist at prices well above the costs of production and distribution plus a reasonable profit, or get along without!

Our nineteenth-century experience taught us the ironic lesson that unregulated competition ultimately kills competition—exactly the opposite outcome that Adam Smith said would be produced by the "invisible hand." We learned that the Founding Fathers had collectively erred in their rejection of federal economic regulation. Competition could not generally survive without some government action to protect competition. To teach this point in economics courses, I've used the analogy of a referee in sports. We need someone with legal authority to make sure that the game is played according to rules that are fair to both sides. In the economic game of setting medical prices for most of the past one hundred years, the most powerful team (organized medicine) has controlled the referee (state boards of medical examiners), and the referee prevented teams with lower payrolls (advanced practitioners) from playing independently. This arrangement made sense when less-expensive teams couldn't play at a safe and acceptable level, but now they can.

Recognizing the unpredicted problems arising from unfettered competition, Congress passed the first federal law against monopolies, the Sherman Antitrust Act of 1890. To this day, the Sherman Act is used to fight against restraints of trade that might lead to uncompetitive prices, restricted choice, and other harms of monopoly. The law has serious teeth. Convicted violators can be sent to jail and/or required to pay fines equal to three times the actual monetary damages caused by illegal monopoly behavior. Republicans and Democrats tend to apply the Sherman Act differently in today's highly polarized and dysfunctional environment, but neither party has expressed any interest (so far) in weakening or eliminating the law. Attorneys General on either side of the aisle find it useful for their purposes, independent of major differences in the parties' attitudes toward regulation.

The Clayton Act was passed in 1914 to strengthen the fight against powerful trusts, complementing the Sherman Act's ability to break up existing monopolies by giving the federal government additional tools for preventing the accumulation of harmful market power. The Clayton Act outlawed practices that might allow a business to become a monopoly, practices such as price discrimination (charging different prices to different customers for the same good, that is, as much as each is willing and able to pay), interlocking directorates ("behind closed door" arrangements that give competing companies opportunities to set non-competitive prices and divide markets), and tied buying contracts (requirements that consumers purchase goods they don't want in order to buy goods they do want). All these monopolistic practices result in consumers paying more and/or buying less than they would in competitive markets.

The Federal Trade Commission (FTC), also created in 1914, serves as a referee with the power to put an end to "false, fraudulent, misleading, and deceptive" trade practices in the medical marketplace. Like the Sherman Act enforcement actions by the Department of Justice, the FTC's activity ebbs and flows with the economic philosophy of the party in control of the White House. All other things being equal, the FTC is more likely to take action against monopolistic behavior during Democratic administrations. However, as a federal agency with a large staff of economists and lawyers specifically assigned to promote competition in the medical marketplace, the FTC has played a significant role in expanding consumer access to health services provided by qualified non-physician practitioners.

Several FTC actions during Republican and Democratic administrations have helped consumers benefit from expanded competition between health professionals. The United States Supreme Court recently supported the FTC approach in *North Carolina Board of Dental Examiners v. Federal Trade Commission*, declaring that occupational licensing boards were not uniformly immune from antitrust law.* The FTC's actions support the position that the actions of professional licensure boards should protect the public, not the members of the profession. The Commission's

---

* United States Supreme Court, No. 13–534. Argued October 14, 2014—Decided February 25, 2015.

2014 assessment of the merits of advanced practice nurses is frequently cited in this regard.*

Before taking a deep dive into a medical monopoly that many doctors still fight to preserve beyond its defensible existence, we need to understand an exception that proves the rule of competition in economic policy. Monopolies can be beneficial under specific circumstances, such as industries with very high fixed costs. Economic theory has historically justified monopolies in natural gas and electric utilities, as long as a public utilities commission approves prices that include a fair return (but no more) on investment. Until the last decade of the twentieth century, "natural monopolies" were given a public franchise to be sole suppliers in defined geographic markets because the high costs of competing infrastructures would lead to higher prices.

Most public utilities were deregulated in the 1990s, beginning with the breakup of American Telephone & Telegraph (AT&T). This dramatic and sudden shift away from public oversight on pricing and services provided a new political context that had to be addressed at some length in the first two editions of *Not What the Doctor Ordered*; I consider it a moot point 25 years later. The debate about deregulation's impact on pricing is probably impossible to resolve because the technologies and products of regulated industries are very different today.

As shown throughout this book, goods and services produced by physicians and advanced practitioners are acceptable substitutes, APs cost less than MDs and DOs, and allowing them to compete increases the overall supply of health care beyond what it would be when physicians are allowed to control access to the competition. The compelling case for ending physician control of APs stands on its own now. No examples from other industries are needed to justify eliminating laws and regulations that deny consumers direct access to non-physician health professionals practicing at the full scope of capabilities defined by their state (i.e., government-authorized) licensing boards.

Economic Perspectives on the Medical Marketplace

It's hard to think of doctors as monopolists. A trusted family physician or the surgeon who saved Grandma's life hardly seems like one of the selfish robber barons whose economic actions necessitated the Sherman Act and the FTC. Doctors really do want to relieve us of pain and suffering. Few of them are in it just for the money, as cynics might want us to believe. Medical doctors are respected professionals, yet they enjoy some unique economic advantages in comparison with accountants, lawyers, architects, bankers, and other "learned" professionals who help us deal with life's serious problems. Let's examine the differences.

---

* Federal Trade Commission "Policy perspectives: Competition and the regulation of advanced practice nurses," March, 2014. This report and others on the same topic are available at https://search.usa.gov/search?query=advanced+practice+nurses&submit.x=0&submit.y=0&submit=Search&affiliate=ftc_prod.

The actions of the medical monopoly as addressed in this book are rooted in third-party insurance, which is not a factor in the other professions. Patients have historically cared little about doctors' fees because someone else picked up most of the tab. With the proliferation of health insurance coverage following World War II—first private (Blue Cross and Blue Shield), then public (Medicare and Medicaid)—doctors no longer needed to vary fees based on what consumers could afford to pay. They could charge everyone the same fee, and health insurance would reimburse them for all of it (or, if not all of it, enough that the balance owed by the patient would usually be waived). How could doctors be in such a nice position? By controlling the boards of directors of the insurance companies, which ensured that health plan managers worked in doctors' best interests. This self-serving arrangement continued well into the 1980s when courts finally ruled it to be anti-competitive. (Physicians can no longer control health insurance companies as physicians, but many continue to "call the shots" as private investors.)

While it would be easy to accuse doctors of manipulating health insurance solely for their own economic benefit, it would not be completely fair. In fact, American physicians were brought into the third-party payer system kicking and screaming. Through the American Medical Association, their powerful trade organization, doctors consistently opposed any third-party intervention between themselves and their patients. The Hippocratic Oath, as we will soon see, stipulates that money should not influence a doctor's decision in choosing the best care for a patient. Private health insurance evolved from its American beginnings in the 1930s as organized medicine's compromise with strong political forces pushing for socialized medicine. It's also significant that health insurance was invented a half-century earlier in Germany. The concept was opposed in general, not least because Germany had been our mortal enemy in World War I. Using insurance to pay for health care might have developed differently in the US if the basic principles had originated in some country other than Germany.

The truce between American medical doctors and health insurance was an uneasy one. Indeed, even when Medicare and Medicaid were first proposed during the mid-1960s to cover people who did not receive private insurance coverage by virtue of employment (i.e., a tax-free fringe benefit in lieu of wage increases that had been outlawed), organized medicine was the most vocal and powerful opponent. Doctors as a group did not want any government intrusion into the "sacred" doctor–patient relationship. Indeed, organized medicine was so strongly opposed to health insurance in general that doctors only embraced it when they discovered they could effectively control the insurance companies through the boards of directors. In virtually every other country, including Germany, the health insurance industry was either heavily regulated by government or government-owned.

In the United States, the health insurance industry—dominated by Blue Cross and Blue Shield plans in the beginning—was created of doctors, by doctors, and for doctors as a defensive move to make sure that government could not tell them how to practice medicine. Does this sound like monopoly behavior? You do not need a PhD in economics to answer this question correctly, although organized medicine deserves credit for tempering its economic self-interest with a sincere belief that a patient's ability to pay should not influence the doctor's diagnosis or choice of therapy. Also, patients accepted this monopoly arrangement because they did not have to pay for it; employers and governments were picking up the tab.

The American doctor may have been forced into third-party payment against his will and professional ethics. However, because there was no competition from outside the medical guild of physicians and surgeons, the resulting insurance system paid whatever the doctor wanted to charge and supported a very good standard of living. In other words, organized medicine initially tried hard to kill the goose that would ultimately lay the golden eggs for its members, but it continued its staunch defense of state medical practice acts and reimbursement practices to make sure that no other health professionals could receive the same economic benefits. Doctors became monopolists unintentionally, but they became monopolists nevertheless, and they continue to fight against APs on many fronts. They established a seller's market, and the old guard does not want any competitors who would sell comparable services for less. Monopoly's defenders are a relatively small and declining force within the overall medical community, but they are still strong enough to prevent competition across the country.

Consumers are understandably bothered by doctors' monopoly power when they stop to think about it. However, they are not used to stopping and thinking about competitive remedies to the problem. Organized medicine manipulates our periodic debates on health reform to address costs and choices of insurance rather than costs and choices of care. Democrats tend to accept the monopoly and propose more regulations to deal with its adverse consequences. I've given up trying to figure out what the Republicans are trying to accomplish in the Trump era, other than oppose Obamacare and eliminate most of its regulations. The party's traditional positions have disappeared, with no consistent or coherent replacements discernible to me at the time of this writing. I'd like to think the resulting chaos in our nation's capital provides an opportunity to forge a new direction in health reform, like ending the medical monopoly in all 50 states.

Today's superior alternative to monopoly—direct competition among all qualified health professionals—doesn't yet have a powerful political champion, but it does have powerful opponents: the monopolists, their financial intermediaries, other provider entities beholden to them, and elected officials they have heavily supported. Consumers all along the political spectrum therefore need to speak up as a group, demanding direct access to advanced practitioners who can independently (i.e., free of physician oversight) provide diagnostic and therapeutic services consistent with the full scope of their skills and licensure. Ensuring competition is a much better solution than providing more to the "same old, same old" insurance that enriches doctors when other health professionals could acceptably meet most of the same needs for less money.

Physicians threatened by my economic prescription for competition should note that I am absolutely not proposing regulations to control physicians' fees or incomes, nor am I proposing any actions that would restrict consumer choice. My goal is to improve consumer welfare by introducing competition among all qualified practitioners, not to regulate what doctors charge for their services or to force consumers to buy from the least-expensive seller. Consumers should be free to choose a physician or an AP for any service that can be professionally, and safely, provided by both. Insurers should be required to reimburse any qualified independent practitioner under financial arrangements that reflect price differences, charging different premiums or imposing co-pays that vary accordingly. As with today's preferred provider organizations (PPO) and accountable care organizations (ACO), premiums will be lower for health plans offering provider panels of less-expensive caregivers, including advanced practitioners.

Just as physicians must not be told what price to charge, they must not be required to lower their fees in response to competition. Physicians should instead be expected to negotiate their own prices in a competitive marketplace, based on the "wiggle and jiggle" of supply and demand. We economists use this quaint English term to remind people that competitive markets are dynamic and uncertain. Long-term price stability in a market, on the other hand, is a common indication of monopoly control. Monopolists try to suppress price competition because its uncertainties make them uncomfortable. They prefer stability; they work to maintain status as price-makers, not price-takers.

The dynamic effect of competitive pricing is a major component of the creative destruction that improves marketplaces over time. Consumers benefit significantly from an array of prices, but price competition is not the only outcome that matters in economic analysis. Giving consumers freedom to choose among similar products is just as important. Monopoly has prevented or significantly hindered consumer access to other benefits that advanced practitioners bring to the medical marketplace. Giving consumers the right to choose among different care models, independent of price differences, is an equally important reason to ensure direct access to independent advanced practitioners. For example, many people suffering from lower back pain do not want to see an orthopedic surgeon because they do not want surgery, but they are willing to be treated non-invasively by a physical therapist—even if price is not a concern. Consumers in many states do not have this option, but they should. Now.

The Changing Measure of the Medical Monopoly

As already seen in a different context, employers (through private insurance companies) and taxpayers (through government health plans) have historically borne the burden of higher prices resulting from doctors' monopoly power. However, the latest round of health reforms is changing the situation for patients with insurance. The Affordable Care Act (ACA) requires that patients pay a greater portion of medical costs than they were paying until recently. Consumers now have "some skin in the game," in current policy jargon. This is arguably the only reform goal shared by a significant number of Republicans and Democrats.

Health insurance still picks up most of the tab for Americans with coverage, including ACA plans, but making consumers pay even a little more strengthens the case for ending the medical monopoly. Here's why. Public and private health insurance made approximately 80% of all payments throughout the second half of the twentieth century. The portion of total costs paid by government and employer-sponsored insurance, known as the actuarial ratio, has fallen from 80% to around 70% since then, so public and private third parties are still paying considerably more than half of doctors' total bills. (A 70% actuarial ratio has become the de facto national standard under the Affordable Care Act, although individual patients can see wide variations in different geographic markets.) Charity, research, and other subsidies have continued to pick up about 10% of all medical expenditures, all other things being equal.

But here's the rub. Patients' overall out-of-pocket obligations have roughly doubled since the ACA was passed in 2010, from 10% to 20% of the total bill, as the actuarial ratio has dropped from 80% to 70%. As a result, even patients with insurance are reducing their consumption of medical services because they cannot afford their rising share of the total costs of care. Disposable personal income has not risen in proportion to the rise in personal responsibility for health care spending. Indeed, it hasn't risen at all for 90% of the population due to income redistribution; all income growth since the Great Recession of 2008 has gone to America's upper 10%.* Most Americans will therefore need less-expensive alternatives if they are to be able to buy any medical services at all. As shown by the economic analysis and cost models presented above, competition is the best way to make care more affordable. Competition is not perfect, but I believe it is the best remedy under today's circumstances.

The Affordable Care Act has almost no mechanisms to tame the rising prices of health care, and its future is highly uncertain. (President Obama talked frequently about why a law was needed to tame the rise in total spending, i.e., prices of goods and services multiplied by quantities purchased. He did not address the rise in prices themselves.) Regulation is an equally dubious approach to getting a handle on prices under the current political situation. Both political parties have shown

---

* Widening gaps in income distribution make it almost impossible for most consumers to pay the increasing portion of health care costs transferred to them by the bipartisan reform goal of "having skin in the game." Federal data on income inequality are available at https://www.census.gov/topics/income-poverty/income-inequality/data/data-tables.html. Discussions of the problem are presented by P Cohen, "Research shows slim gains for the bottom 50 percent," *The New York Times*, December 6, 2016, p. B1; B Appelbaum and R Pear, "Median household income grew again, but slower, last year," *The New York Times*, September 13, 2018, p. B2; and P Kiernan, "Workers claim a shrinking slice of the pie," *Wall Street Journal*, February 25, 2019, p. A2.

little regard for enforcing laws or regulations.* For example, I can't think of a single major provision of the ACA that has been implemented as enacted or regulation that has been consistently enforced as promulgated. Indeed, many parts of the original law and subsequent regulations have been abandoned altogether.

The doubling of patients' out-of-pocket responsibility for payment is surely enough to make them care more about physicians' charges, but a typical doctor's bill provides little or no definitive information about effective prices of the services provided. It seldom makes any economic sense at all.† An explanation of benefits (EOB) statement usually shows what the doctor charged the insurer and what the insurer paid the doctor, after opaque adjustments for contractual allowances and other arrangements made between the two parties. (Truth be told, most of my doctor friends don't understand EOBs either.) The bottom line on a typical EOB statement is presumably what that the patient owes in addition to the insurance payment, but it is often followed by a curious notation not to pay that amount because it is only an estimate. Although itemized bills are generally incomprehensible, the total amount due is what matters to the patient. It may be ambiguous for any given doctor–patient encounter, but it is unquestionably rising overall.

If you find this situation confusing, then I am explaining it clearly. Today's medical pricing is inherently hard to understand. It is not supported by any rational policy or sensible system. In fact, doctors have almost no information about the actual costs of the services they provide or the prices that patients pay. Fees charged are meaningless in terms of conventional economic analysis, and different consumers pay different amounts for the same service based on differences in their insurance coverage. We are also learning that drug prices are totally irrational and that the prices of diagnostic services are extremely complicated. Therefore, health reform driven by "skin in the game" thinking doesn't make much sense either. How can health policy wonks expect "informed consumers" to choose doctors, buy drugs, or shop for diagnostic tests on the basis of comparative pricing when final prices are almost impossible to know in advance of consumption?

I could easily show off my skills as a medical economist by explaining how rational prices are set in a competitive market—which you might expect because this book is about eliminating the medical monopoly—but it wouldn't really matter. In fact, it isn't even relevant to the future of competition in the medical marketplace.

---

* Although the focus of this book is to enable competition between physicians and other comparably qualified caregivers, there's lots more to be said about promoting competition in other areas of the health care delivery system. Readers who would like to know more about the broader range of antitrust issues will find a good overview in TL Greaney and B Richman "Promoting competition in healthcare enforcement and policy: Framing an active competition agenda," American Antitrust Institute Series on Competition in the Delivery and Payment of Healthcare Services, 2018, https://www.antitrustinstitute.org/wp-content/uploads/2018/09/AAI_Healthcare-WP-Part-II_6.18.18.pdf.

† R Pear, "Hospitals post their prices: Try to decipher them," *The New York Times*, January 13, 2019, p. A14.

Why? Itemized fees for specific services are disappearing, slowly but surely, as reimbursement reform shifts from volume to value. Payment is being bundled around episodes of care and disease entity management, not quantity of services, so what matters most in the future is the total cost of providing services. And, as shown above by conventional economic analysis, input substitution in production is a (if not *the*) critical key to reducing total cost.

The medical marketplace is likely to experience the same general transformation that occurred in telecommunications when AT&T's monopoly was dismantled. Advancements in communications technology ultimately caused metered minute-by-minute charges for roaming and long-distance to disappear. Over the course of a decade, line-by-line itemization of our phone calls was replaced by a flat monthly charge. As fee-for-service billing declines in health care, charging for a specific service will become correspondingly less important.

Who provides the service becomes more important, which will increase demand for any health professional who can do what a doctor does for less money. Data in the previous section showed that labor costs of advanced practitioners are about half the cost of physicians—but efficient input substitutions cannot be made in about half of the states because medical monopoly gets in the way of using advanced practitioners for services they can provide at least as well as physicians. Paying physician prices for work done at considerably lower cost by advanced practitioners is contrary to the reform imperative of reducing overall spending on health care—one more reason for all states to recognize advanced practitioners as independent practitioners, ASAP.

Although economic analysis of monopoly's harms focuses on production costs and consumer prices, convenience can also be an important consideration. If monopoly power keeps a certain good or service out of a geographic market, a consumer who wants it must incur the additional costs (e.g., travel time, shipping charges, downtime while waiting for delivery) of buying it somewhere else. Several examples of this problem were brought to my attention as I conducted interviews for this book, particularly by independent advanced practitioners who treated patients from neighboring states. A growing number of consumers who want to purchase care directly from advanced practitioners must travel to another state if medical monopoly restricts access to APs at home. When their state of residence does not recognize the prescribing authority of the neighboring state's APs, these consumers are either forced to return to the other state to get prescriptions refilled or find a physician who will approve the prescription in their home state—at extra cost and considerable inconvenience, either way. (It's analogous to the market failure that causes many American to buy medication from Canadian and Mexican pharmacies.) Enabling competition will save a lot of money for consumers who live in states where doctors still restrict access to advanced practitioners. The next chapter reviews the relevant lessons of history and shows how not to repeat them as states take action to end the many harms of medical monopoly.

Chapter 3

The Medical Marketplace: Learning Lessons of History

So much for economic analysis, for now. A brief historical analysis of medical care delivery in the United States also helps reveal the benefits of allowing advanced practitioners to compete with physicians. This history is something very different from expectations based on recent experiences. Unless you have studied it already, you probably assume that medical care has always been under the control of uniquely qualified professionals who spent years studying a systematic science of human health—in other words, archetypal doctors. If you assume that doctors have always been in charge because it could not be any other way, then you definitely need to read this chapter. Seeing that health care not only can—but now must—be organized in some other way is essential for successful health reform in the United States. Receiving medical care has not always meant "going to the doctor," nor should it mean this in the future.

The prevailing concept of "going to the doctor" is essentially a twentieth-century creation. It had a different meaning in the nineteenth century, so there's no timeless force that requires it to mean the same thing in the twenty-first. The human race has somehow managed to get through at least the last thousand years without relying on an exclusive and immutable guild of professionals who identified themselves as "the doctor." Nothing in human history or sacred scripture suggests that the world will come to an end if we challenge the assumption that health services should only be provided by a doctor or someone working under the control of a doctor. We have every right to expect a properly trained professional, of course, but not necessarily a medical doctor. Therefore, I feel perfectly comfortable asking you to join me in challenging this assumption.

To do so, we need to understand the history behind American doctors' common assertion that they alone should be in charge. The following brief history of health care explains why our system is what it is today—with my sincere appreciation for the doctor's role in making it much better than it would have been without their dominance in the twentieth century—and why it can and should be different now without their accustomed control. Above all, this history shows that medical care exists in a constant state of evolution, and there is no reason to believe that the evolution stopped for all time when American doctors eliminated professional competition in the early 1900s.

Ancient Roots: Religion and Medicine

In antiquity, the delivery of medical care was often inseparable from religion. The doctor played the same leading role as the priest or priestess. Others, from exorcists and astrologers to herbalists and bloodletters, played supporting roles. While the techniques they used generally seem crude and unscientific to our modern minds, a few early practices were surprisingly advanced. For example, early "surgeons" cut a hole in the skull to release evil spirits, much like a modern neurosurgeon opens the skull to release pressure and remove tissue that is causing harm. Trepanation shows that interventional medicine has been around for at least 5,000 years, and history suggests its early practitioners had religious status.

Priests and priestesses dispensed medical care in temples in the Mediterranean area. Evidence of healing practices is found in many other parts of the world, particularly India and China, over the next 2,500 years. However, clearly identifiable roots of modern medicine are found in Classical Greece (500–300 BCE). Unlike their predecessors, the Greek physicians were not holy men. They were lay practitioners who addressed health problems from scientific perspectives, not from religious beliefs. Indeed, their concepts occasionally contradicted religion's teachings. Their theories about human health may seem rudimentary by today's standards, but they were derived from methods and principles that laid the foundations for today's medical science. One of the most prominent Greek physicians, Hippocrates, is well known to any modern physician. (See box, "The Hippocratic Oath and Today's Doctors.")

THE HIPPOCRATIC OATH AND TODAY'S DOCTORS

Every medical doctor still takes the Hippocratic Oath, written by Hippocrates of Kos in the fifth century BCE, upon graduation from medical school. What is its relevance to medicine as practiced in the United States at the beginning of the twenty-first century? The Oath itself is a short, discursive document that dictates how physicians ought to behave. Some of its key directives include:*

- Honor and respect one's teacher, and teach the "Art" of healing to one's own sons and one's teacher's sons "without fee or stipulation," as well as to "disciples bound by a stipulation and oath according to the laws of medicine, *but to wnone others*" [italics mine].
- Refuse to assist in suicide or abortion.
- Live and practice medicine "with purity and with holiness."
- Abstain "from every voluntary act of mischief and corruption, and ... from the seduction of females or males, of freemen and slaves."
- Maintain patient privacy.
- "I will follow that system of regimen which, according to my ability and judgment, I consider for the benefit of my patients, and abstain from whatever is deleterious and mischievous."

The Oath is most often summed up as: "Above all, do no harm."

All medical doctors educated in the United States have taken the oath, but the care they provide obviously deviates to varying degrees from its precepts. Doctors do not lose their licenses for performing abortions or assisting suicide (even though they are breaking laws in many states), medical school professors make very nice incomes teaching the "art" of medicine, some very good clinicians are bad people, some seduce females or males, etc.

The Hippocratic Oath, administered only to physicians, is sometimes used to defend the unique qualifications and ultimate authority of doctors. Other health professionals are considered subservient to doctors because they are not part of the fraternity bound by this 2,500-year-old pledge. Given the substantial differences between the practice of medicine today and the obligations imposed by the Oath, I simply do not see how being admitted to the brotherhood of Hippocrates can be used as a reason to prevent others from striving to be in charge of doing comparable good for people in need.

With proper training and commitment to professionalism, as defined in Chapter 4, followers of other clinical traditions should be allowed to diagnose and treat patients without a follower of Hippocrates looking over their shoulders and charging extra for providing the supervision! Hence, I have real difficulty with any attempt to justify physicians' monopoly on the basis of unique ownership of an ancient oath that is violated on a daily basis. It's hypocritical. We, the people who need expert care, should urge doctors to either abandon or update the Oath and accept the fact that it does not define a superior status only a doctor can attain.

---

* This version of the oath is from Erwin Ackerknecht, *A Short History of Medicine* (Baltimore: Johns Hopkins Press, revised edition 1968), p. 57.

The theory and practice of medicine did not advance appreciably during the Roman Empire, although Galen (130–201 CE), a Greek physician and surgeon who had trained on gladiators, exhibited a major influence on medical thinking that lasted until the Renaissance. However, two Roman innovations—public works and social administration—contributed significantly to the health of the population. For example, aqueducts supplied clean water for public fountains and baths, draining swamps eliminated many pathogens, and sewer systems reduced many diseases caused by urbanization. The Roman state also established a form of health insurance and hired physicians, perhaps the world's first system of socialized medicine.

The Middle Ages advanced some of the foundations laid by the Greeks and Romans, but the study of medicine returned for a while to the hands of priests and monks who relied more on mysticism and religion than on science. At the same time, the study of medicine took hold in the Arab world with the ascendancy of Islam. A medical encyclopedia written by a Persian priest, Avicenna (980–1063 CE), became a standard resource throughout the Western world for centuries to come. Medical studies moved out of monasteries and into universities by the twelfth century. The Church decreed that clerics could no longer engage in bloodletting or other surgical procedures, which led to them being performed by lay practitioners, especially barbers and "quacks of every description." This tradition endured for the better part of a millennium. In Zurich in 1790, for instance, there were "only four academic doctors, but thirty-four barber-surgeons."* Rossini's famous opera, "The Barber of Seville," is historically accurate in portraying the barber as the family doctor in the early nineteenth century.

As it did in art and science, Renaissance medicine reflected the conflict between Church doctrine and the secular belief that humans had the power to change the world. The latter worldview opened a new direction for medicine, beginning the serious study of anatomy that had been discouraged by the Church. Surgery, still separate from the non-invasive practice of medicine by university-educated physicians, gained some respectability, and barber-surgeons began to compete with midwives in the practice of obstetrics. (Until very recently, American medicine was shaped by this male takeover of a function performed for centuries by females in other most cultures.)

The advancements of fifteenth- and sixteenth-century science led to an explosion of scientific and medical knowledge in the seventeenth century. The circulatory, respiratory, and lymphatic systems, as well as bacteria and cells, were all "discovered." Diseases were studied more than ever before, but effective treatments remained elusive. University-trained physicians still had one foot in earlier eras, and the practice of medicine was open to anyone who claimed the ability to provide diagnosis and treatment. This competition—unfamiliar to Americans, for reasons we'll now examine—never completely disappeared in Europe.

---

* E Ackerknecht, *A Short History of Medicine, op. cit.,* p. 89.

The American Way of Medical Care

Until the end of the nineteenth century, medical care in North America was provided by a hodgepodge of healers with widely varying backgrounds. University-trained physicians were just one among many. Indeed, being a medical school graduate in America was very rare until well into the 1800s. The study of medicine led only to an undergraduate degree, if any degree at all, and could be completed with a minimum of effort at many schools. More likely than not, medicine was learned through apprenticeship with a practicing physician who may or may not have had any formal training.

The United States was still a predominantly rural nation, and the criteria for giving (and receiving) medical help often had more to do with location than with training. In the cities, however, there were a few formal medical practices managed by university-trained physicians. While most of our nation's early doctors were trained in Europe, especially Scotland and Germany, more and more were educated in this country once the first American medical school was established in Philadelphia in 1765. Some attempts to organize and even license physicians were made in more populated states in the late 1700s, but the efforts generally floundered.

The state of American medicine remained disorganized until the mid-nineteenth century, a direct reflection of the laissez-faire policies of Jacksonian democracy (named after Andrew Jackson, who was elected in the 1820s and 1830s on a campaign platform that shunned almost all forms of government regulation) and the country's rapid expansion westward. In 1846, a group of physicians banded together to form what became the American Medical Association—the AMA—but its early impact on medical care was minimal. Not only did those who called themselves "doctors" remain divided and intensely competitive in their individual practices, but they also competed with the many lay practitioners, mostly women, who provided much of the medical care of the day.

A few key developments during the nineteenth century served to advance medical science and thereby turn medicine into a learned profession. (We need to remember that bloodletting and intestinal purging were still the primary treatments for a host of ailments well into the 1800s.) Advancements such as vaccinations, anesthesia, antiseptics, and sterile surgery procedures all nurtured the development of modern medicine in the mid- to late-1800s. Louis Pasteur's discovery of the microbial cause of infectious disease did not occur until 1864. Prior to this remarkable advancement, health care practitioners had no definitive understanding of the physical mechanisms that led to illness, nor could they prove any cause-and-effect relationship between their care and changes in their patients' health.

Many "medical schools" proliferated in late nineteenth-century America, offering a host of philosophical approaches to diagnosis and treatment. These schools bore little resemblance to the high-quality academic health centers that we have today. They were more like trade or technical schools, with students gaining admission upon completing the equivalent of high school. The schools offered as little as a few months to a year of basic courses, which were often repeated for a second year. Although many of these schools were attached to general colleges or universities, students commonly paid their tuition fees directly to the professors—usually doctors needing a little extra income. The students were expected to go on to an apprenticeship after the classroom instruction, although this applied and (presumably) supervised learning did not always occur.

Given the disorganized general state of affairs and the low incomes that resulted from such a highly competitive market, where virtually anyone could work as a doctor, organized medical societies like the AMA began pushing states toward basic standards for physician licensing. This movement began in the 1870s, but the United States Supreme Court did not officially recognize the right of a state to license doctors until 1888. Giving states the power to restrict who could be a doctor was the first step toward giving medical doctors their monopoly power. Within 30 years, every state had some sort of medical licensing law.

While licensing physicians did serve to protect the public from "diploma mill" quacks and charlatans, licensure also placed the control of who could and could not practice medicine into the hands of university-trained physicians. These doctors gained not only the power to police themselves but also the power to establish the new order of medical care in the United States—giving one of the meanings to this book's title, ordering the medical marketplace according to doctors' wishes. The "losers" were not just bogus or poorly trained (i.e., not university-trained) doctors, but experienced lay practitioners such as midwives who were, because they were women or ethnic minorities, all but excluded from the institutions of higher education dominated by white males. In fact, one of the AMA's early positions was to oppose the "ignorant meddlesome midwife," both as an abortionist and a caregiver.*

Despite this consolidation of control by the medical profession, the medical schools that proliferated across the country during the latter 1800s were only loosely regulated. The AMA, which had reorganized and grown to represent half of the physicians in the country, commissioned Abraham Flexner of the Carnegie Foundation to examine all the medical schools in the United States. His report, released in 1910, condemned all but a handful of schools as being substandard. While many schools were already in a weakened condition due to the new state licensing laws and other changes to the medical profession, the Flexner Report thrust medical education into a period of reform and consolidation, firmly under control of the AMA. Within five years, the number of medical schools in the US

---

* S Faludi, *Backlash: The Undeclared War Against American Women* (New York: Crown, 1991), p. 413; and the Boston Women's Health Book Collective, *Our Bodies, Ourselves* (New York: Touchstone, 1992), p. 692.

had dropped by one-third, from 131 to 95.* By the mid-1920s, that number had dwindled even further.

Only a few dozen medical schools remained to train the kind of doctor with the AMA's stamp of professional approval. Competition was neutralized in the name of educational reform. This consolidation served to homogenize medical education into an institution of, by, and for upper-class white males. It also served to define doctors who met that criterion as the sole source of medical care in the country. In the process, five of the seven black medical schools closed, as well as two of the three medical schools established for women. In the schools that did survive, no more than 5% of the student positions were allocated to women.

The philosophical thrust of the revamped medical schools was even more limiting. As Rocio Huet-Cox has written:

> The Flexner Report served, in essence, to establish a highly durable model for medicine—disease-oriented and mechanistic, centrally based in the hospital or office, and focused on the individual patient. In this model, the sick or injured individual comes to the solo practitioners for rational assessment of an illness. The physician then attempts to "cure" the patient with the diagnostic and therapeutic tools placed at his disposal by biomedical research and technology.[†]

Medical schools, and thus doctors, came to embody the *allopathic* approach to medicine, that is, one where there is no need for intervention until a problem occurs, whereupon it is addressed in a systematic and scientific way.

Some alternative views of disease and treatment gradually faded away. Two of the more prominent alternative practitioners coexisting with mainstream physicians during the latter half of the nineteenth century were the eclectics and the homeopaths. The former served mainly to oppose some of the aggressive treatments of the day, such as bloodletting, purging, vomiting, and toxic drug therapy. Instead of accepting these therapies, eclectics practiced herbalism as much as mainstream scientific medicine. Homeopathic doctors advocated treating disease by administering minute quantities of natural substances that were known to cause the same or similar symptoms as the disease. As a widely accepted form of medical practice, it quickly lost favor within the first two decades of the twentieth century, arguably because of the licensing and educational reforms imposed by mainstream scientific medicine.

---

[*] P Starr, *The Social Transformation of American Medicine* (New York: Basic Books, 1982), p. 120.

[†] V Sidell and R Sidell, *Reforming Medicine: Lessons from the Last Quarter Century* (New York: Pantheon Books, 1984), p. 131.

The Physicians: Allopaths and Osteopaths

Allopathy, the clinical foundation of mainstream American medicine since the educational reforms of the early twentieth century, is based on the belief that the physician's role is to create within the patient a physical environment to fight a diagnosed illness or injury. Consequently, allopathic physicians use active and invasive interventions, such as drugs and surgery, to counteract the factors that are believed to cause disease. Physicians who graduate from an allopathic medical school are designated by the MD degree. Osteopathy is based on the same conceptual foundations as allopathy, but it additionally emphasizes the relationship between organs and the musculoskeletal system. Therefore, like chiropractors but unlike allopaths, osteopaths are trained to use manipulation as part of their approach to healing, but not all include it in their regular practices. Physicians who graduate from a college of osteopathic medicine receive the DO degree.

Osteopathic medicine is now generally considered as acceptable as allopathic medicine. Allopaths and osteopaths are both defined as physicians in state medical practice acts, with the same privileges and scopes of practice. Students attend three or four years of medical school, allopathic or osteopathic, and take the same examinations to obtain state licenses. Doctors of both orientations commonly practice together without any ill feelings between the two professions (or, at least, no more animosity than exists within each profession separately). Bitter interprofessional divisions of the early twentieth century took a long time to disappear, but the distinction between the two philosophies no longer seems to be a significant problem. The number of medical students in osteopathic schools has grown by approximately 85% over the past decade; one in four medical students now attends an osteopathic school.* Osteopathy's impressive growth would not have occurred if organized medicine (e.g., the AMA) opposed it. Indeed, it is a sign of progress because many allopathic physicians still treated osteopaths as unqualified competitors when the previous editions of this book appeared in the 1990s.

I have been hoping the allopathy–osteopathy rapprochement indicated that organized medicine was developing a more open-minded attitude toward advanced practitioners, but this sadly does not seem to be the case. Allopaths have apparently stopped believing that osteopaths are encroaching on their turf, but the American Osteopathic Association (AOA) has now joined the American Medical Association in opposing advanced practitioners. The AOA has officially asked its members *to tell lawmakers* about patients who have been harmed by non-physicians.[†] I find this very disturbing for three reasons.

---

* American Osteopathic Association, Osteopathic Medical Profession Report, as reported in "Surge in DO students could help ease physician shortage"; https://www.modernhealthcare.com/article/20180112/NEWS/180119947.

[†] "Scope of practice update: New HHS report promotes expansion for non-physician providers," *The DO*, December 12, 2018; https://thedo.osteopathic.org/2018/12/scope-of-practice-update-new-hhs-report-promotes-expansion-for-midlevel-providers/.

■ First, as explained at length in the next chapter, members of a licensed health profession should police their peers, not members of other professions. All health professions have an ongoing obligation to improve quality of care by exposing inappropriate prescribing or unnecessary diagnostic tests, but osteopaths and allopaths will find plenty of examples of dubious practice in care provided by members of their own professions. Physicians shouldn't waste time tattling on fully trained professionals who are licensed under other clinical models that meet the criteria of independent practice. Osteopaths really ought to understand this point, having argued for so many years that they should not be judged by allopathic physicians. It was only a decade or two ago that many allopathic physicians were telling patients that osteopathic care could be wasteful or harmful.

■ Second, patients are not always qualified to decide whether they have been harmed by care, which the AOA curiously defines in economic terms of unnecessary service rather than clinical measures of real physical harm, such as missed diagnoses, botched procedures, iatrogenic (i.e., care-induced) infections, etc. Deputizing patients in a campaign to discredit competitors clashes with a phrase commonly used by the medical profession, "Doctor knows best." If physicians believe that patients aren't as smart as doctors, how can they entrust patients to judge or make meaningful comments on care provided by other fully qualified health professionals? Sure, lots of unnecessary care is delivered—the consensus within the medical profession is that over 30% of all medical spending is wasted—but doctors frequently disagree on whether any single intervention is wasteful or necessary as "defensive medicine." Besides, doctors point out that they provide many services against their better judgment because patients demand things like antibiotics for viral infections or immediate imaging studies when watchful waiting would be medically appropriate. Many patients also believe that an appropriate diagnostic test was unnecessary when it doesn't reveal the possible problem. Most patient reports to legislators would be unsubstantiated anecdotes, with potential to do more harm than good. Scientifically trained physicians should be embarrassed to put patients in this position.

■ Third, reports of negligent practice should be made to the state-appointed boards that have statutory authority to regulate the professional practicing negligently—not to legislatures. Licensure boards have appropriate policies and procedures for handling reports from both professionals and patients, including investigators to see which complaints have demonstrable merit that requires corrective action. Legislators, on the other hand, tend to take complaints at face value and use them for political gain. Malpractice litigation is also an appropriate action when serious harm is done. In other words, legislators have no collective ability to assess deficient professional practices. That's why they create regulatory boards and professional liability laws. Health professionals should use these established legal mechanisms to protect public safety. Sending patients to complain to legislators is not what we should expect of a health professional; it is what economists would expect of a monopolist.

Osteopathy was able to survive as an independent profession in a few states where it had a strong presence at the time of the Flexnerian reforms. Medicine's suppression of nursing, on the other hand, was national. Nurses across the country were declared to be "the doctor's handmaidens" and were removed from any further consideration for the right to practice independently of physicians. The implicit assumption was that nurses (women) could not exist without doctors (men), and that was that.* Nursing's only bright spot in the formative years of American medical care came when Florence Nightingale pioneered the concept of the "clean" hospital. Despite this innovation that saved countless lives and transformed the hospital from a place where poor people died to a place where all people regained health, her accomplishments on behalf of nursing never elevated her profession above the doctor-subservient role it has traditionally played.

One of the primary goals of this book is to correct that injustice to nursing and other health professions, to bring history up-to-date with today's realities. Fortunately, it's an easy task *conceptually* now that the scientific and professional foundations of today's advanced practitioners have become at least as strong as those of physicians. However, it's a difficult task *politically*. One clear lesson of history is that doctors will not willingly perform this public service on their own, as just shown by osteopathy's monopolistic emulation of allopathy. Organized medicine, correspondingly expanded in size, is still fighting competition on grounds that are no longer defensible.

The Golden Age of American Medicine: The 1920s to the 1960s

By the 1920s, the allopathic doctor was firmly in the driver's seat of American medicine. Practitioners of alternative clinical approaches had either joined up or shut down, non-physician practitioners had been placed in support roles, and lay practitioners had been driven into the shadows. Within just a few decades, the medical marketplace had gone from totally unregulated to highly regulated—following orders of allopathic doctors implemented via organized medicine (aka the AMA).

State medical practice acts defined the practice of medicine, limiting it to individuals who had graduated from medical schools accredited according to the standards of university-trained practitioners. Specific details of the medical practice acts varied from state to state, but the net impact on medical marketplaces across

---

* For an example of this sexism and its role, see RL Van Nest, "The life and trial of Dagmar Nelson—part 2," *AANA Journal*, 2006; 74(4): 261–265.

the country was the same. Physicians were in control, first by legislating who could provide care and then controlling how and what they got paid for doing the work. The AMA, one struggling medical society among many in the mid-1800s, effectively gained control of American medicine by the early 1900s.

Not that other practitioners were ignored ... states also began passing acts to regulate practices for the other health professions, including nursing, dentistry, pharmacy, optometry, podiatry, physical therapy, occupational therapy, and audiology. The non-medical state practice acts were carefully written so as not to encroach on doctors' ultimate authority. Indeed, in more than a few states, the scopes of practice of these non-medical practitioners were contained within the medical practice acts and enforced by the boards of medical examiners, leaving no doubt who was in control. Doctors were clearly "captain of the ship," a concept carefully explained and analyzed in the next chapter because it needs to be applied for the new realities of the twenty-first century.

Doctors' authority was not unopposed, however. Socialized medical insurance was a major goal in most European countries, and attempts were made in the United States to promote various forms of practice that placed physicians in the position of being employees of—and thus subservient to—a larger organization such as a corporation, fraternal organization, or consumer cooperative. The official AMA party line was that the doctor should remain free of all outside authority, should work only on a fee-for-service basis, and should at all costs protect the sanctity of his personal relationship with each patient. As proof, organized medicine strongly opposed the formation of Kaiser-Permanente, now one of the country's most successful and respected health systems, when a prominent West Coast industrialist created it to deliver health services to his employees in the 1920s. (I met physicians who believed that Kaiser was a subversive organization, part of the Communist plot to overthrow the United States, when I joined the faculty of the University of Colorado School of Medicine in 1973. I am not making this up!)

State medical practice acts provided the framework for doctors' defenses against challenges to their professional authority. The laws were written at the behest of physicians, allowing doctors to determine the rules of medical practice rather than giving other entities the power to write guidelines for them. Doctors made sure they were the only ones who sat on state licensing boards and medical review panels. When state practice acts needed to be changed, doctors usually drafted the bills for legislators to pass. When regulations needed to be written for other health care providers and for hospitals, organized medicine tended to take care of that task, too. Legislators followed doctors' orders and received generous campaign contributions in exchange for their obeisance.

This situation contrasts significantly with standard approaches to regulated public utilities, as established in economics and law. In virtually every case but medical practice, the relevant regulatory body consisted predominantly of outsiders appointed by elected officials. In the case of medicine, doctors secured the power to regulate themselves under the guise of being a learned profession, one so special that outsiders could not possibly know enough to regulate it in the public interest. It was a classic case of putting the fox in charge of the hen house.

The same professional autonomy was preserved in the case of medical insurance. As noted in the preceding economic analysis, medical doctors in the 1920s and 1930s fought strenuously against the concept of third-party coverage on the grounds that it intruded on a "sacred" doctor–patient relationship. (The word *sacred* almost always appeared in this context, reinforcing the long-standing image of doctors as gods.) But realizing that "the best way to beat 'em is to join 'em," doctors deflected the threatened loss of control by establishing Blue Cross to pay hospitals and Blue Shield to pay physicians. Again, organized medicine manipulated state legislatures to secure special treatment, including non-profit status and exemption from insurance laws that required control by outside directors. With this special treatment, the physician-controlled "Blues" cornered the market on health insurance, too.

Periodic campaigns for socialized medicine likewise provided a challenge for American doctors. Teddy Roosevelt proposed government-controlled health insurance in 1912 as the Progressive Party candidate for president. The proposal was raised again as part of the New Deal program during the 1930s, but physician opposition ultimately caused it to be left out of the Social Security Act in 1935. It reappeared under both the Truman and Nixon administrations, only to be branded as socialism by the AMA and other groups with a vested interest in the status quo. Doctors' independence and their authority over American health care remained intact. Indeed, the medical monopoly became so strong that doctors had effectively broadened their fiefdom to the entire health care delivery system. Of course, maintaining control is a lot easier when you do not have any competition.

Organized medicine did not meet its match until Lyndon Johnson became president in 1963, following the assassination of John F. Kennedy. A Democratic Congress and a strong Democratic president combined forces in 1965 to create Medicare and Medicaid, unprecedented programs to provide health care to the nation's elderly and poor. Doctors, of course, vigorously fought against both programs for the usual reasons: the threat of socialized medicine, government interference with the sacred doctor–patient relationship, and loss of the patients' right to choose their doctor. The compromise that ultimately made passage acceptable to the AMA was designating "The Blues," still controlled by physicians, to administer the programs.

Doctors were bruised politically, but not harmed economically. It did not take long for them to learn that this new infusion of federal money into "their system" turned charity patients (i.e., patients who could not afford to pay for care) into paying patients—starting an unprecedented journey to higher incomes, increased social status, and guaranteed employment. Most older physicians I know think of the three decades following Medicare and Medicaid as the "golden age" of American medicine—even though the medical profession initially did just about everything possible to prevent the programs from being created.

In economic theory, competition from acceptable non-physician caregivers could have led to a more balanced distribution of income at the time. However, physicians had made sure they were "the only game in town," and—to be historically fair—doctors were the only health professionals qualified to oversee the delivery of health care. As a perfect example of the law of unintended consequences, the first programs to train qualified competitors began at about the same time. Doctors' rapid acceptance of Medicare and Medicaid unwittingly and ironically led them to help improve the skills of the health professionals who are now qualified to bring efficiency to the medical marketplace through competition.

Drawing the Fein Line

In 1967, two years after enactment of Medicare and Medicaid, Harvard economist Rashi Fein published *The Doctor Shortage*,* projecting that the United States would face a severe shortage of doctors by the mid-1980s. This book bore the imprint of the prestigious Brookings Institution and received a great deal of attention during the final years of the Johnson administration and President Nixon's early years. Congress responded by passing laws to double the number of physicians in practice by 1985, making unprecedented sums available to expand existing medical schools and to establish new ones. With Medicare and Medicaid already boosting the demand for medical care far beyond original projections, preventing the doctor shortage became one of the nation's top priorities. (I began my academic career at the University of Colorado School of Medicine in 1973 under a new federal law that earmarked funds to add health economics to the curriculum. The dean opposed renewing the grant that funded my first year on the faculty, arguing that the Hippocratic Oath precluded teaching economics to doctors. I survived by focusing my teaching on statistics and research and ultimately spent nearly 20 years on the faculties of two medical schools.)

Because of the fear that our country would not be able to increase the number of medical doctors fast enough, other health professions volunteered to help. In particular, nursing and dentistry jumped on the bandwagon and began to expand their respective roles in patient care. New training programs with new curricula proliferated throughout the 1970s and 1980s. Federal money was readily available for any accredited academic health center that wanted to join the campaign to alleviate the doctor shortage predicted by Professor Fein. Programs were started to educate not only more physicians but many other health professionals as well. Two official terms were coined to describe the 100+ categories of new or enhanced professions: allied health providers and physician extenders. The titles of all these new professions clearly reinforced the intended subservience to physicians.

Within a few years, allied health providers and physician extenders were ready to take over some of the doctors' traditional tasks. Feeling secure in their status as "captains

---

* R Fein, *The Doctor Shortage: An Economic Diagnosis* (Washington, DC: The Brookings Institution, 1967).

of the ship" and fearing shortage-induced overwork, physicians were willing to delegate some of their clinical tasks for the first time. The medical profession as a whole was on a roll, fueled by the country's willingness to spend extravagantly on health care in response to the very real increases in demand created by Medicare and Medicaid.

Meanwhile, other factors were influencing nursing, the largest of the allied health professions. Driven by the growing feminist movement and economic necessity, more and more young women were choosing a career instead of the traditional housewife role, and many saw nursing as an appealing choice. On the practical side, nursing education was a much less drastic commitment of time and money than medical school. But more importantly, at a time when professional equality of the sexes was still a new concept, nursing was attractive because it was historically a woman's profession. And it was among the most respected professions in the United States. (It still is; nursing had the highest rating for honesty and ethics in Gallup's 2018 ranking of professions. Members of Congress were at the bottom, below telemarketers and car salespeople.*)

PROFESSIONAL MODELS OF NURSING AND MEDICINE—VIVE LA DIFFÉRENCE

Each health profession should have a clearly articulated model that states the fundamental principles and concepts its practitioners apply to patient care. In this context, the nursing and medical models are not the same, reflecting significant differences in the historical development of the two professions. While the allopathic physician is clinically aggressive, invasive, and symptom-oriented (i.e., focused on the disease), the professional nurse concentrates on an individual's mental, physical, and emotional well-being (i.e., focused on the patient). Nurses' training emphasizes personal contact, listening, and caring—in short, a more holistic approach. The difference is often summarized in a saying that doctors treat diseases from a base of organ-specific knowledge, while nurses treat patients by applying general models to individual circumstances. Both approaches are built on very good foundations and meet essential needs, and neither can solve all our health problems on its own.

Health care theorists have argued that the doctor model is inherently "masculine" and the nursing model "feminine," the doctor model "active" and the nursing model "passive," etc. Of course, a sexist differentiation is consistent with medicine's suppression of women at the beginning of the twentieth century. However, some analysts expect the medical model to become less masculine now that the majority of medical students are women. I'd like to think that the real issue is a medical school applicant's orientation to medical science and human caring, not his or her sex. If slightly more

---

* Gallup, "Nurses again outpace other professions for honesty, ethics," December 2018; https://news.gallup.com/poll/245597/nurses-again-outpace-professions-honesty-ethics.aspx.

women meet the criteria for admission, slightly more than half the students in medical school should be women, but medical science should be gender neutral. This point holds for all the professions and their training programs.

Men and women are different in many scientifically demonstrable ways, but the differences should be respected in ways that do not diminish any individual's opportunities to achieve his or her full potential as a human being. I apply the same philosophical outlook to differences between physicians and nurses. The two professions are different, desirably so. *Vive la différence* ... let nurses be nurses and doctors be doctors, male or female. We need both! American health care will be better when competition allows physicians, nurses, and other APs to work not only to the full extent of their licenses but also to fully express their professions' differentiating characteristics (i.e., professional models).

I absolutely do not want nursing and medicine to merge into a single profession. We need competition between health professions, offering us a range of scientifically supported possibilities, not a bigger monopoly. Consumer choice must not be limited because one profession claims superiority over all the others and therefore controls them. The same point applies to competition between physicians and other APs. Physical therapists should not start treating back pain like orthopedic surgeons, certified nurse midwives should not start managing pregnancies like obstetricians, psychologists should not adopt the psychiatric model, etc. Consumers, having different needs and different preferences, deserve choice between all science-based models of care.

Enrollments in nursing programs began to swell in the 1970s. Up till then, the vast majority of nurses had completed two-year or three-year diploma programs that were more apprenticeship than academic in structure. Most of these programs were hospital-based and administered under the tutelage of doctors. Graduates of the programs received a nursing diploma, not a college degree, usually conferred in a "capping" ceremony led by (who else?) a doctor. The event clearly reinforced the image of a nurse as the "doctor's handmaiden."

However, the massive infusion of federal funds for health education fueled an unexpected revolution in nursing. Doctors effectively controlled hospital-based nursing diploma programs, but they did not control the schools of nursing within public and private universities. Academic leaders in the nursing profession began to push for full four-year nursing programs leading to a bachelor of science in nursing, the BSN degree.* Even master's and doctoral degrees became widely available for

---

* For several years in the late 1970s, I served as strategic planning consultant to the Roles and Functions Committee of the American Nurses Association (ANA). The nurses involved in this work were extremely committed to defining the background and skills of the professional nurse, one firmly rooted in the nursing model. Many of the educational reforms in nursing education during the 1980s were a direct result of the extensive work done by members of this committee.

the first time in the late 1970s as nursing professors shifted their focus from teaching historical theory and practice to doing research—dramatically expanding the scientific foundations of nursing.

Overall, nursing education experienced renewal comparable to the Flexner-era transformation of medical education. In particular, nursing moved to four years of university education as the new standard for entry into professional practice—the same length of basic undergraduate training that doctors had used a half-century earlier to prevent any other health professionals from becoming captain of the ship. (We'll explore the current significance of this point in two later chapters. I experienced it firsthand as a medical school professor invited to teach research and statistics courses to graduate students in the nursing school. Nurses wanted to equal physicians in scientific training, but within the nursing model.)

The enhancement of nursing education was initially accomplished with the tacit blessing of doctors who readily acknowledged the need for more and better-trained nurses. However, doctors were undoubtedly expecting the nursing schools to train more handmaidens, not self-confident professionals who were taught to provide care according to the nursing model. Aghast at what it had allowed to happen, the AMA proposed in the early 1990s to establish its own programs for nurse-technicians who would be trained to follow doctors' orders. The plan received no support outside the medical profession and was quietly withdrawn in mid-1993 when the AMA had to turn its attention to fighting Bill and Hillary Clinton's new battle for health reform. The failure of this AMA effort to put nurses back in their place may mark the beginning of the end of the unique reign of doctors, "not with a bang, but a whimper."*

While federal health policy in the 1970s was focused on averting a domestic crisis in medical care delivery—an insufficient supply of doctors to meet the demands of Medicare and Medicaid patients—the Vietnam War was creating an even greater demand for health care professionals. The doctor shortage was particularly acute in the armed forces because of medical student deferments and the lack of volunteer enlistments for an unpopular war where doctors on the front lines faced a 50/50 chance of coming home in a box. As a result, the military began to train its own medics and corpsmen in many medical skills, including some complex procedures (e.g., restoring airways, removing ruptured appendixes, stabilizing erratic heart rhythms, cleaning serious wounds) that had previously been performed only by doctors.

The stateside return of these military-trained medics after the war created a new challenge for the health care delivery system. Many had little more than a high school education, yet they had been trained—well trained—to do many things that only doctors had done before. The physician's assistant (PA) movement was the result. Several medical schools began to train civilians (many of whom were former medics or corpsmen using their veterans' educational benefits) to perform a number

---

* TS Eliot, "The Wasteland."

of advanced procedures as PAs, provided they were trained in a medical school and worked under a doctor's supervision.

Even more substitutes for medical doctors were created when Congress passed several National Highway Transportation and Safety Acts in the late 1960s and 1970s. These laws set up a system of emergency medical technicians (EMTs) and paramedics trained specifically for emergency pre-hospital care of seriously injured persons. Until this system was established, most ambulance services were operated by funeral homes—establishing a rather morbid conflict of interest, in retrospect. The creation of emergency medical services (EMS) systems provided the newly trained professionals with the skills to stabilize critical patients at the scene of an illness or injury before transporting them to definitive medical care at a hospital, a real life-saving improvement over the "scoop and run" approach that prevailed before the creation of EMS.

Paramedics have since proven beyond all doubt that someone besides a doctor can save a life. More than a few of my good physician friends have told me over the years that they would prefer being treated by a paramedic, rather than a physician, at the scene of a serious accident. Their reasoning illustrates the importance of different clinical models. A paramedic's goal is to stabilize the patient for transport to an appropriate setting for treating the problem; a physician is more likely to try to treat the problem at the site of the emergency, without the life-saving resources of a hospital or other adequately equipped facility.

SALUTE TO MILITARY HEALTH CARE

Some of the most important advances in civilian health care, including clinical specialties and technologies, were invented in the US armed forces. The roles of nurse anesthetists, emergency medical technicians/paramedics, physician assistants, physical therapists, and some mental health practitioners might not exist without the military's historic commitment to taking care of soldiers' special needs.* Transformational medical technologies, like telemedicine and life-saving transport systems, also wouldn't be as advanced as they are today if the Department of Defense hadn't assumed responsibility for their research and development.

An excellent example of the military's leadership in innovation is the Telemedicine and Advanced Technology Research Command (TATRC)[†] at Fort Detrick, MD, a major center for scientific and technological work

---

* For an excellent discussion of the military origins of one of the advanced practice professions featured in this book, physical therapy, see M Moffat, "The 1996 APTA presidential address: Three quarters of a century of healing the generations," *Physical Therapy*, 1996; 76(11): 1242--1252.

[†] http://www.tatrc.org/www/default.html.

that ultimately improves health care for all Americans.* The military has also developed leading educational methodologies, simulation training in particular, that are now used in just about every academic health center in the United States. The Uniformed Services University of the Health Sciences (USUHS) offers nationally recognized programs in the education of health professionals.[†] The 59th Medical Wing at Wilford Hall/San Antonio-Lackland Air Force Base (AFB) is one of the military's many regional training centers for allied health practitioners and many clinical specialties.[‡]

Other good examples are too numerous to mention here, but any one example is well worth studying because the military's ongoing contribution to civilian health care deserves more recognition than is generally given. I expect many readers are surprised by how many of the everyday health services discussed in this book were born and bred in military medicine. However, military health care is also very important to the case for independent practice, for three other reasons:

■ First, it proves that many clinical skills traditionally associated with physicians can be performed just as well by highly specialized caregivers who did not go to medical school. As noted above, a doctor isn't the only caregiver qualified to stabilize a seriously injured person for transport to definitive care at a hospital. Paramedics—created by and for the US military and then adopted for civilian use—do the job at least as well as physicians, and they are adequately trained and certified to perform this specific service without physician supervision. Some relatively uncomplicated surgical procedures (e.g., appendectomies, C-sections) are successfully performed in military operational settings. Hence, military health care is a model for the full scope of civilian practice. It demonstrates why training and competence, not terminal degree (a degree for entry into practice), should define who is qualified to deliver unsupervised health care. If this arrangement is good enough for our men and women in uniform, why isn't it good enough for the rest of us? (Legislators and regulators should ask this question to any doctors who are lobbying to maintain the medical monopoly.)

■ Second, the armed forces' overall excellence in health care for active duty personnel shows that a doctor does not need to be in charge of everything. Military rank, not academic degree, defines who has ultimate authority on health units. The officer in charge of a clinical

* https://www.detrick.army.mil.
† https://www.usuhs.edu.
‡ https://www.59mdw.af.mil/About/Fact-Sheets-and-Documents/Display/Article/466715/59th-medical-wing/.

service, having worked up through the chain of a health command, is chosen for leadership on the basis of his or her demonstrated management skills. Corporals report to sergeants (who were once corporals), colonels report to brigadier generals, etc. The colonel can be a physician, and the commanding general a nurse anesthetist or clinical psychologist. The key point here is that nurses don't necessarily report to physicians, physical therapists report to senior officers who may or may not be physicians, etc. Demonstrated knowledge and cumulative experience concerning the job to be done, not the professional degree, define who does what in military medicine—and the system works very well.

■ Third, in the military's rank-based system, health professionals have no degree-dependent income or other superior market power to protect. A general can't economically exploit a colonel by personally keeping part of the operating budget that pays for the colonel's work. Military health professionals therefore don't waste time fighting to protect their income. They earn their pay based on time in rank. Those in administrative positions surely spend time protecting budgets for their clinical units and commands, but that's a necessary task of health systems management, not a telltale sign of medical monopoly. In other words, the military model shows that a health system can perform very well without one health profession extracting a monopoly rent from income earned by another. So why do legislators and regulators in so many states still condone the practice in civilian health care? Let's ask them … and the physicians who cajole them to do so. The honest answer will reveal one more unnecessary reason why civilian health care costs so much more in the US than anywhere else.

In conclusion, military medicine does great things without requiring that a doctor be captain of the ship. In fact, military medicine realized well over a century ago that physicians could not meet all its needs and therefore created many of the advanced practitioners who could do so much more in civilian health care if freed from the constraints of medical monopoly. Thank you, US armed forces, for your innovative leadership.

At approximately the same time, a nationally respected pediatrician, named Dr. Henry Silver, decided that nurses could be trained to provide a good deal of pediatric care in a fully professional and competent manner. (Dr. Silver became a colleague of mine at the University of Colorado School of Medicine; we had adjacent offices for a few years, so some of his thinking must have passed through the wall.) He knew that the vast majority of professional nurses were women and mothers who knew a lot about kids. Dr. Silver also saw no direct correlation between pediatricians' specialty training, three years of caring for high-risk infants in large teaching hospitals, and the most common pediatric services provided in a doctor's office, such as dealing with earache, performing routine physicals and well-child assessments, and monitoring growth and development.

In 1965, believing the use of medical specialists for primary care was a misallocation of resources, Dr. Silver and the dean of the University of Colorado College of Nursing, Dr. Loretta Ford (to whom this book is dedicated) created the nation's first post-baccalaureate program to train non-physician caregivers for advanced practice. Drs. Silver and Ford determined that bachelor degree-trained nurses were well prepared to learn basic childcare, so they set up a revolutionary master's degree program for pediatric nurse practitioners at the College of Nursing—revolutionary because, as already noted, all previous programs to solve the doctor shortage were created at Schools of Medicine to train "physician extenders" who could only practice under the supervision of a physician.

The Colorado demonstration program quickly became a big success. Pediatricians liked it because the first advanced practice nurses provided excellent primary care for kids with routine health problems, liberating the doctors to treat seriously ill children who needed specialty services. Perhaps most importantly, from today's perspective of patient-driven care, mothers of kids with normal ailments quickly expressed a preference for the pediatric nurse practitioners when given a choice of caregivers. The Colorado State Legislature soon updated the state's medical practice acts, giving these qualified non-physicians the legal authority to diagnose and treat patients without physician supervision. The rest is history—the nurse practitioner movement was born. And so were the battles over direct consumer access and independent practice authority!

Nursing schools across the country began offering advanced training that led to a master's degree in basic nursing skills. Many graduates of these new post-baccalaureate programs became the first family nurse practitioners. Though trained to diagnose and treat a number of illnesses from the perspective of the nursing model, advanced practice nurses often found themselves limited by a state's medical practice act. These nurses had at least as much training as physicians in a broad base of primary health services, in addition to the nursing model's focus on patients (in contrast to the medical model's focus on disease). However, in almost all instances the nurses with advanced training had to work under the supervision of a physician. They almost always had to work in a physician's office for a salary. Physicians billed insurance for the services and got to pocket the difference between the professional fee and the salary they paid the nurses to do the work. Physicians took classes to learn how to make this arrangement work to their financial benefit, with the promise that it was highly profitable—one well worth protecting, as any monopolist would tell you.

As a late-1970s concession to meeting the needs of Medicare and Medicaid patients, nurse practitioners and other new non-physician caregivers began to win the right to practice independently of physicians. Open-minded legislators in a few states began asking the same questions being asked by the growing numbers of new, well-trained professional nurses, "Why is the practice of medicine in this country reserved only for doctors? We can provide many of these services just as well, if not better. Why can't we be allowed to do the jobs we are trained to do?" In other words, "Why can't we practice without medical supervision at the full scope of legal authority granted by the State Board of Nursing?" Doctors' economically self-serving answers were no longer convincing in many state legislatures.

As this historical review has shown, a national response to address the impending doctor shortage with non-physician practitioners was accelerating by the mid-1970s. The momentum was not being successfully contained by organized medicine in many jurisdictions for a variety of reasons. By the early 1980s, a few more states began loosening the power of medical practice acts and allowing selected non-physician practitioners to practice independently of doctors, giving consumers the right to see these newly trained professionals without a doctor's order. The number of permissive states has grown in subsequent years, but more than half still put outdated roadblocks in the way of consumers who could have benefited from direct access to advanced practitioners trained to provide services without the unnecessary, cost-increasing supervision of a physician.

Beyond the Doctor Shortage

The year 1983 was a watershed year in health care finance. Before then, almost all third-party insurance reimbursement was paid to hospitals on a cost basis. Hospitals would bill insurers according to the full costs they had incurred to provide the invoiced services. Insurers sent back the requested payment retrospectively, after care was delivered, no questions asked. Of course, payments would be questioned if fraud was suspected, but wasteful spending or bad management never got in the way of the general principle of reimbursing a hospital's total costs. This wasteful arrangement ended in 1983 when Congress unexpectedly passed legislation to create a prospective payment system (PPS) for Medicare reimbursement to hospitals.

This dramatic shift in federal policy—from retrospectively and fully reimbursing incurred costs to paying a fixed, prospectively determined amount that may not cover all costs —was an expression of Congressional disgust with the uncontrolled growth in medical spending financed by American taxpayers. It was the first serious federal reform to limit spending on health care. Hospitals and doctors did not have to make any sacrifices under the old, cost-based reimbursement mechanism because the government was effectively writing blank checks. The new system was intended to impose some cost-consciousness by putting a lid on payment. If a provider couldn't find a way to survive on fixed payments by lowering costs of production, that became the provider's problem under PPS.

The prospective payment system was also Congress's way of controlling the size of the health care "pie" by determining in advance exactly how much the federal government was willing to spend on medical goods and services, in contrast to the retrospective system that paid whatever the providers charged. Reimbursement was further simplified by lumping thousands of hospital-based procedures into a few hundred diagnostic-related groups (DRGs). Hospitals put up quite a fight against the change in policy, but Congress ultimately prevailed and forced hospitals to accept the new system of payment—which history has subsequently shown was not the same as forcing hospitals to reduce their spending. They quickly learned to "game the system," billing for higher levels of services and exploiting other loopholes in the new rules and regulations governing reimbursement.

Congress went after hospitals before it went after doctors because inpatient services accounted for roughly 40% of all dollars spent on health care, roughly twice the level of spending on physician services, and because organized medicine fought harder than hospitals when Congress decided to bring an end to unlimited, unpredictable spending on health care. However, the same general approach to restraining reimbursement was applied several years later to physicians under a Resource-Based Relative Value System (RBRVS). Physicians quickly referred to it as "Really Bad Reimbursement Very Soon"; hospitals had already started calling the DRG system "Da Revenue's Gone." RBRVS, developed under a federal contract with a Harvard medical economist named William Hsiao, theoretically based payment to physicians on the actual costs of producing services rather than the old system that did not have any relationship to costs of production.*

Before RBRVS, doctors were comfortably accustomed to being paid "usual, customary, and reasonable" (UCR) fees—a benefit they had secured by controlling the leading private health plans. Insurers looked at the profile of all fees for a particular service and paid any submitted fee up to a certain cut-off point, commonly the 90th percentile. This system may seem salutary for refusing to pay the "unreasonable" fee in the top 10%, but it did not require any competition between doctors. New doctors would look around to see what established doctors were charging, and then set their fees near the top of the range, but hopefully below the 90th percentile. If a fee was rejected because it was too high, it was reduced and resubmitted until it fell just below the threshold.

Hence, UCR reimbursement consistently and predictably increased the overall level of fees. (By statistical definition, adding any value above the average raises the average.) Led by the doctor-controlled "Blues," the health insurance industry paid submitted fees, with a token rejection of the highest charges. A truly competitive market would never support such a one-sided financial arrangement. Doctors were free to charge more or less whatever they wanted, confident that no other health professional would drive fees down by submitting a below-average bill for the same service. This outcome should not have surprised medical economists. It's perfectly consistent with monopoly behavior.

Even though the Hsiao study was generated by a reasonable goal of bringing reimbursement in line with actual costs, something UCR fees did not do, it was

---

* WC Hsiao et al., "Estimating physicians' work for a Resource-Based Relative Value Scale," *New England Journal of Medicine*, 1988; 319: 835–841.

conducted in a highly political environment and has been criticized for the resulting methodological flaws. (Even Professor Hsiao expressed dismay at how bureaucrats translated his recommendations into payment policy.*) In addition to bringing fees in line with actual costs, RBRVS was also supposed to transfer some income from highly paid proceduralists, such as surgeons, to primary care physicians whose services had been undervalued by surgeon-controlled insurance companies.

INCONSISTENT LESSONS FROM THE 1980S AND 1990S

The DRG reimbursement system was based on a model of health care quality developed by a Yale professor, John Thompson. Thompson's model had nothing to do with payment systems, but his innovative research was being widely discussed when health policy wonks were looking for a new way to structure payment. The bureaucracy appropriated his quality assessment model and tried to make it fit the payment system, which probably helps explain why PPS failed to stop the increase in hospital spending. (Like Bill Hsiao, John Thompson sought to distance himself from a policy that was associated with his name but implemented with no direct relationship to his actual work.)

Even worse, historical charges were used as the basis for DRG payments, even though they had no demonstrated relationship to actual costs of production. No analysis of actual costs was ever performed by the policy community. The new system just repackaged the inefficiencies of the historical payment mechanism, akin to putting lipstick on a pig. What politicians set out to do had very little in common with what policy-makers and regulators ultimately did. In my opinion, if you were to read everything about PPS and DRGs and spend hours trying to make sense of everything, it still would not make sense to you—not in the historical context of the 1990s, nor two decades later. Trust me, I've tried.

Public pronouncements to the contrary, most members of Congress did not care whether PPS and DRGs were fair to doctors. Elected officials voted for the changes because they believed doctors and hospitals had taken advantage of Medicare and Medicaid. I spent a lot of time in Washington policy circles at the time that these reforms were imposed, and I believe most Members of Congress truly wanted to give patients better access to health care and to end the constantly rising, completely unpredictable increases in the cost of health care. In spite of my cynicism toward the eventual outcomes, I draw one hopeful conclusion from the health reform battles of the 1980s and 1990s: organized medicine did not get everything it wanted. Politicians and bureaucrats were able to change some important rules of the game over strong opposition from the health professionals who played *and* refereed it.

---

* WC Hsiao et al., "Assessing the implementation of physician payment reform," *New England Journal of Medicine*, 1993; 328: 928–933.

By learning how to bill for the most profitable services and otherwise "gaming the system," hospitals and doctors have made lots of money under PPS and RBRVS payment reforms that were supposed to hold their incomes in check. A whole industry of reimbursement consultants developed to help providers make money while staying one step ahead of regulatory interpretation and legal enforcement. Intelligent observers would therefore be on very firm ground if they questioned the wisdom of basing future health reforms on payment reform. Ending the medical monopoly would be a far more productive way to begin putting downward pressure on prices in health care.

Indeed, economic studies generally suggest that any reductions in costs of care since the 1980s and 1990s have not come from payment reforms, but from competition between sites of care (inpatient vs. outpatient; traditional vs. retail and virtual), productivity enhancement (e.g., information and communication technologies, Lean manufacturing, Six Sigma), and scientific advances (e.g., genetics, pharmacology, precision medicine). Doctors have embraced these forms of competition. Indeed, they have led innovation in these sectors as successful entrepreneurs. We therefore have proof that doctors can do just fine when pressed to compete—one more reason why state legislators should remove the remaining barriers to competition from advanced practitioners created in response to the doctor shortage.

Physicians are perfectly capable of dealing creatively and constructively with competition, but a vocal minority will still put up quite a fight to suppress it. Medicine's professional organizations and political action committees will continue making major campaign donations to get politicians' attention. They will continue making undocumented charges ("Trust me, I'm a doctor") that advanced practitioners provide inferior quality of care. They will continue to divert public attention from the fundamental cost and quality issues already addressed in this book. Legislators and regulators must therefore demand that doctors present a comparable body of studies to counterbalance hundreds of peer-reviewed publications that show advanced practitioners are at least as competent as physicians within their defined scopes of practice. This professional literature on APs is extensively referenced in the remaining chapters. Given that I am unable to find any studies that physicians might use to defend their assertions, it should not take long to pass legislation that eliminates the medical monopoly. There's really nothing to debate.

The Mirage of Managed Care

The battle over the Clinton reforms lasted longer than necessary because opposition forces were slow to recognize the importance of competition as a viable solution. For most of 1993, Senator Bob Dole and other Republican leaders attacked "Hillarycare" with the argument that our country did not need another big government program. This position did not faze reformers sequestered in the White House because they had not decided to propose a big government program. (In fact, we now know that they had not decided much of anything.) When Bill Clinton finally introduced his incongruous reform plan near the end of the year, Republican opponents prolonged the debate over it with the equally absurd position that there was no health care crisis to solve. That is, reform was unnecessary because the health system was working just fine.

Realizing after a few months that most Americans were not buying the "no problem" argument, Republicans discovered a position that ultimately helped defeat the Clintons' reform package: yes, there was a health care crisis, but the market could take care of it. A new concept called managed care—an amalgam of capitated health maintenance organizations (HMOs) and discounted preferred provider organizations (PPOs)—was reportedly lowering the cost of health care in markets as diverse as Minneapolis-St. Paul and Los Angeles-San Diego. It could presumably work its wonders just about anywhere else if government would just get out of the way. The conventional wisdom of managed care said that savvy buyers and aggressive brokers operating on the buyers' behalf would make health care less expensive.

After wandering for nearly two years in the desert of unfocused government reforms, voters and legislators alike were relieved to see something so seductively simple on the horizon. Managed care glimmered like an oasis in the desert, if purchasers would just develop demand-side power to counteract supply-side monopoly. Competition between health plans, not regulation of providers, would presumably achieve the goals of health reform. On the basis of this vision, the nation's focus shifted almost overnight from government-driven reform to private sector competition between managed care organizations. Sadly, competition between managed care organizations didn't then, and doesn't now, resolve the adverse economic consequences of doctors' control over qualified competitors.

Managed care defies simple definition. It is not a standardized, universally meaningful term. A common insider saying, "If you've seen one managed care program, you've seen one managed care program," is telling. Original managed care and its subsequent variations encompass a variety of operating principles, but, in general, the common element is an imposition of some form of restriction on the delivery of care: a gatekeeper, a formulary, a mandatory treatment protocol, a dollar cap on coverage, a limited panel of providers covered by the plan, etc. These changes often posed ethical conflicts for caregivers, physicians and advanced practitioners alike.*

Although managed care is often positioned as the remedy for traditional fee-for-service (FFS) reimbursement, it has not eliminated FFS. One long-standing version of managed care, the preferred provider organization (PPO), still pays

---

* CM Ulrich, KL Soeken, and Miller N., "Ethical conflict associated with managed care: Views of nurse practitioners," *Nursing Research*, 2003; 52(3): 168–175.

service-specific fees to many or most of its participating providers, but with discounts. Another, the health maintenance organization (HMO), collects premiums and agrees to be at risk on a capitated basis (i.e., fixed payment per member per month), but many of its participating providers are still paid fees for billed services. The latest variant, an accountable care organization (ACO), is still a work in progress. A few ACOs have achieved impressive reductions in the costs of care they provide, often with extensive use of advanced practitioners, but most have failed. Government efforts to advance the concept of ACO have been unfocused and inconsistent.

Managed care reforms, therefore, have not solved the FFS cost problem as promised by their proponents. Nor have they uniformly pressured doctor-driven PPOs, HMOs, and ACOs to provide direct consumer access to APs in order to pass along the lower costs. Since its inception in the 1990s, managed care has effectively provided a subtle but perverse incentive to preserve the medical monopoly and FFS. Managed care provider organizations commonly provide services with less-expensive APs while charging doctors' higher fees—pocketing the difference as excess profit. It's a classic case of a monopoly rent, a major market failure in terms of economic theory. (It's also a classic case of exploitation of labor in Marxist economic theory, but I'll say no more on this point.)

Touted as the hope for health reform during the mid-term elections of 1994, managed care became its hype (i.e., deception) by the end of the decade, but it has never really disappeared. It did not eliminate old problems; it did create new ones. The rate of increase in health care spending declined for a few years after the mid-terms, but it quickly returned to historic levels. However, the darker side of 1990s-style managed care and its various iterations is the fact that the number of employees covered by health insurance fell substantially even as the number of employees rose to an all-time high. Managed care did nothing to move our country toward the Clintons' goal of increasing access to care through less-expensive insurance coverage.

Further, state legislatures and the US Congress were pressured to pass many laws in 1996 and 1997 to counteract managed care's common practice of denying coverage for pre-existing medical conditions. (In my opinion, one of the Clintons' biggest strategic errors was putting so much emphasis on the problems of the uninsured. Focusing attention on *insured* Americans who were being denied services under managed care plans would have been much more successful politically.) In addition, media coverage has exposed considerable greed and incompetence in the managed care business. Fraud by providers is a widespread, ongoing problem. Finally, total spending on health care continued to rise as managed care plans gained market share during the 1990s. All other things being equal, total spending on medical services should have fallen if managed care were accomplishing its promised objectives. Instead, considerable money was transferred from hospitals, doctors, and patients to investors and financial executives. Moneyed interests came out ahead on health reform in the 1990s; consumers fell further behind.

Transition to the Twenty-First Century

Health reformers' efforts to deal with the undesirable economic consequences of medical monopoly culminated in the 1990s with managed care. It did not live up to its expectations then and hasn't since. Medical services were as overpriced after managed care as they were before it. We still need competition in the medical marketplace, which, in economic terms, means we need to give *informed* consumers the choice to buy directly from all *qualified* sellers in markets where no buyer or seller has enough power to restrict allocation of resources and control the prices of health-producing goods and services.

In spite of managed care's shortcomings in practice, it rests on a powerful idea in theory. Managed care was intended to attack the long-standing problem of paying providers without questioning whether the care was truly necessary or competitively priced. If care could be managed so that unproductive services were eliminated, either less money could be spent on health care without reducing individual and social well-being, or a healthier population could be produced for the same total spending. (In terms of economic analysis, this is efficiency.) Unfortunately, health care providers in the 1990s did not have many tools to eliminate waste from the system.

Fortunately, the rapid development of information technologies and sophisticated analytics over the past two decades make this possible today. For example, and to organized medicine's credit, a dozen medical specialty associations have created a great program called Choosing Wisely (www.choosingwisely.org). It provides excellent information to help consumers identify medical services that are not generally worth the money paid for them. A strong and consistent body of medical literature suggests that roughly one-third of all dollars spent on medical services cannot reasonably be expected to improve the patient's health.[*]

As explained in *Paradox and Imperatives in Health Care* (second edition), we could improve the health of Americans if we reallocated this wasted money to cost-effective care.[†] To facilitate the necessary shift from unproductive to productive utilization, we must eliminate the medical monopoly that diminishes consumers' ability to make clinically and economically wise choices. Twentieth-century laws that protect the doctor as captain of the ship must be updated to reflect competitive alternatives created over the past 50 years. Traditional American medicine is no longer the only vehicle to get the medical marketplace where it needs to be, and physicians are no longer the only professionals qualified to steer the course. Let's now explore the history and implications of this important concept.

---

[*] Using Medicare data, the Dartmouth Institute for Health Policy and Clinical Practice has done pathbreaking work in this area. Important information at its findings for the US is available at https://atlasdata.dartmouth.edu.

[†] This concept is fully developed in JC Bauer, *Paradox and Imperatives in Health Care: Redirecting Reform for Efficiency and Effectiveness*, second edition (New York: CRC Press, 2015).

Chapter 4

Captain of the Ship: Legal Foundations of Independent Practice

The American public interest was generally well served when unscientific caregivers were driven out of business early in the twentieth century. By exposing glaring deficiencies in the knowledge and skills of practitioners who had not graduated from a university-level program, Abraham Flexner and other reformers of the era built solid clinical foundations for the doctor-driven health system we know today. However, for reasons explained in the previous chapter, a new class of comparably trained competitors began to emerge following the creation of Medicare and Medicaid (1965) and the end of the Vietnam War (1975). The subsequent professional development of these independently competent non-physicians—collectively categorized as *advanced practitioners* (AP)—eliminates the historical justification for allowing physicians to control APs through state medical practice acts. Therefore, the medical monopoly is clearly an impediment to accomplishing the fundamental goals of health reform.

As the historical analysis has shown in previous chapters, early twentieth-century physicians did not conspire to raise prices or otherwise diminish consumer welfare. Sick or injured Americans benefited from the disappearance of the charlatans who peddled unproven cures, often worse than the conditions they pretended to cure. Medical doctors could reasonably have expected their incomes to improve in the absence of competition from quacks, but the historical record shows that physicians were fundamentally dedicated to improving health care. Given their allegiance to scientific principles and patient welfare, the early twentieth-century medical doctors did not deserve to be lumped with their industrial contemporaries, the robber barons, whose motto was "buyer beware." The doctors' proud credos were "do no harm" and "heal thyself." In the spirit of protecting patients and self-improvement, university-trained physicians argued, with good reason, that they should be given superior authority as "captain of the ship."

The "captain of the ship" doctrine, a legal principle originating in maritime law, was used to place the medical doctor in command of everyone involved in treating a patient. It makes all other health care providers subject to the doctor's orders and supervision. The principle is not inherently self-serving, however, because in return for being granted full and final authority, the captain accepts responsibility for work done by members of the crew. If caregivers other than the physician make mistakes that harm a patient, the physician-cum-captain accepts liability for the negligent acts of the others (who may also have legal liability, depending on the circumstances). Just as the captain of a seagoing vessel has ultimate responsibility for the ship's entire crew, the legal doctrine put everyone on the health care delivery team—nurse, pharmacist, technician, therapist, and aide—under the doctor's command and control.

The principle reflects more than the common business practice of one person, "the boss," being in charge. Bad things tend to happen when the crew starts working against the captain's orders; mutiny on the high seas is a crime for good reason. But the doctors' case for "captain of the ship" authority has been additionally based on the premise that doctors are uniquely qualified to be in charge of the entire crew because they have more education than any of the other members. Doctors have long made a big point that they go to medical school for four years, at least a year or two more than the training programs of the other health professionals who work with and for them. It is directly reflected in the common phrase, "doctor knows best." Physicians almost always mention the longer duration of their education when seeking to justify authority over nurses and other health professionals.

Having more training was a defensible argument well into the twentieth century, but it is no longer valid for several reasons. First, APs are now trained in graduate (i.e., post-baccalaureate) programs of comparable length, at the same academic health centers where the medical schools are located. Further, medical schools are beginning to eliminate the fourth year of MD and DO programs. A growing number of medical educators believe that learning objectives can be met in three years by eliminating a considerable amount of redundant content, particularly in the basic sciences, that is included in the traditional four-year curriculum. Academic leaders are also cutting specialty rotations unrelated to the general knowledge required of a physician. Medical education, like medical practice, is finally addressing its long-standing inefficiency (i.e., waste), with extra pressure coming from medical students who believe they learn little of value in the fourth year while incurring tens of thousands of dollars in extra tuition debt.

But last, and definitely not least, length of training programs is no longer an appropriate measure of competence to provide health services—rendering irrelevant the argument that physician control is necessary because doctors have more years of education than anyone else on the ship. The vocal minority of doctors in organized medicine still like to argue that APs require supervision because they have less training, but my extensive research for this book (all three editions!) has not produced a single scientific article to support the premise that total years of education correlates with clinical superiority or supervisory authority. APs actually have a lot more training than doctors in many clinical areas where their scopes of practice overlap, and, as we will see, peer-reviewed publications consistently show that APs are at least as qualified as physicians within the overlapping areas.

Given significant differences in clinical models defined by professional licensing boards, APs also provide beneficial health services that doctors do not provide at all. For example, many medical specialties use surgical approaches to treat problems that APs address just as effectively without surgery for many patients. Some surgeons argue that a physician must decide whether surgery is needed before offering non-surgical options, including referral to an AP. Patients absolutely should understand their options, but an AP is trained to evaluate individuals' needs and required to refer patients for surgery when indicated. The real issue for both physicians and APs is making appropriate referrals—which is not related to years of training.

Allowing physicians to control access to APs not only deprives patients of a reasonable choice between surgical and non-surgical treatment options; it also makes consumers pay more for health care because surgery is almost always more expensive than the non-interventional alternatives. This historical bias toward surgical care is one of the most important reasons to eliminate laws and business practices that allow physicians to restrict informed consumer choice. Americans pay a high price for it, with no evidence that we get correspondingly better outcomes in return.

In spite of changes in the circumstances that once justified medical monopoly, many doctors still defend their traditional authority in the same old ways. Perhaps the most blatant example of this outdated power grab is organized medicine's persistent pressure on state legislatures and boards of professional practice to disallow other professions from delivering services that doctors consider to be within the scope of the practice of medicine. It's surely a major reason why the well-known journalist told me back in 1993 (see pages 1–2) that neither she nor anyone else would ever want to see an independent nurse practitioner or clinical pharmacist for health problems. Like so many Americans, she believed that doctors were the only practitioners with the requisite knowledge to diagnose disease and prescribe treatments. In the journalist's mind, only *the* captain of *the* ship could know everything that needed to be known and set things right when someone else did something wrong. Why? Because the doctor told her so.

For example, orthopedic surgeons have prevented podiatrists from performing specific foot operations in many markets, even though the same procedures are taught in podiatry schools and performed quite competently by podiatrists in other states where orthopedists do not have the power to prevent direct consumer access to podiatrists. In many states where nurse practitioners are allowed to diagnose an illness without medical oversight, physicians still control a nurse practitioner's (NP) ability to write the prescriptions to treat it—even though the state board of nursing grants independent prescriptive authority to NPs *and* requires them to maintain current pharmaceutical knowledge via continuing education programs comparable to those taken by physicians. (Physicians cannot claim that their programs are more rigorous. In my experience as a presenter at continuing education programs for advanced practice nurses and for physicians, nursing programs actually tend to enforce higher quality standards for faculty and content.) In the case of certified nurse midwives (CNMs), many are only allowed to deliver specific services under the supervision of a doctor, even though the CNMs are more extensively trained in providing them. In my own ongoing struggles with lower back pain in Illinois, I had to get a prescription from a physician (generating an extra fee for the office visit) so that a doctorally trained physical therapist could provide the treatment that worked for me. I did not need a doctor's order to get the same care from an equally qualified physical therapist when I previously lived in Colorado.

WHO'S ENTITLED TO BE CALLED DOCTOR, REALLY?

The MD or DO is an undergraduate degree in American institutions of higher education, and a high school diploma is the only degree required for acceptance into medical school. (Most students admitted to medical school have a baccalaureate degree, but this is due to the intense competition for entry into one of the highest-paying professions in the US.) Admission to traditional graduate schools requires a BS, BA, or other undergraduate degree, but medical schools are not graduate schools. Rather, they are a cross between a university and a technical school. The first two years focus on the academic study of basic and medical sciences; the third and fourth years of medical school provide "hands-on" experience with rotations through a variety of clinical specialties. Medical schools do not provide the equivalent of a graduate school's in-depth focus on a specific academic discipline, nor the advanced original research required for a PhD or ScD.

Why then, do MDs and DOs not only claim the title of doctor, but recognition as "a real doctor" when in the presence of those who only finished graduate school? When I joined the medical school faculty at the University of Colorado in the mid-1970s upon completing a PhD in medical economics, I was regularly reminded by some MD colleagues that I was not a "real doctor," even though I had spent as many years in graduate school as they had spent in medical school. A few faculty peers pointedly addressed me as Mr. Bauer.

Not surprisingly, American physicians' appropriation of "doctor" is commonly linked to the medical monopoly they created in the twentieth century, and it is unique to the United States. Physicians in other countries have traditionally been awarded undergraduate degrees after completing four years of medical education, such as MB for Medical Bachelor in Great Britain, and they have been addressed as "mister." ("Doctor" is generally reserved for university professors in Europe.) They had no exalted status; they always faced competition from other health professionals and earned middle-class incomes. They never benefited from anything like the Flexner Report that allowed American doctors to monopolize not only the medical marketplace but also a professional title to go with it. Perhaps this international difference in the use of "doctor" helps explain why Americans spend almost twice as much on health care as Europeans, with no better health to show for it. Just saying.

More examples of doctors' exclusionary market behavior against advanced practitioners are presented in subsequent discussions of specific health professions (e.g., nursing, pharmacy, physical therapy, and mental and behavioral health). The key point at this stage of analysis is that consumers pay higher prices and/or have reduced access to care in the states where physicians still exercise authority over APs. Given the complete absence of scientifically valid evidence that the captain of the ship doctrine improves consumer welfare in today's medical marketplaces, it's time for consumers in all states to have direct access to APs who are free to provide the full scope of services authorized by their professional licensing boards. This essential path to reform is obvious, but it is not easy.

Like their counterparts in other industries, some leaders of organized medicine and individual physicians work hard to preserve the monopoly powers associated with being *the* captain of *the* ship. Cartoons in the first and second editions of this book illustrated the point with images of the "USS *Allopathic Medicine*" patrolling the sea and shooting down any other vessels that dared set sail. (See next page.) Allopathic medicine's ship was, of course, much bigger than any other health profession's ship, and it was able to keep the entire sea clear of intruders for most of the twentieth century because no one dared challenge it. However, by the end of the previous editions, cartoons showed several other professions successfully launching seaworthy boats in safe harbors (i.e., in consumer-friendly states) that were not controlled by monopoly-defending physicians. Let's look at the concepts that not only made this progress possible in many states but now make it imperative for the future well-being of Americans all across the country.

Professionalism and Autonomous Authority

Being captain of the ship that controls the sea is different from being a professional. For example, university professors are professionals, but they do not have the self-designated authority to prevent others from teaching or researching within their fields of academic expertise. Certified public accountants are at the top of the professional hierarchy of financial scorekeepers, but they cannot unilaterally prevent other accountants and bookkeepers from preparing our taxes. Architects are the professionals associated with designing buildings, but they do not have the power to prevent engineers or contractors from making houses, much less the power to oversee their work. Likewise, attorneys have special roles in the judicial system, but they cannot claim the power to prevent a real estate agent from managing the sale of a property or an arbitrator from resolving a dispute outside a court of law.

Physicians are, in effect, the only learned professionals who have continually placed themselves at the top of the hierarchy of all workers within the profession *and* established the right to control the work of others. There are, of course, exceptions that prove the rule in the medical marketplace. Dentists, optometrists, podiatrists, and chiropractors have managed to maintain considerable autonomous authority within the legally defined scope of practice of their respective professions. In some instances, they have protected their independence by agreeing not to provide specific services that physicians defined as the practice of medicine, rather than agreeing to provide the services under the supervision of a physician. However, patients can see them without a referral from a physician, and physicians do not have the authority to review their patient records or co-sign their prescriptions.

Advanced practitioners now deserve comparable status as autonomous caregivers with sole authority to control their practices. They have attained full professional status by developing their own clinical models, establishing their own educational requirements, setting their own publicly accountable licensure and certification procedures, defining and enforcing their own standards of professional ethics (i.e., acceptable practice), and setting their own standards for quality assurance. The result is now an acceptable quality of care provided by advanced practitioners who were, until recently, categorized as *allied health practitioners*—a euphemism I dislike almost as much as *mid-level practitioners*. Today's advanced practitioners have become fully qualified to do what they do, without physician supervision; *allied* and *mid-level* imply inferiority and subservience that is no longer appropriate. After all, would you want to fly on a commercial airliner if the first officer was called a mid-level pilot? The captain probably has more years of experience, but the first officer has the same training as the captain and is just as capable of flying the plane on his or her own.

Lawmakers and regulators are not alone in confounding autonomous authority and professionalism. Health policy specialists have generally deferred to physicians' claims of professional superiority, perpetuating the economic harms of medical monopoly in the process. If those responsible for shaping health reform are really serious about improving quality and reducing costs, they will shift their preoccupation from changing the way we pay for care to enabling competition between all the practitioners who are qualified to provide it. Let's therefore look at the seven criteria that physicians used to justify their authority over others in the twentieth century. We'll quickly see that APs are just as qualified to be ships' captains—an essential step on the American path to health reform for the twenty-first century.

Seven Foundations of Professional Authority and Autonomy

Abraham Flexner's 1910 report for the Carnegie Foundation did more than expose wide quality variations among the many commercial and academic institutions that trained doctors. It notably narrowed the definition of medical care to the science-based, disease-oriented, AMA-endorsed approach taught in universities and it gave physicians captain of the ship authority over all other practitioners under medical practice acts. The monopoly power inherent in this arrangement was defensible at the time because non-medical doctors were harming consumers, physically and fiscally. The need to protect public safety outweighed concern about the economic powers—uncompetitive prices, excess profits, restricted choices—that physicians would predictably reap and strenuously protect when competition was eliminated.

Legal structures to regulate the medical monopoly developed at different rates and in different ways on a state-by-state basis, but they were based on seven reasonable principles that have stood the tests of time. This section explores the principles that physicians have used over the past century to justify their authority to issue orders that all other caregivers must follow. These foundations of professional autonomy are as valid today as they were when elaborated in the Flexnerian era, but medical doctors are no longer the only health professionals who meet them.

The principles explained in this chapter were drawn from extensive research for the first edition of *Not What the Doctor Ordered*. They incorporate key observations made by the scholars whose histories of American health care are referenced in previous chapters. This seven-part formulation received many favorable comments over the past 25 years and has reportedly been useful in state-level efforts to define defensible and consistent criteria for independent practice, so I have retained it for this edition (with updated commentary, of course).

It is somewhat surprising to me that other health industry specialists have not published similar checklists, given that so much has been written on the evolution of state medical practice acts and physicians' authority over other health professionals. I have not been able to find any other general frameworks. The National Council of State Boards of Nursing has published a consensus model specifically for professional nursing,* but independent practice authority must be granted to advanced practitioners of all health professions that qualify under criteria that evolved from Flexner-era reforms. The required steps to independence are illustrated by this cartoon of the captain—a doctor, of course—standing proudly at the helm of the good ship, USS *Allopathic Medicine*:

Let's look at each of these steps to independent practice in enough depth to guide legislators, regulators, and other officials responsible for updating laws and regulations to ensure direct consumer access to advanced practitioners in states where competition is still constrained by medical monopoly. Any health profession that meets all these requirements deserves the legal right to full independent practice authority. By the way, the seven steps are not presented in any rank order. All are equally necessary to justify independent practice by any health profession … including physicians!

1. Advanced Education

As the preceding review of history has shown, education was the common denominator of reasons for medicine's claim to authority as captain of the ship. Spending

---

* https://www.ncsbn.org/aprn-consensus.htm.

more years in university-based scientific training than any other type of doctor, allopaths arguably knew more than the others and, therefore, possessed the superior knowledge expected of a person in charge. By comparison, many non-medical doctors learned their trade in informal apprenticeships, often with no classroom attendance or required readings. Even some allopathic medical schools did not meet the minimum standards expected of a four-year academic program. There were many "diploma mills" where a doctor could get a degree in just a few months, often without spending any time in a laboratory or at the bedside. As Flexner reported after visiting well over 100 programs that trained doctors of various professional persuasions, the quality of education varied from generally inadequate to "utterly wretched." A few "good" schools offered adequate facilities and required four years of post-baccalaureate, college-level education, plus some practical training for an MD degree.

The traditional four-year requirement is based on the curriculum adopted in 1892 at Johns Hopkins, the university program Flexner placed at the top of his ranked list of American medical schools. Four years of training probably was adequate, given the medical knowledge of the day. However, the breadth and depth of medical science has increased dramatically since then, to the point that no one—not even a doctor—can know it all. The length of time at medical school would surely be several decades by now if the duration of training had increased in proportion to the increase in knowledge about human health. But it remained at four years until a few medical schools recently lowered it to three. This movement to a shorter program is expected to grow for reasons discussed in the first section of this chapter.

Whether it takes three years or four, completing medical school is the absolute legal requirement for becoming an allopathic or osteopathic physician, which also makes it the basic criterion for becoming a captain of the ship. Physicians would like us to believe it means they have seven or eight years of college education—four years of undergraduate education plus three or four years of medical school, but even this premise is not necessarily true. Here's a little-known fact: a bachelor degree is not a universal requirement for admission to medical school. (I learned this when several of my college classmates entered medical school after their junior year.) It's also been possible to become a medical doctor with only six years of university education at a few universities with a "fast track" curriculum. (An old friend entered one of these programs at Jefferson Medical College right after high school, receiving his MD degree six years later and going on to become one of the country's leading cancer treatment specialists ... even though he had no more years of university education than a master's-trained nurse who would have been required to work under a physician's supervision at the time.)

As a result of these trends in health education over the past several decades, physicians and advanced practitioners now complete professional training programs of comparable length. It's possible to become a physician with six years of university education, the same minimum requirement for becoming an advanced practice nurse. (Most nursing programs have already established a seven-year doctoral requirement, and others are in the process of doing so.) It now takes seven years of university studies to become a doctor of clinical pharmacy, a doctor of clinical psychology, or a doctor of physical therapy. Hence, defenders of the medical monopoly can no longer claim that physicians should control advanced practitioners solely because physicians have more training than any other health professionals. The claim is simply no longer true.

If a physician can become "captain of a ship" in six years, why isn't an advanced practitioner with just as much education equally qualified for independent practice? The fair and reasonable answer is obvious. Physicians and APs are now comparably qualified not only for entry into practice but also for the right to be in charge of their own practices—not subject to control by someone trained in a different health profession. Difference in years of education is no longer a valid basis for perpetuating the medical monopoly because there really isn't a difference. Therefore, no American should be denied the right to seek care directly from APs on the premise that physicians have more education. Legislators, regulators, and policy-makers must act accordingly by eliminating any impediments to full practice authority that are based on this outdated argument. The common minimum standard for independent practice authority is six years of accredited, university-level education that meets the licensure requirements of state boards of practice for recognized health professions.

Of course, those physicians who still want to control APs will strenuously disagree, saying that they have more education than APs when physicians' additional training—a specialty residency for most, plus a sub-specialty fellowship for many—is taken into account. The point is technically correct because residency and fellowship add between three and seven years (depending on the medical specialty) to the time required for entry into practice, but the point is also irrelevant. Completion of medical school, not total years of training, is the historical foundation of doctors' monopoly power as captain of the ship. In the many states where APs must practice under physician supervision, a licensed physician with only a three- or four-year medical school degree has legal authority to control consumer access to advanced practitioners who may have several more years of professional education. (I am not making this up. I know of many nurse practitioners around the country who are legally required to have their practice records and prescriptions reviewed by lesser-trained physicians.)

Physicians' long-standing claim to control advanced practitioners has also become irrelevant for another reason—the emergence of significant differences between the clinical models that underpin state practice acts for independent health professions. As previously explained, nursing and medicine were closely aligned when the Flexner Report initiated educational reform a century ago. Doctors played a major role in defining the role of nursing back then; they were qualified to supervise nurses because they knew what nurses were expected to do. However, nursing began to develop as a free-standing academic discipline in the

1960s. Physicians were no longer involved in defining the education-based criteria for judging a nurse's performance, and the medical model has become so complex in the meantime that it now demands a doctor's full-time attention. How, then, can physicians claim to be qualified to supervise nurses and other advanced practitioners who are trained in different clinical models? To flip a phrase doctors have used for many years: if a physician wants to be in charge of advanced practice nurses (or other APs), s/he should have gone to nursing school (or pharmacy school, or physical therapy school, etc.).

Physicians usually get paid for supervision, directly or indirectly, even though they do not have formal training in how to supervise APs and spend little or no time actually doing it. (Any physician who disagrees with this assertion needs to challenge it with credible evidence; I've never seen any, after several decades of studying of how physicians spend their time at work.) Economists call this type of unearned income a *monopoly rent* because it results from economic power rather than productive labor. Medical monopoly's advocates realize that defending monopoly rent is a tough sell, so they suggest instead that economic payment for supervisory authority is appropriate compensation for the extraordinary expenses they incur to become physicians. The two previous editions of this book detailed the high cost of becoming a physician, which some doctors argue is a big investment that justifies a high return.

An updated cost analysis is not included in this edition because the claim is indisputably true. Becoming a physician has historically cost a lot more than becoming an advanced practitioner, but this fact does not in any way justify depriving consumers of direct access to independently qualified health professionals who cost less than physicians. Forcing consumers to pay monopoly prices for health care is a very poor way to compensate physicians for the high costs of medical education. Physicians' legitimate problems with overregulation and dysfunctional reimbursement must be resolved, but not at the consumers' expense. Liberating APs to practice to the full extent of their training is the more productive and less-expensive step toward improving the efficiency and effectiveness of American health care.

Medical education's comparatively high cost is therefore a "red herring" with respect to the medical monopoly, but it is closely linked to another serious problem with American health care: overspecialization. Physicians' control of reimbursement in the postwar years enabled a rapid development of medical specialties in American medicine. Private health insurance plans started paying higher fees for given services when provided by a specialist, and Medicare and Medicaid started picking up the costs of graduate medical education to train the specialists. The revered general practitioner (GP), the physician who did everything *and* made house calls, had all but disappeared by the 1980s—and overspecialization of American medicine has been identified ever since as one of the main reasons (along with fee-for-service reimbursement and wasteful production) for our singularly high costs of health care.

Overspecialization at the expense of primary care has not occurred in countries without a medical monopoly, which covers just about every other country in the world. Comparative international data suggest not only that spending more on primary care produces healthier populations, all other things being equal, but that spending more on specialty care can actually reduce health of the population. Primary care also costs less than specialty care and produces more health per dollar spent. You don't need a PhD in medical economics to translate these facts into desirable changes in health policy. Because advanced practitioners are much more likely to provide primary care than physicians, we need to ensure that *all* Americans have direct access to APs. Ending the medical monopoly is therefore a missing link in health reform, in terms of both cost and quality.

Flexner-era reformers could not have foreseen how eliminating competition would lead to overspecialization; medical specialties did not yet exist. However, some thoughtful leaders warned against making medicine overly scientific at the expense of pursuing a more humanistic approach. Others feared that the disappearance of schools that did not fit into the elitist traditions of the Ivy League universities favored by Abraham Flexner would eliminate the medical colleges catering to Americans of color, women, and poor students. These fears of social injustice came true. The medical profession quickly grew into its comfortable position as a group of white, upper-class men armed with science to fight illness and injury. The profession has made considerable progress since the 1980s toward becoming humanistic and representative of the American population, but much more work needs to be done. Fortunately, the advanced practice professions have been relatively inclusive as they developed educational standards on a par with those of medicine. Ensuring direct consumer access to equally qualified APs, therefore, addresses other social goals that were lost when physicians eliminated insufficiently educated competitors.

2. Ongoing Certification

Completing the degree for entry into practice is not the end of a health professional's education. Every field is changing so fast that any caregiver must constantly learn new concepts and skills. The half-life of knowledge in human health sciences is estimated to be somewhere between two and four years. A top graduate from one of the most prestigious health profession schools would be incompetent just a few years later if s/he didn't continue to learn new principles and unlearn some old ones. (Just think how often a new miracle drug or favored health behavior is suddenly found to be bad for us.) Professional schools under these circumstances really cannot provide much more than the scientific and clinical foundations for lifelong learning. Continuing education is absolutely essential to help all practitioners keep up with advances in their fields, plus expanding their awareness of best current practice in related areas.

Because a so-called terminal degree (that is, a degree for entry into practice) from an academic health center says less and less about a graduate's competence over time, periodic recertification must be one of the key requirements for being captain of a ship. Any caregiver who has not continually updated his or her professional knowledge is simply unqualified to treat patients, much less control the work of other health professionals practicing different clinical models. Physicians were slow to impose this obvious requirement on their own profession, but they generally do a good job at it today. A few pages were dedicated to analysis of this problem in the earlier editions, urging physicians to get more serious about ongoing certification. They have made considerable progress since then, in my opinion, so the point can now be addressed in a few paragraphs.

Twenty-five years ago, most physicians were required to attend continuing education courses, but they were not rigorously tested to see if they had learned anything. A doctor who slept through a course got just as much credit as one who paid attention. Having been an instructor in these programs for nearly 50 years, I can assure you that attendees' engagement with the courses varied considerably from the 1970s through the 1990s. It was not uncommon for doctors to sign an attendance sheet at the beginning of the presentation and then head for the golf course or the bar. Continuing education was frequently sponsored by pharmaceutical companies or other special interest organizations and presented in upmarket resorts; the programs were commonly described as "boondoggles." No longer. Physicians now attend each entire session and pay attention. They also pay their own way, thanks to a belated resolution of the serious ethical problems inherent in allowing for-profit vendors to provide doctors with continuing education at little or no charge, with lax expectations for participation and marginal measurement (if any) of learning.

Medical specialty societies now have conscientious governing boards, which include at least one representative of the general public. They provide guidance for overseeing continuing education and evaluating the competency of their members every few years according to current standards of practice. The exams include written, oral, and observational components and have developed a reputation for being rigorous, even difficult. The recertification process is not without its critics, many of whom have valid points and offer sensible suggestions for improvement, but it works well enough under the circumstances and is getting better. It is a sign of significant progress in maintaining the competency of medical doctors, systematically and accountably.

Physicians' exemplary progress in this area over the past two decades does not mean that they should also control the recertification of APs. All advanced practice professions must be required to enforce continuing education standards at least as stringent as those now in effect for the medical specialties, but without physician supervision. Medical oversight could easily be used to protect physicians' monopoly power, limiting competition by making it difficult for APs to validate their continuing education even though they had stayed current professionally. Medical organizations have been known to require that a physician teach an AP's recertification course, but under circumstances that did not attract physicians to do it. Hence, each independent health profession should be subject to equally stringent requirements for ongoing professional education *managed by the profession itself.*

The challenge is to maintain a good general model for meeting this requirement, one that each profession can apply to its own practitioners.

3. Scientific Base

Adherence to scientific principles was a major criterion that allopathic physicians used to justify their educational, clinical, and economic monopoly in the first half of the twentieth century. Unscientific approaches to care were eliminated or driven underground by state medical practice acts in the early decades of the twentieth century. (Having taught scientific research and statistics at two medical schools for nearly 20 years, I firmly believe in science. The other requirements for independent practice authority may be somewhat relative, but science is absolute. A health profession without solid scientific foundations should not be licensed to provide services, in my opinion, even if it meets all the other criteria.) Thanks to the work of Pasteur and other scientists in the second half of the 1800s, plus the simultaneous development of statistical analysis, the Flexner-era rejection of unscientific practices allowed medicine to base its practices on methodical, quantitative observation to understand whether and why they worked—and then report the results in peer-reviewed journals.

Scientific medicine's competitors deserved to be put out of business a century ago because they could not demonstrate that their clinical practices were beneficial—or, at the very least, that they did more good than harm. Today's physicians could use a similar argument about supervising advanced practitioners *if* APs' practices were not firmly based on scientific evidence, but such is *not* the case. The advanced practitioners covered in this book are equally well-grounded in human health sciences. They learn the same biochemistry, physiology, anatomy, genetics, and pharmacology as their medical school-trained counterparts. Indeed, students from all the professional schools, at many academic health centers, take the same science classes together, from the same professors, using the same textbooks, and passing the same examinations. (Again, I speak from personal experience. Integrating basic sciences across the schools of medicine, nursing, dentistry, and pharmacy was one of my major assignments as Assistant to the Chancellor for Academic Planning and Programs at the University of Colorado Health Sciences Center back in the 1980s.)

Physicians could fairly claim superior scientific knowledge in the not-too-distant past, but their counterparts in other professions have caught up. There's no longer any case to be made that physicians need to oversee the scientific knowledge of APs. Each of the health professions covered in this book has its own research programs, for example. All receive financial support from the National Institutes for Health (NIH) and numerous other federal agencies that fund basic research in the health sciences. Advanced practitioners are also employed in large numbers by drug companies and other research organizations. The work done by APs and their research partners is published in a broad array of peer-reviewed journals. Multidisciplinary research is common. In the interests of public safety, legislators and regulators should demand proof of these scientific activities of any health profession that seeks the right to independent practice.

WHAT IS A SCIENTIFIC BASE?

An essential indicator of any health profession's scientific legitimacy is a cumulative body of literature published in peer-reviewed journals that adhere to internationally accepted principles of research method and statistical analysis. The articles' findings must be based on unbiased data collected from random, controlled experiments and analyzed by accepted methods that estimate the probability that any observed difference is caused by the experimental effect (e.g., the drug, surgical procedure, or other treatment being studied).* The publications' reviewers and editors should subscribe to ethical principles that ensure professional and public accountability. The articles' authors must fully disclose any conflicts of interest, especially financial.

Allopathic medicine's scientific literature has had its problems; the quality of research has not always met the expectations set by Abraham Flexner. Poorly conceived and/or ineptly managed studies became rather common by the 1980s and 1990s—giving me lots of good examples of bad research to use as teaching material in my medical school lectures. Thanks to the efforts of a few dedicated editors, prominent medical journals have improved the overall quality of the literature since then. They now provide a benchmark for other health professions' publications.† Any profession seeking to be captain of its own ship should be represented by journals that publish scientific studies comparable to those found in the *Journal of the American Medical Association*, the *New England Journal of Medicine*, *Annals of Internal Medicine*, *Science*, *Nature*, and the *British Medical Journal*.

Although the overall quality of medical literature has risen to acceptable levels, recent exceptions raise serious questions about the future. The most troubling to me is the number of authors, some very prominent, who have not only failed to reveal their financial ties to the companies whose drugs or devices they are studying, but who have also manipulated results for personal gain. Their transgressions range from eliminating data that don't support their selfish interests to fabricating data that do. The punishment is usually a slap on the wrist, not the banishment—even imprisonment—they deserve for the massive damage done. For example, our nation's opioid tragedy was created by well-known physicians who violated scientific principles in their research, with

---

* For a clear and detailed overview of scientific research, see the first three chapters of JC Bauer, *Statistical Analysis for Decision Makers in Health Care: Understanding and Evaluating Critical Information in Changing Times*, second edition (New York: CRC Press, 2009).
† For an excellent summary of core practices in all professional journals, see https://publication-ethics.org/core-practices.

the clear intent of becoming wealthy in the process. The rising acceptance of "alternative facts" and other misinformation in politics is surely enhanced by dishonesty within the medical research community. If leading scientists can get rich and powerful by lying, why bother with telling the truth? Sadly, then, a body of supportive literature is no longer a sufficient measure of a health profession's scientific base. The profession must also be able to prove it takes rigorous steps to ensure that research and publications are not biased by personal gain.

In contrast to the devastating impact of fraud and greed, good things are likely to come from new technologies that enable the collection of better data. Researchers now have more powerful tools to study the causes of ill health and find effective ways to manage them. Multi-dimensional analysis of data from multiple sources (e.g., electronic health records, insurance companies, individual health monitoring devices) is starting to identify optimal care, helping clinicians and patients make informed decisions on clinical effectiveness and economic efficiency. Traditional retrospective studies based on small random samples will increasingly be replaced by the real-time analysis of population data. Precision health care—personalized, predictive, and preventive—is in the early stages of development, but it is growing fast. Adapting its clinical model to the evolution of science is a daunting and exciting challenge for every independent health profession.

A strong scientific base is not only important in determining the legitimacy of a profession's interventions, but also in identifying ineffective or harmful treatments. Doctors would like us to believe that we always benefit from their ministrations, but medical care is not always helpful. Indeed, much care is unnecessary because the human body has remarkable curative powers of its own. A significant portion of the ills that cause a person to see a doctor are self-limiting; they will resolve in due course with or without medical intervention. (Physicians have an old saying that a patient who gets care from a doctor will get over a common cold in just a week. On the other hand, a patient who does not seek a doctor's care can expect the cold to last for a whole seven days.) Until researchers find a cure for the common cold, for instance, there is no reason to seek professional help, unless the symptoms persist for an unreasonably long time or quickly develop into something serious. Advanced practitioners are as well trained as physicians in recognizing signs and symptoms that merit professional care—and they are subject to the same legal obligations to refer patients whose needs are outside their scope of practice.

Although we are taught to think that we should see a caregiver for common colds and other minor ailments, just in case there's something serious going on, health care itself can cause harm. Illness or injury caused by health care is sufficiently common to merit a formal name, *iatrogenic disease*. It's not all due to professional negligence. In fact, most iatrogenic disease occurs as a result of scientific ignorance. The caregiver is following standards of practice, but the standards are wrong. Medical history is littered with accepted treatments that have subsequently been found to be ineffective or even harmful. Drugs once in favor and widely available, such as cocaine and thalidomide, have done far more harm than good. Many drugs and procedures in common use today are likely to be discredited in the future for the same reason.

This problem reinforces the critical need for ongoing scientific research in every health profession. We should expect that some treatments once supported by research will be discredited by subsequent studies, especially as new data and information technologies expand our awareness of all costs and benefits for individual patients. For example, orthopedic surgeons and physical therapists use different methods for treating lower back pain, both supported by valid research within their respective clinical models (surgical vs. non-surgical). Rather than spending time challenging the other profession's different approach to care, each should be constantly engaged in research to improve its own methods. The deficiencies of physicians' competitors 100 years ago no longer justify controlling the APs who are now equally devoted to good, ongoing research. A profession's commitment to science is one of the most important justifications for independent practice authority.

In the absence of something better than real science, we should remember the Hippocratic Oath's charge to doctors, "Above all, do no harm." All independent health professionals—be they physicians or advanced practitioners—should be held equally accountable to this principle, and scientific method is the best tool we have to judge a caregiver's performance accordingly. It has generally served allopathic medicine well, and it should be applied equally to physicians' competitors.

4. Coherent Clinical Model

Modern, mainstream medicine is not much more than 150 years old. Until Louis Pasteur discovered the bacterial cause of some illnesses in the 1860s, doctors did not have scientific foundations for understanding diseases and knowing how to treat them. Doctors' practices were based on subjective experience rather than objective analysis. Diagnosis was made by sensory perception, and treatments were often based on ideas that are barbaric by today's standards. Several schools of medical thought could exist simultaneously, based more on theory than fact, because so little was known about how the body works and how it was affected by pathogens.* Different schools followed different models in approaching the same disease.

For example, the school of homeopathy (from the Latin word, *umere*, "to be moist") relied on the analysis of the body's secretions for clues about the cause of an illness, and herbalism sought cure through ingestion of dried plants believed to have specific medicinal properties. Chiropractic, established in 1895, explained disease as the result of a misaligned nervous system and delivered treatment through

---

* Specific designations of these schools are taken from WS Haubrich, *Medical Meanings: A Glossary of Word Origins* (San Diego: Harcourt Brace Jovanovich, 1984) and *Mosby's Medical and Nursing Dictionary*, second edition (St. Louis, MO: Mosby, 1986).

realignment of the spine. Osteopathy began about the same time and also concep-
tualized disease as a function of misalignment, though in various parts of the body
in addition to the spine. In addition to sharing spinal manipulation as part of their
respective clinical models, today's osteopaths and chiropractors also focus on preventive medicine, a clinical concept that allopathic medicine all but ignored until
recently. In spite of allopaths' strenuous objections, osteopathic and chiropractic
models survived the Flexner era, although on relatively smaller scales. Chiropractic
is arguably the exception that proves the rule of medical monopoly. Organized
medicine has successfully pushed homeopathy and herbalism into the fringes of
the medical marketplace. Osteopathy has evolved into the mainstream largely by
assimilating with allopathy, as previously noted. The advanced practice professions
covered in this book developed throughout the rest of the twentieth century, as
explained and contrasted with the medical model in other chapters.

The takeaway from this short section is that a coherent clinical model (as
defined in the sidebar, "Professional Models of Nursing and Medicine—*Vive la
Différence*," pages 50–51) is one of seven criteria that all states should use when
giving consumers direct access to health care practitioners. Allopathic medicine
is no longer the sole, scientifically based paradigm for understanding and treating
illness and injury. We've gone beyond the time when organized medicine could
legitimately argue that competition existed because patients were free to select the
doctor of their choice. (This reminds me of Henry Ford's promise that people could
buy a Model T in any color they wanted, as long as it was black.) Consumers must
now have the right to choose among all independently qualified health professionals who have a coherent clinical model *and* meet the six other conditions for being
captain of a ship. I'm not passing judgment on the different models, just saying
that there must be a coherent one so that consumers know what general concepts a
specific health profession's practitioners are expected to bring to patient care.

5. Professional Liability

Together, a scientific base and coherent clinical model effectively set the boundaries
of appropriate clinical practice for a profession's licensed practitioners. Those who
step outside these boundaries can be guilty of professional negligence, commonly
called malpractice, in accord with American tort law. They are subject to corrective
action (e.g., additional education, supervised work) and/or punishment (e.g., fines,
revocation of license to practice the profession) proportional to the extent of devia-
tion from acceptable practice and harm to the patient who received negligent care.

As "captains of the ship," physicians have not only accepted liability for themselves but for the members of their crew as well. (Accepting responsibility for negligent acts in the past, however, is different from ensuring appropriate performance
in the future—Quality Assurance, the seventh criterion for independent practice.)
Doctors' professional associations do not intervene in the judicial process to defend
a doctor who has obviously practiced negligently, nor do they attempt to evade

responsibility when a subordinate commits an error that does harm. To its credit, the medical profession does not have a "buyer beware" skeleton in its closet, as is the case for many American monopolies.

Just as physicians accept professional liability, so must other health professionals who have earned the privilege to practice independently. The same rules apply to all captains of all ships. Indeed, physicians should be freed from liability for care provided independently by other health professionals they controlled in the past. It should lower doctors' malpractice costs, which are very high in some medical specialties. To the extent that malpractice laws need to be reformed—which can be the case—the reforms should likewise apply to all. Creating competition for doctors should not create any profession-specific malpractice issues. Indeed, physicians would have a legitimate complaint if alternative practitioners were held to any lower standards of liability.

The launching of new ships captained by advanced practitioners may give the appearance of creating new liability problems because physicians often end up treating patients who have been under the care of an AP. Advanced practitioners should always refer patients for care that is not within their licensed scope of practice, but doctors argue that the referrals are too often made too late, that is, after a patient's condition has deteriorated due to a delay in appropriate care. For example, a certified nurse midwife who is fully qualified to manage a normal pregnancy from start to finish will need to transfer to an obstetrician's care an expectant mother who develops high-risk symptoms during the course of the pregnancy. Or a physical therapist who is fully qualified to diagnose and treat a sprained ankle may discover a bone defect that requires the prompt attention of an orthopedic surgeon. However, failure to make the necessary referral on a timely basis constitutes malpractice for the advanced practitioner, not for the physician who takes the referral. Physicians are wrong to argue that supervising APs prevents or solves the problem. Rather, the appropriate solution is holding advanced practitioners accountable to the same referral standards that apply to physicians, letting licensing boards and courts do their respective enforcement jobs as necessary.

Failure to refer can be a serious problem when it happens, but it is not confined to the non-physician practitioners some doctors still feel the need to supervise. Physicians make similar mistakes, including failure to refer, probably as often as APs.* Many a physician friend has told me about other medical doctors who practice beyond the limits of their competence, either providing care incorrectly or missing obvious diagnoses that ultimately result in harm to a patient. This paradox is particularly evident in the case of prescribing medication. Physicians in about half the states maintain at least some control over nurse practitioners' prescriptive

---

* Ideally, this experience-based opinion would be documented, but I am not aware of published research on this topic. If anyone can cite scientific studies of failures to refer, they should be introduced into the discussion. In the meantime, absence of evidence is not a sufficient reason to accept physicians' self-serving argument that they should supervise advanced practitioners.

authority, asserting that advanced practice nurses aren't adequately trained to prescribe medication on their own. Yet these same physicians will often complain about the drugs prescribed for their patients by other physicians. (It must be fairly noted that these disagreements often reflect reasonable differences of doctors' opinions and patients' preferences, but some are the result of serious errors that cause harm.)

Beyond paradox, there's hypocrisy when doctors argue they need to control APs to prevent negligent acts—acts that physicians are also known to commit. The real need is to hold all health professionals reasonably accountable for appropriate practice and to punish obvious deviations from acceptable performance. The solution is good malpractice law that is equally applicable to all independent health professionals, physicians and advanced practitioners alike. I've never seen any scientific evidence that physician supervision of APs solves the problem it presumably addresses. Hence, whenever physicians ask legislators and regulators to extend medical control over other health professionals, public officials should respond by asking physicians how to strengthen and generalize (i.e., make equally applicable to all health professions) the state's professional liability laws instead.

The process of generalizing professional liability for all independent practitioners would provide states with a good opportunity to update the general concept of negligent practice. It has gotten out of hand in many jurisdictions, to the point that a malpractice judgment does not necessarily mean a practitioner was negligent. (Nor, by the way, does a clean slate mean that a practitioner has never made an egregious error. Most malpractice in health care goes undetected and/or unreported.) Juries occasionally sympathize with patients who experience bad outcomes, regardless of other facts that may exonerate the caregiver. Health professionals should only be found guilty of negligence when they fail to do the right thing, that is, when they do not adhere to accepted standards of practice.

Due to the vagaries of human health and the resulting uncertainties in appropriate responses, a poor outcome is not necessarily proof that a caregiver did anything wrong. For example, many bad outcomes result from patients' self-destructive behavior and/or non-compliance with professional advice. All independent health professionals should be liable for the appropriateness of their actions within the scope of practice granted to them by the state, not for the results of their care. As previously noted in other contexts, the ongoing revolution in medical science and technology creates constant change in the standards of care against which health professionals should be judged. Clinical practice guidelines, outcomes-based protocols, and performance improvement programs are always evolving, constantly creating new concepts of appropriateness for all health professionals within their particular scope of practice.

Economic considerations are also entering the picture, with significant implications for defining and enforcing appropriate practice. For example, a clinical practice guideline might designate drug therapy as the initial course of treatment for all patients with common clinical characteristics and diagnoses, only allowing patients to progress to surgery when pharmacotherapy hasn't worked because a drug is generally as effective and considerably less expensive than an operation. We're not too many years from the time when precision medicine will immediately identify destination therapy—the intervention likely to work best, based on each patient's unique combination of disease characteristics, genetic factors, and social determinants of health—but sequential or step approaches are still part of the "art" of medicine. Just like physicians, advanced practitioners are trained to follow rules in the evolution of each patient's care. They should also be legally liable for following the rules. Therefore, health reform should focus on making sure we have good rules to guide appropriate (i.e., non-negligent) practice, applicable to all the independent health professions. Physician oversight of APs is no longer needed when the laws and regulations regarding professional liability are clear, reasonable, and uniformly applied.

MALPRACTICE AND ADVANCED PRACTITIONERS

If advanced practitioners were as unqualified for independent practice as some medical associations and protectionist physicians would have us believe, malpractice data would prove the need to keep them working under doctors' orders. And if out-of-court settlements and legal judgments against advanced practitioners were significantly greater in volume and/or value than those against physicians, we might even question whether APs should be licensed to practice at all. Even though defenders of medical monopoly are unable to produce peer-reviewed articles and other scientifically valid evidence demonstrating the inferiority of advanced practitioners, adverse malpractice data would raise legitimate concerns about giving them full scope-of-practice authority.

Well, APs have gained extensive practice rights in almost half the states over the past 50 years—cumulatively providing enough patient care that we would see an overall increase in the number and dollar value of malpractice judgments against them if they were not able to practice competently on their own. The good news for consumers and purchasers of health care is that advanced practitioners' malpractice experience is extremely favorable.* Relatively few claims are filed against APs, the rate of adverse judgments is comparatively low, as is the dollar value, and malpractice insurance costs them less and has remained relatively stable over time. In other words, physicians can't legitimately argue that professional liability is a reason to prevent

---

* Reducing or eliminating restrictions on nurse practitioners has even been shown to reduce physicians' costs of malpractice. BJ McMichael, BJ Safriet, and PI Buerhaus, "The extraregulatory effect of nurse practitioner scope-of-practice laws on physician malpractice rates," *Medical Care Research and Review*, 2018; 75(3): 312–326.

advanced practitioners from having equal rights to practice independently within the full scope of their professional licenses.

Malpractice data do not suggest that advanced practitioners are perfect. They occasionally make errors, large and small, just like the physicians who would like to supervise them. However, APs' overall malpractice experience is absolutely no worse, as measured in terms of the volume and value of successful claims against them. In fact, it is arguably much better. Some physicians will counter that the comparison is unfair because physicians deal with more complicated patients and have deeper pockets—which make them more attractive targets to greedy plaintiffs' lawyers. I sympathetically agree with doctors on these points, but they are red herrings that have nothing to do with APs' qualifications to practice independently. State legislators and regulators should turn a deaf ear to the "more complicated patient" and "deeper pocket" arguments as they work to end the medical monopoly. However, the points are relevant to malpractice reform in general and deserve attention from that perspective.

Physicians probably won't mention that one of the other main reasons for malpractice suits against them has nothing to do with the quality of care they provide. Many patients sue because they are disgruntled with the way they were treated in personal and business interactions, using professional liability as the vehicle for compensation because they can't sue a doctor for being uncommunicative, condescending, or arrogant. Advanced practitioners generally do a better job of listening to patients and trying to help them deal with non-clinical aspects of the relationship, which makes patients less likely to sue APs even if clinical care was legally deficient. In defense of physicians, I don't think that professional liability should be related to personality. Some excellent doctors have very flawed personalities. In defense of advanced practitioners, however, I think that consumers should be able to take interpersonal relations into account when they choose a caregiver—one more reason why patients should have direct access to all qualified practitioners.

6. Professional Ethics

The ethics of a profession are the shared guidelines that define acceptable conduct for its members. Medicine's original code of conduct was the Hippocratic Oath, with the famous dictum "Above all, do no harm." By the mid-1900s, its written code of ethics dealt almost entirely with how physicians should relate to one another rather than how they should relate to patients. With pressure from our legal system, it unofficially evolved by the end of the twentieth century to be "Above all, do whatever is necessary to keep the patient alive." (This is my formulation, but I believe it is generally accurate.) Fortunately, it is finally taking into account the patients' wishes and resources, and patients don't always want to be kept alive at all costs. Relatively new concepts like patient-centered care, shared decision-making, patient experience, and customer satisfaction (as defined by the customer!) have gained considerable attention in the past few years, and they seem to have staying power. Indeed, pro-consumer initiatives have become key differentiators for some of our country's most respected health care systems. They are new baseline standards for professional conduct.

The professional ethics of American medicine now exist on several levels that continue to evolve. The foundation is the doctor–patient relationship. Despite the historical lack of published guidelines defining it, the majority of doctors have achieved acceptable marks in this domain. However, the doctor–patient relationship is being complemented, if not replaced, by the institution–patient relationship as health plans contract more with health systems and less with doctors. This shift is not surprising because private practice (i.e., physician self-employment), the "sacred" right doctors strenuously defended throughout the twentieth century, is rapidly declining. More than half of all physicians are now employed by organizations, a trend likely to continue as drug chains, health plans, and technology companies compete with hospitals and health systems to employ doctors. These same business entities also employ the majority of advanced practitioners. Hence, the future of professional ethics is likely to be determined by institutions at least as much as by individual health professions. Corporate policies will increasingly define how caregivers are supposed to perform in their relationships with each other, as much as with patients.

How states deal with the consequences of this shift from self-employment to institutional employment is important, but it is a different issue than how they use professional ethics as a criterion for granting independent practice authority to advanced practitioners. Legislators and regulators should examine not only how the health professions (including medicine) define each member's obligations to other caregivers and patients, but also to society—an area where the medical monopoly has let us down. Physicians have enjoyed an enormous increase in income and social status, while access to their services has become a function of a patient's ability to pay. As Jacques Barzun said, "The modern professions have enjoyed their monopoly so long that they have forgotten it is a privilege given in exchange for a public benefit."* Many physicians are detached from the original mission of healer and caregiver and are using the system primarily as the means toward a well-funded lifestyle. Many doctors' ethics are influenced by self-serving conflicts of interest, such as prescribing drugs and ordering diagnostic services in which they have a financial interest (a practice known as self-referral).

"What every profession should bear in mind," Barzun warned, "is the distinction between a profession and a function. The function may well be eternal, but the profession, which is the cluster of practices and relationships arising from the

---

* J Barzun, "The professions under siege," originally published in *Harper's Magazine*, 1978.

function at a given time and place, can be destroyed—or can destroy itself—very rapidly." All the independent health professions need to take this risk seriously, constantly evaluating their obligations to patients and to society. Physicians need to improve their code of ethics and adherence to it. The Hippocratic Oath no longer ordains superior status in the hierarchy of health professions; it defines professional obligations instead. No less should be expected of the advanced practitioners. Each health profession should have a code of ethics that defines its practitioners' obligations to patients and to society—clearly, publicly, and accountably. Lawmakers and regulators should require each profession to have an ethical code as an indication of what it offers in exchange for the state-granted privilege of independent practice.

7. Quality Assurance

Professional peer review was the standard method for evaluating quality of care from the mid-1960s through the 1980s. The process was as simple as it sounds: doctors evaluated the performance of other doctors. It operated under the joint assumptions that (1) doctors and only doctors know what is best for each patient, and (2) the only person qualified to judge one doctor's work is another doctor. All too often—to the extent peer review was happening at all—it perpetuated a "good old boys" network due to an inherent conflict of interest. Initially, peer review only happened when something went blatantly wrong, so very little care was ever scrutinized by a peer. Physicians staunchly defended independent practice, which meant freedom from intrusion by other physicians almost as much as independence from any person or organization outside the profession.

Physicians called upon to evaluate each other's work ultimately had to decide whether their allegiance was to the physician who delivered the care in question or to the patient who received it. Back then, quality assurance raised questions about objectivity because the physician being evaluated was a fellow member of the guild, often a co-worker and even a good personal friend. As further proof that traditional peer review was designed by doctors for doctors, the legal system provided weak protection for those who reviewed their peers. Giving negative evaluations could easily result in being sued. Immunity for negative "good faith" reviews did not start protecting peer reviewers in most states until the 1980s.

Peer review's last problem, and certainly not its least, is that medicine is not an exact science. Differences in patients with the same underlying disease and symptoms can lead to justifiable deviations from specific standards of care, complicating the task for peer reviewers who were not present when decisions were made. Yes, mistakes are made, but decisions that look like mistakes in hindsight might have been defensible at the time. All things considered, the process of peer review was deeply flawed when the first two editions of this book were published. I seriously questioned how physicians could claim the power to evaluate other health professionals when they had so many problems evaluating themselves.

To their credit, physicians finally began to develop new and better methods for evaluating medical care. The next generation of quality assurance mechanisms was made possible by information technologies that help determine which treatments work best for specific diseases. Objective, data-driven formulation of best practices replaced subjective peer assessments as the basis for evaluating quality by the end of the 1990s. Safety became an additional requirement of quality assessment in the early 2000s because the best treatment is still a bad treatment if provided unsafely, such as transmitting an avoidable infection, administering a medication via the wrong route, or allowing the patient to fall off the operating room table.

The newest variable in the quality equation is precision medicine, that is, customizing therapy to individual variations in patients (e.g., genetics, health histories and behaviors, environments) and specific characteristics of their disease (e.g., molecular signature, functional proteomics). Within the next decade, quality assessment will most likely grow to encompass economic considerations as well, as more purchasers decide that they can no longer afford to do everything—and more patients decide that they do not want to do everything, even if they can afford it. The electronic health record (EHR) also plays an important role in supporting meaningful quality assessment. Good EHRs evaluate information to determine if appropriate tests were performed, which drugs were prescribed, if potential side effects were taken into account, if the right procedures were followed, what the patient was told, what the patient wanted, how the patient responded, etc. And a good EHR sends caregivers timely notifications of discrepancies between best practices and actual performance.

A profession's quality assurance mechanisms should also be educational. Evaluation tools should not only identify practitioners who deliver care outside expected norms but also indicate appropriate changes to correct the deviations. Professional literature has taken a major leadership role in recent years to accomplish this goal. Many journal articles now include self-assessment tests that go far beyond the traditional practice of simply showing whether answers are right or wrong. The new approach—especially effective in online publications—follows wrong answers with targeted instruction so that readers can learn from their mistakes.

I can no longer claim, as I did 25 years ago, that physicians shouldn't be given power to evaluate others just because they cannot evaluate themselves. Doctors have actually gotten pretty good at it, especially in partnership with many hospitals and health systems. To give credit where credit is due, much of the impetus for getting serious about quality assurance came from physicians. However, nursing leaders have made equally impressive gains within their institutional and organizational domains, as have their counterparts in the other health professions. Any health profession that seeks independent practice authority should be required to demonstrate how it assures the quality of care provided by its members. The professions covered in this book should ably meet the requirement and can apply quality assurance mechanisms of their own.*

Although doctors now have good mechanisms for assessing themselves, there are still three other reasons why they cannot use quality assurance as an argument to justify monopoly power (i.e., authority over licensed practitioners from other health professions).

■ First, physicians have their hands full just policing their own profession. Doctors will be the first to tell you that they are so busy meeting regulatory requirements and other demands of modern practice that they don't have enough time to take care of their own patients. This being the case, they certainly don't have time to monitor APs, much less other physicians. And, as previously noted, physicians are not generally trained to provide supervision constructively. They are capable of identifying deficiencies in care provided by others (as seen from their individual perspectives), but very few have the skills or time to assure quality by improving the performance of the caregivers being observed.

■ Second, mechanisms of quality assessment are well-developed, constantly improving, widely available, and applicable to all the health professions. Physicians do not have a monopoly on the tools of quality assessment; any other health profession has unfettered access to them. If there ever was a time when physicians could argue they were leaders in quality assessment, with an obligation to oversee the application of their expertise in other fields, that time has passed. The appropriate action now would be collaboration on quality assurance in interprofessional forums where physicians and advanced practitioners work together to improve quality assurance tools and techniques that all can use.

■ Third, the fundamental concepts of quality need to be applied within the discrete clinical models of the different health professions. For example, an MD would use clinical concepts of the allopathic specialty, psychiatry, to judge mental health care provided by a PhD clinical psychologist. This would be inappropriate because, as you will see in the next chapter, psychiatry and

---

* Excellent examples of quality assurance programs for advanced practitioners are provided by the National Conference of State Boards of Nursing (NCSBN) (https://www.ncsbn.org/boards.htm), the Federation of State Boards of Physical Therapy (http://www.continuing-competence.org/), the American College of Clinical Pharmacy (ACCP) (https://www.accp.com/docs/positions/guidelines/Saseen_et_al-2017-Pharmacotherapy__FINAL.pdf), and the American Society of Health-System Pharmacists (ASHP) (https://www.ashp.org/-/media/assets/pharmacy-practice/resource-centers/inpatient-care/entry-level-competencies-needed-for-pharmacy-practice-in-hospitals-and-health-systems.ashx). The NCSBN also publishes a very useful collection of general principles that apply to all advanced practice registered nurses: The Consensus Model for APRN Regulation, Licensure, Accreditation, Certification and Education (https://www.ncsbn.org/aprn-consensus.htm).

psychology use different—yet equally defensible—concepts for diagnosing and treating mental health problems. A psychiatrist cannot know if a psychologist is consistently providing appropriate mental health care because the psychiatrist is not trained in psychology, and vice versa. (OK, maybe a few dozen doctors are trained in psychiatry *and* clinical psychology, but they have much better things to do than supervising caregivers; they are of greatest value as researchers and innovators.)

All three points put a new spin on physicians' long-standing, forcefully stated assertion that only a physician should evaluate a physician because medical training is required to do the job correctly. It is perfectly defensible, but ironically, it goes both ways. Advanced practitioners must evaluate APs within their scope of practice, and they have the tools to do it on their own. Allowing physicians to supervise the process in other health professions only gets in the way and wastes time and money.

Building on Today's Foundations

I expect that few, if any, readers find fault with the seven principles on which physicians have defended their special status as "*the* captain of *the* ship" (italics mine) for the past century. These well-established foundations of independent practice are not what is wrong with the health care delivery system or the medical marketplace. They make sense, and the medical profession generally conforms with them—yet we all know there are bad doctors currently in practice. (Having spent 50 years working closely with physicians, I have never met a physician who couldn't identify at least a few allopathic and/or osteopathic peers they believe to be incompetent.)

If doctors are unable to ensure the quality of care provided by all members of their own profession, how can they possibly claim that their oversight is needed to guarantee the quality of care in other health professions? The obvious answer underscores a central premise of this book: physicians have no right to control consumer access to advanced practitioners by arguing that the other health professionals occasionally make mistakes. There's simply no longer any reason for lawmakers and regulators to believe that physician supervision ensures quality of care provided by advanced practitioners. It's time to empower new ships with new captains and treat all ships equally.

We will now examine other health professions qualified for independent practice authority under the same criteria that organized medicine used to establish the medical monopoly—with a keen eye on how creating competition will make health care more accessible and less expensive without reducing quality. We'll see how giving full practice authority to advanced practitioners will accomplish the goals of health reform without increasing taxes and creating bureaucracies. We'll also be reminded that the required changes must be made locally because practice authority is controlled by each state. States created the medical monopoly, and states must end it—as two dozen mostly have. Given the failed politics in Washington, DC, local action is the only way to get anything done. Health reform, like health care itself, is local. We don't need to wait for Congress. Indeed, we are wasting our time if we do. Consumers deserve choice sooner rather than later.

Chapter 5

Advanced Practitioners: Health Professionals Whose Time Has Come

Advanced practitioners were not well-known when *Not What the Doctor Ordered* first appeared in 1993. I had to invent a generic term—qualified non-physician practitioners (QNPP)—to identify them as a group and create scenarios to describe the services they provided. Fewer than ten states had granted the full scope of practice authority that allowed APs, mostly nurse practitioners and nurse anesthetists, to practice independently of physicians. They still faced strong opposition from organized medicine and encountered great difficulty trying to compete in the medical marketplace. Individual physicians were as likely as not supportive of APs, but the medical establishment decidedly was not.

Most advanced practitioners still ended up working in clinical settings controlled by doctors who ostensibly reviewed their work under "collaborative practice" agreements. Physicians profited from this supervisory role, even though there was no body of evidence to support its value and not much evidence that they actually performed it. Even in states where consumers had the right to seek care directly from advanced practitioners, there was a catch-22. Most APs could only get paid if they billed through a doctor's practice. Insurance procedures were not generally updated to require payments directly to APs, even though they were legally qualified for reimbursement as independent health professionals. Patients were still being charged fees that included the costs of an unnecessary middleman. (For what it's worth, tying the sale of two products is an illegal monopoly practice under federal antitrust law.)

Reimbursing advanced practitioners' services through payments to physicians has definitely hindered full awareness of APs' value to health care delivery. It fails to recognize the productivity of an AP who is 100% busy providing patient care, quite possibly in his or her own private office, but linked to the physician under whose provider number the services would be billed. Some physician organizations fight to preserve this unfair and deceptive accounting arrangement because it gives an economic advantage to doctors under today's performance-based compensation systems—adding one more item to the list of reasons for eliminating vestiges of a twentieth-century monopoly in the medical marketplace.

The American markets for television and telephone services provided useful economic analogies of monopoly at the time of the first and second editions of this book. Three networks controlled Americans' home screens at the beginning of the 1990s, as they had since the introduction of commercial television five decades years earlier, and they used their economic power to control the emerging competition from satellite and cable channels. One of our country's most powerful corporations (American Telephone & Telegraph, commonly known as Ma Bell) handled all our phone calls over a wired network and fought hard not only to prevent the creation of other telephone companies but also to prevent the commercialization of portable devices using wireless and cellular services. Fortunately, deregulation during the 1990s allowed new competitors to reinvent the respective marketplaces by the end of the decade. An expanded choice of products, services, and prices would not be available to us today if lawmakers and regulators had continued to cave in to dire warnings and other self-preservation efforts of ABC, CBS, NBC, and AT&T.

A comparable transformation of the medical marketplace is overdue because health care has changed in comparable ways since the 1990s. Web searches allow us to get medical information that only a doctor could give us back then. Most physicians now work for a health system or group practice, and self-employment in private practice is about as common as a landline telephone. We can monitor our own health indicators in real time without seeing a doctor. We can still go to a doctor's office, but new sites of care, like free-standing urgent care centers and retail clinics, have proliferated over the past 25 years.* We are even beginning to have viable choices in telemedicine services that eliminate traditional barriers of place and time.† Major corporations with no health care experience but deep pockets (e.g., Amazon/Berkshire Hathaway/JPMorgan Chase, CVS, Wal-Mart, Google) are positioning to shake up the marketplace. Finally, several health insurance companies, most notably United Healthcare and its Optum subsidiary, are using their "big data" to create unprecedented business models for reinventing the health care delivery system.

---

* Advanced practitioners are playing a significant role in these developments. See J Morrissey, "A doctor at your fingertips and on your doorstep," *New York Times*, February 24, 2019; p. B5.

† JC Bauer and MA Ringel, *Telemedicine and the Reinvention of Health Care: The Seventh Revolution in Medicine* (New York: McGraw-Hill, 1999).

The success of these transformational initiatives will require the extensive use of advanced practitioners, but results will fall far short of potential as long as organized medicine controls these acceptable substitutes (i.e., potential competitors). Monopoly power in any industry—including health care—perpetuates inefficiencies, increases costs, diminishes innovation, reduces consumer choice, and generally wastes resources that could be put to better use. Legislators and regulators in all states must therefore eliminate legal barriers that prevent advanced practitioners from offering their knowledge and skills directly to consumers without physician supervision. Until state authorities take definitive action to ensure direct consumer access to all qualified caregivers, a small but vocal guild of physicians and medical organizations will continue using scare tactics to create a negative view of competition. (The AMA likes to give the impression that it speaks for all physicians, but only one in four actually belongs to the organization, and it is far from unified.*)

This chapter presents detailed information about the capabilities of six health professions now fully qualified to compete in the medical marketplace. It does not present any valid evidence to the contrary because, to the best of my knowledge, none exists. My research for this book was assisted by two professional research librarians and includes information I gathered in interviews with over 60 experts in health care: professors from academic health centers, association leaders, and practicing health professionals around the country (including physicians). All my inquiries explicitly requested positive *and negative* information supported by scientific research. Not a single negative assessment of advanced practitioners was produced in response to my requests for all relevant details—including requests to medical organizations that oppose competition and direct consumer access. If I had been able to identify any peer-reviewed publications favoring medical oversight for any reason, they would be included in the discussion and cited as references.

The history of the advanced practitioner movement provides additional support for state-level actions to enable competition between all comparably qualified health professionals. If physicians' fears of APs were valid, some states that had already granted full scope of practice authority surely would have rescinded it in response to negative results. This simply hasn't happened. Indeed, health experts and consumer advocates from states with independent practice experience have enthusiastically testified in states that were considering it, helping counter the dire warnings of local medical associations and physician-supported political action committees (PACs) with economic interests to protect.

I expect that some other health professions would argue for inclusion in this chapter. Although the six specialties featured here meet the criteria of independent practice, this book was not intended to be an exhaustive study of all that might qualify. I made an editorial decision that adding comparable information about

---

* J Graham, "Like a slap in the face: Dissent roils the AMA, the nation's largest doctor's group," *STAT*, December 22, 2016; https://www.statnews.com/2016/12/22/american-medical-association-divisions/.

more professions would make the book too long for its intended audience—public officials with the power to bring state practice acts into the twenty-first century, plus policy analysts and consumer advocates whose interventions are needed to make change happen in the political arena. If other health professions feel qualified for independent practice, I encourage them to take the "captain of the ship" model and move forward. The medical marketplace always needs creative destruction. I'll be satisfied if this book helps bring it about in ways I could not foresee.

Nurse Practitioners (NPs)

Nurse practitioners are an ideal antidote to medical overspecialization—arguably the #1 problem that makes American health care so absolutely expensive and relatively inefficient in international comparisons. Having controlled the medical marketplace over the past century, our physicians have created excellent medical specialties that, not coincidentally, produce excellent incomes for physicians. Wealthy patients from all over the world come to the US for specialty care because no other country does it better. Americans who can afford it have no reason to go elsewhere. Medical tourism (i.e., Americans going to other countries for health care) has flourished in recent years as a way to save money, not to get better specialty care. The irony is that other countries spend around half what we do per capita on health care and have healthier populations. The difference is that their health systems devote the majority of resources to primary care; we spend the bulk of our money on specialty care, for historical reasons already elaborated in Chapter 3.

The obvious policy solution is to make physicians shift from specialty care to primary care, right? Wrong, I argue as a medical economist. Physicians in practice today should not be punished for resource misallocations they did not create. I only have an axe to grind with those still working to protect the outdated monopoly. Specialty care isn't bad per se, and trying to remediate medical overspecialization would almost certainly create more problems than it would solve. (Don't ever forget the power of the law of unintended consequences, which explains why the biggest cause of problems is solutions!) Due to two powerful market forces beyond the physicians' control—aging of our population and aging of our physicians—supply and demand in the market for specialty services will probably be about right for the foreseeable future as aging medical specialists retire faster than we can replace them.

Further, having spent 50 years working to reallocate health care resources for more efficient and effective outcomes, I don't think that medical specialists could be turned into generalists fast enough (if at all) to make a difference. The *only* economically and clinically feasible solution is enabling nurse practitioners, plus other advanced practitioners featured in this chapter, to work to the full extent of their scopes of practice without being required to follow doctors' orders. Our national policy imperative is to end the medical monopoly in all 50 states, ASAP. No other approach to meeting the needs for primary care could be accomplished as quickly or at less cost, especially because the costs of training an advanced practitioner are much less than the costs of training a physician. Looking at the cost-effectiveness of nurse practitioners with state-specific data will provide one of the most compelling reasons for giving them full scope of practice authority in states that have not already done so.

Nurse practitioners excel at primary care, and their profession is positioned to meet the need for it.* The vast majority, 87% of all 270,000 NPs, are licensed in primary care; 78% deliver primary care in their practices.† According to studies published by the US Office of Technology Assessment‡ and the Agency for Healthcare Research and Quality,§ primary care nurse practitioners perform between 75% and 90% of the services provided by primary care physicians, and they perform them at least as well.⁵ NPs provide a full range of services, including:**

- Ordering, performing and interpreting diagnostic tests such as lab work and x-rays.
- Diagnosing and treating acute and chronic conditions such as diabetes, high blood pressure, infections, and injuries.
- Prescribing medications and other treatments.
- Managing patients' overall care.
- Counseling.
- Educating patients on disease prevention and positive health and lifestyle choices.

NPs work in a variety of different physical locations associated with primary care (e.g., private offices, clinics, retail pharmacies), and the number of practice locations will grow substantially when they gain full practice authority and receive

---

* National Governors Association, "Policy paper: The role of nurse practitioners in meeting increasing demand for primary care," December, 2012; http://www.nga.org/files/pdf/1212NursePractitionersPaper.pdf; and Robert Wood Johnson Foundation, "Charting nursing's future: The case for removing barriers to APRN practices," March, 2017.

† American Association of Nurse Practitioners, 2018 Fact Sheet; https://www.aanp.org/about/all-about-nps/np-fact-sheet).

‡ US Congress, Office of Technology Assessment, "Nurse practitioners, physician assistants, and certified nurse-midwives: A policy analysis," *Health Technology Case Study No. 37*, Pub. No. OTA-HCS-37 (Washington, DC: US Government Printing Office, 1986); http://ota.fas. org/reports/8615.pdf.

§ US Department of Health & Human Services (DHHS), Agency for Healthcare Research and Quality (AHRQ), *Primary Care Workforce Facts and Stats No. 2* (Rockville, MD: AHRQ, 2011); http://www.a hrq.gov/sites/default/files/publications/files/pcwork2.pdf.

⁵ ET Kurtzman, BS Barnow, JE Johnson, SS Simmens, DL Infeld, and M Fitzhugh, "Does the regulatory environment affect nurse practitioners' patterns of practice or quality of care in health centers?" *HSR: Health Services Research*, February, 2017; 52:1, Part II:437–458.

** https://www.aanp.org/about/all-about-nps/whats-a-nurse-practitioner.

direct insurance reimbursement.* According to historical studies of their general geographic distribution relative to physicians, nurse practitioners are also much more likely to increase their presence in rural areas and minority communities once they are freed from physician oversight.[†] Last, and not least, patients are highly satisfied with the care provided by nurse practitioners. No other health professionals have higher overall consumer ratings—a fact that should compel health systems to support full practice authority because patient satisfaction is fast becoming key to financial success. Hospitals and other provider organizations have tended to sit on the sidelines during political battles over full practice authority, not wanting to offend nurse practitioners but fearing financial repercussions from opposing doctors. The financial gain produced by fully engaged nurse practitioners may now be greater than the loss of income from an obstructionist doctor or two. At the bottom line, nurse practitioners create satisfied patients, and satisfied patients generate revenue (which, of course, helps explain why physicians have wanted to control them).

All available evidence supports nurse practitioners from all relevant perspectives,[‡] even though they are strongly opposed by a vocal minority of physicians. Based on my close professional association with nurse practitioners since the mid-1970s, supplemented by extensive interviews conducted for this book in 2018, I have never seen or heard any evidence to support some physicians' alarmist claim that nurse practitioners want to become physicians without going to the trouble of attending medical school. Quite the contrary. Nurse practitioners understand and accept responsibility for referring their patients to physicians when necessary, but they take pride in providing primary care to the full extent of their training and licensure as nurses who are trained to care, as opposed to physicians who are trained to cure. This comparison implies no bias in either direction. I have consistently supported care *and* cure. We need experts in each domain; what we don't need is cure-focused physicians controlling care-focused nurse practitioners. (Full disclosure: in addition to having been a tenured medical school professor, I am an honorary fellow in the American Association of Nurse Practitioners.)

Nurse practitioners pay close attention to empathetic communications, patient education, social determinants of health (e.g., housing, food, employment, safety),

---

* JA Graves, P Mishra, M Pranita, RS Dittus, R Parikh, J Perloff, and P Buerhaus, "Role of geography and nurse practitioner scope of practice in efforts to expand primary care system capacity: Health reform and the primary care workforce," *Medical Care*, January, 2016; 54(1): 81–89.

† PI Buerhaus, CM DesRoches, R Dittus, and K Donelan, "Practice characteristics of primary care nurse practitioners and physicians," *Nursing Outlook*, March-April, 2015; 63(2):144–153.

‡ For overviews of nurse practitioners' positive contributions from several policy perspectives, see J Traczynski and V Udalova, "Nurse practitioner independence, health care utilization, and health outcomes," *Journal of Health Economics*, 2018; 58: 90–109; https://www.ncbi.nlm.nih.gov/pubmed/29475093; and MM Kleiner, A Marier, KW Park, and C Wing, "relaxing occupational licensing requirements: Analyzing wages and prices for a medical service," *Journal of Law and Economics*, May, 2016; 59(2); https://www.nber.org/papers/w19906.pdf.

behavior change, conflict resolution, and other interventions that prevent health problems from progressing to stages necessitating referral to a physician. Medical specialists who receive these referrals tend to support full NP practice authority because nurse practitioners provide basic services that doctors do not have time to do, do not want to do, or do not know how to do. (Most family practice physicians and many pediatric and internal medicine specialists also deserve recognition for providing patient-focused primary care, which ironically makes them second-class citizens within the specialized world of medical care. I have good-naturedly accused primary care physician friends of wanting to practice nursing without attending nursing school.)

Although predominantly recognized for their work in office-based settings, nurse practitioners are also making major contributions to inpatient care. They have become very successful at providing pre- and post-operative services on hospitals' specialty units, for example, allowing surgeons to spend more time operating on patients (their unique, high-value expertise) instead of making bedside rounds (something an advanced practice nurse can do at least as well). Nurse practitioners excel in preparing patients for home and follow-up care, including coordination with social workers, physical therapists, and mental health professionals. In focus group interviews conducted for this book, several hospital executives told me that nurse practitioners were particularly well-respected for their skills in patient education. Whereas most physicians would simply tell a patient to quit smoking, get exercise, and lose weight—sadly, all that's required of them for compliance with federal quality reporting programs—nurse practitioners actually help patients find customized smoking cessation programs, teach them how to build needed physical activity into their daily lives, and give them recipes for meals matched to their health needs.

Nurse practitioners are also being used quite successfully in hospital-based medical residency programs, ably complementing interns and residents whose work week is limited to 80 hours. (Incongruously, NPs in some states are required to get a doctor's approval to provide services they are teaching medical residents to perform.) NPs have quickly developed training and certification programs in response to growing demand for new skills, such as inserting central lines and chest tubes. Nurse practitioners are also federally qualified to provide annual physical examinations and other mandated health services for workers engaged in many high-risk activities (e.g., navigating sea-going vessels, driving 18-wheel trucks, operating nuclear power plants).

The resulting improvements in cost, quality, and outcomes from all these services in all these settings are substantial—but only fully realizable in states where nurse practitioners can practice independently. Even if the status quo-defending doctors could produce research-based evidence that physician supervision is required to ensure the quality of some nurse practitioners' services (which, I repeat, they have not been able to do), the economic gains of granting full practice authority to nurse practitioners would surely be enough to tip the cost-benefit analyses in their favor, with appropriate procedures to deal with the exceptions.* No matter how you look at the bottom line, it's time to end medicine's economic monopoly all across the country. Giving full practice authority to nurse practitioners is an excellent place to start. They are very busy taking care of patients, so consumer advocates, community activists, business leaders, and health system executives should be leading the charge.

Certified Registered Nurse Anesthetists (CRNAs)

Although there are far more nurse practitioners than certified registered nurse anesthetists, CRNAs have been around a lot longer ... almost a century longer. Their story illustrates perfectly the harmful economic effects of doctors' ongoing efforts to control comparably qualified competitors and the public benefits of competition from advanced practitioners. In particular, it shows why antitrust enforcement—government action very different from health reform—and coordinated changes in states' professional practice acts are needed to expand consumer choice and end the medical monopoly when acceptable alternatives are available.

The story begins with the development of anesthesia as a clinical science in the period between the Civil War and World War I. (Anesthesia is, ironically, the only medical specialty where the Founding Father is a woman. The enduring title, "mother of anesthesia," was conferred on Alice Magaw in the 1890s by Dr. Charles Mayo, one of the physician brothers who founded the Mayo Clinic.[†]) Nurses administered almost all anesthesia in the United States until medical doctors began exerting control over all other providers of health services early in the twentieth century, as detailed in Chapter 3.

Nursing's early leadership in anesthesia makes perfect sense because anesthetic services require the professional skills at which nurses excel: monitoring patients, making critical decisions, and taking decisive action (including administration of medication). Nevertheless, state medical societies began challenging nurse anesthetists' right to practice around the time of the Flexner Report (1910), promoting legislation that prevented anyone other than a physician from administering anesthesia. Doctors' efforts to eliminate or control the competition included discrediting nurse anesthetists in the eyes of the public.[‡]

---

* For example, a comparative study of Medicare patients found savings of 29% ($207 difference) when care was provided by nurse practitioners. J Perloff, CM DesRoches, and P Buerhaus, "Comparing the cost of care provided to Medicare beneficiaries assigned to primary care nurse practitioners and physicians," *Health Services Research*, August, 2016; 51(4): 1407–1423.

† https://sharing.mayoclinic.org/2015/01/26/celebrating-nurse-anesthetist-education-alice-magaw-1860-1928-mother-of-anesthesia/.

‡ For a well-documented review of events during this period, see testimony of Gayle McKay, CRNA, before the House Judiciary Committee on February 28, 1996.

Fortunately, anesthesiologists (physicians who specialize in anesthesia) have failed repeatedly in their attempts to completely eliminate competition from nurse anesthetists. CRNAs are licensed to practice in all 50 states, and they currently administer more than half of all anesthesia in the US. CRNAs provide the majority of anesthesia services in rural hospitals and are the main anesthesia providers for the US military. The profession's malpractice premiums are comparatively low, even falling in many states due to ongoing improvements in education, drugs, equipment, and techniques. Perhaps most importantly, published studies have consistently shown that the quality of care provided by nurse anesthetists is at least equal to the quality of care provided by anesthesiologists.[*,†] There is no statistically significant difference in patient outcomes based on the degree of restrictions placed on CRNAs by state scope of practice laws.[‡] Comparable quality should not come as a surprise because CRNAs and physician anesthesiologists (often called MDAs) complete comparable accredited anesthesia education and training programs after at least four years of preparatory training in their respective nursing and medical schools and share the same standards for practice.

If you were observing a professional administering anesthesia, you wouldn't be able to tell from the surgical garb or the tasks performed whether the health professional at the head of the operating room table was a CRNA or an MDA. Even if you knew he or she were a CRNA, chances are good that they are the only anesthesia professional in the room. So why am I including CRNAs among the advanced practitioners who need to be freed from the medical monopoly? Because the restrictions on their practice add unnecessary costs of two anesthesia professionals per patient and serve no valid purpose to improve outcomes. Physicians haven't been able to control what CRNAs do, but they have been remarkably successful in controlling how CRNAs get reimbursed—to the financial benefit of anesthesiologists, of course. On average in 2017, anesthesiologists earned approximately $100,000 more than CRNAs according to the US Department of Labor[§] and nearly $200,000 more according to the Medscape Physician Compensation

---

[*] Cochrane Database of Systematic Reviews, "Physician anaesthetists versus nurse anaesthetists for surgical patients," July, 2014; https://www.cochrane.org/CD010357/ANAESTH_physician-anaesthetists-versus-nurse-anaesthetists-for-surgical-patients. See also DC Simonson, MM Ahern, and MS Hendryx, "Anesthesia staffing and anesthetic complications during cesarean delivery: A retrospective analysis," *Nursing Research*, 2007; 56(1): 9–17.

[†] B Dulisse and J Cromwell, "No harm found when nurse anesthetists work without supervision by physicians," *Health Affairs*, August, 2010; 29(8), https://www.healthaffairs.org/doi/10.1377/hlthaff.2008.0966.

[‡] B Negrusa, PF Hogan, JT Warner, CH Schroeder, and B Pang, "Scope of practice laws and anesthesia complications: No measurable impact of certified registered nurse anesthetist expanded scope of practice on anesthesia-related complications," *Medical Care*, October, 2016; 54(10): 913–920.

[§] United States Department of Labor, Bureau of Labor Statistics, May 2017 National Occupational Employment and Wage Estimates, United States; https://www.bls.gov/oes/current/oes_nat.htm#29-0000.

Report.* How can anyone rationally justify this major difference in compensation for the same work?

Anesthesiologists have effectively managed to justify their monopoly rent—the extra $100,000 to $200,000 they earn each year—as compensation for "supervising" CRNAs. Unable to prevent state legislatures from licensing CRNAs to provide services that were originally performed by nurses, anesthesiologists have used scare tactics with health insurance companies and government programs to make sure that the money flowed under their control as much as possible. This arrangement lets MDAs charge extra for services provided by CRNAs operating under their "medical direction." (For example, Medicare Part B payment regulations have allowed MDAs to charge 50% of their full fee for services simultaneously provided by up to four CRNAs working in four operating rooms. Earning as much as a 200% premium for providing no clinically necessary services is nice work if you can get it, and apparently you can get it if you have monopoly power.) In addition, Medicare's conditions of participation (CoP) wouldn't pay hospitals and other sites of surgical care for anesthesia services provided by a CRNA unless the CRNA was supervised by a physician—who could be a physician with absolutely no training in anesthesia.

This policy created an untenable situation for small and rural hospitals in areas where MDAs did not want to practice. In addition, many surgeons did not want to "supervise" CRNAs due to unfounded fears of additional liability—creating a catch-22 for hospitals that couldn't get reimbursed for CRNA's services because there was no anesthesiologist serving the area. (i.e., because hospitals couldn't afford to pay for an MDA *and* a CRNA when only one anesthesia professional was needed to provide the service). In 2001, this problem led to a Medicare rule change that exempted facilities in states where the governor determined that physician supervision was an impediment to patient access to anesthesia services. Fewer than 20 states (mostly rural) have exercised the "opt out" provision, allowing Medicare coverage for services provided by unsupervised CRNAs. The fact that Medicare providers cannot be reimbursed for unsupervised CRNAs' services in a majority of states attests to MDAs ongoing monopoly power—monopoly power that is unjustifiable because all studies show no relationship between location, supervision, and quality. Anesthesiologists are no better than CRNAs, but they lobby hard to earn a lot more.

The difference between an anesthesiologist's fee and the cost of the CRNA who actually provides the service might be justifiable if supervision were necessary, but it isn't. This situation is a textbook case of exploitation of labor. It is a sign of unwarranted economic power that makes consumers pay more than the price that would prevail in a competitive market. It is also a textbook example of "featherbedding," the discredited labor practice of using more workers than is necessary. Thanks to

---

* Medscape Physician Compensation Report, 2018; https://www.medscape.com/slideshow/2018-compensation-overview-6009667.

modern technology and excellent training, CRNAs do not need medical "supervisors" any more than railroads needed brakemen and conductors in a caboose after automation took over their functions. (I thought about removing the railroad analogy from this edition. It probably means nothing to younger readers; cabooses disappeared about the time I wrote the second edition. The example remains because it illustrates how monopoly power gets in the way of realizing the net economic benefits of technological progress. Unions protected caboose crews' high-paying jobs for several decades after they were replaced by automated sensors and speed governors.)

Eliminating anesthesiologists' unfair competitive advantage is a "low-hanging fruit" among actions that can be taken right now to reduce the costs of health care without reducing quality or accessibility. Lawmakers and regulators also have one more reason to let CRNAs (and other APs) compete without supervision and be paid directly for their services—the non-partisan policy imperative for getting consumers "with skin in the game" to make price-conscious choices. Consumers in every state should have the unrestricted right to choose between an anesthesiologist and a CRNA when they are shopping around for surgical services. Any patient should be free to pay an anesthesiologist's higher price, but many will make a rational economic decision to buy the service of comparable quality from a CRNA at a lower price. This economic consequence of competition is why many anesthesiologists work so hard to protect the status quo. It's also why health reform needs to focus on ending monopolies.

Certified Nurse Midwives (CNMs)

Even though nurse practitioners and nurse anesthetists receive most of the attention in public policy debates about full practice authority for advanced practice nurses, certified nurse midwives deserve equal recognition. CNMs are far fewer in number (12,000) than NPs (270,000) and CRNAs (43,000), but they offer comparable potential to improve quality and reduce costs of health care when freed from the unnecessary clinical and economic constraints placed on them at the behest of the medical monopoly. Their clinical expertise is management of normal pregnancies and deliveries—the number one health service provided in the US and, therefore, a top priority for reform.*

In addition to managing normal, low-risk pregnancies from beginning to end, nurse midwives also provide extensive reproductive health services and primary

---

* Detailed information on certified nurse midwives, including an extensive bibliography of published research findings on nurse midwifery, is presented in American College of Nurse-Midwives, "Midwifery: Evidence-based practice," April 2012; http://www.midwife.org/acnm/files/ccLibraryFiles/Filename/000000004184/Midwifery-Evidence-Based-Practice-March-2013.pdf.

care (e.g., performing health exams, writing prescriptions, teaching nutrition, and educating patients and parents). More than half of all CNMs are employed by physician practices or hospitals. CNMs are carefully trained to refer patients to physicians whenever a patient has needs outside their scope of practice. Nearly 95% of CNM-attended births occur in hospitals, with the small remaining portion split between free-standing hospitals and birth centers.* Certified nurse midwives, known in a few states as nurse midwives, are not to be confused with lay midwives or the home-birth movement. Lay midwives are absolutely not qualified for independent practice according to the criteria established in this book, and home births are still outside the realm of commonly accepted practice.

We pay a high price for the way childbirth is handled in our medicalized, monopolized health care system. Hospital-based deliveries by physicians are not the norm in other countries with less-expensive perinatal care and better overall outcomes. Most babies elsewhere are delivered by nurse midwives in free-standing maternity hospitals and specialized birthing centers—reflecting the "foreign" view that pregnancy is not a disease requiring doctors and hospitals. Average birth-related costs in the US are staggering: $18,329 for commercial payers and $9,131 for Medicaid in a recent year. If a C-section was involved, they rose to $27,866 and $13,590 respectively. Hospital-based services accounted for 70% to 84% of all costs.[†]

The US is not #1 in birth-related spending—Japan is—but the total costs of prenatal care and hospital delivery in the US are anywhere from half as much again to several times higher than in other comparable countries.[‡] Unfortunately, we don't have anything to show for all the extra spending. Our infant mortality rate is higher than in any comparable country.[§] International comparisons on this subject are a bit misleading because some of the difference is explained by factors unrelated to the way perinatal care is managed. Catching up with the countries that spend less and do better will require social progress independent of health reform, but we can make major economic and clinical gains simply by freeing CNMs to do what they do so well.

Substituting CNMs for obstetricians whenever possible will provide consumers with cost reductions comparable to those associated with direct access to NPs and

---

* http://www.midwife.org/acnm/files/ccLibraryFiles/Filename/000000005948/EssentialFactsAboutMidwives-021116FINAL.pdf.

† Truven Health Analytics ,"The cost of having a baby in the United States," January 2013; http://transform.childbirthconnection.org/wp-content/uploads/2013/01/Cost-of-Having-a-Baby1.pdf.

‡ The International Federation of Health Plans, 2015 Report, quoted in "The cost of childbirth across the globe" https://www.coynecollege.edu/news/cost-childbirth-across-globe/.

§ B Sawyer and S Gonzales, "How does infant mortality in the US compare to other countries?" Peterson-Kaiser Health System Tracker, July 7, 2017; https://www.healthsystemtracker.org/chart-collection/infant-mortality-u-s-compare-countries/#item-infant-mortality-rates-u-s-among-non-hispanic-blacks-higher-average.

CRNAs. Obstetricians earn on average between \$235,200* and \$300,000† in comparison with an annual average salary of \$103,000 for CNMs.‡ Using the economic model previously presented in "Advanced Practitioners and the Costs of Care,"§ this difference in earnings alone translates into approximately a 40% reduction in the cost of normal perinatal services when performed by a certified nurse midwife rather than an obstetrician (or, in some geographic areas, a family practice physician). The economic benefits of direct consumer access are not limited to pregnancy care; CNMs also provide many other women's health services.

Although I worked extensively with nurse practitioners and certified registered nurse anesthetists in the 1970s and 1980s, I knew little about certified nurse midwives prior to writing the first two editions of this book. Site visits to several pathbreaking birth centers back in the 1990s convinced me that CNMs were among the most underutilized health resources in the US, largely due to opposition from state and national medical associations and from local obstetricians. It was a classic case of medical monopoly. Women were not only paying doctors' prices for reproductive primary care and normal birthing services that CNMs provided at least as well for less money; they were also denied the right to choose between two equally defensible models of care—physicians specialized in treating things gone wrong and nurses focused on making sure things go right (and referring their patients to physicians if things go wrong).

As should be perfectly clear by now, I defend both approaches. We need medical and nursing models for birth-related care, but *vive la différence!* Hence, I am pleased to report that I found widespread acceptance of CNMs by local obstetricians and family practice physicians while making site visits and conducting interviews for this edition in 2018. CNMs' attitudes toward physicians were also highly favorable. The mutual hostility I observed 25 years ago seems largely to have disappeared, with each profession recognizing and respecting the other in areas where CNMs have full scope of practice authority.

So why are CNMs still subject to physicians' control in so many states? Because there's still a vocal minority of physicians who want to prolong the "golden age" of health care that doctors enjoyed in the second half of the twentieth century. State

---

* United States Department of Labor, Bureau of Labor Statistics. May 2017 National Occupational Employment and Wage Estimates, United States; (https://www.bls.gov/oes/current/oes_nat.htm#29-0000).

† Medscape Physician Compensation Report 2018; https://www.medscape.com/slideshow/2018-compensation-overview-6009667.

‡ United States Department of Labor, Bureau of Labor Statistics. May 2017 National Occupational Employment and Wage Estimates, United States; https://www.bls.gov/oes/current/oes_nat.htm#29-0000.

§ See pages 24–27 for details. The estimated difference in unit costs assumes that a CNM's annual salary is approximately 40% of an obstetrician's salary, which yields total estimated prices of \$100 and \$61 (\$35 + \$26). This conservative estimate is on the low end of estimates given to me when I conducted national interviews for my research.

officials responsible for bringing clinical practice acts into the twenty-first century in these markets must be prepared to resist the traditionalists' outdated, self-serving objections. Consumer advocates shouldn't have to look far to find doctors who will testify to support of CNMs. My research found that obstetricians who had first-hand experience with nurse midwives were among their strongest supporters, noting in particular how CNMs in the community allowed them to spend more time with medically complicated patients and less time responding to calls.

Clinical Pharmacists (PharmDs)

Few, if any, health professions have changed as much as pharmacy over the past several decades. The activities of today's clinical pharmacists in states with full scope of practice bear little resemblance to the tasks their counterparts performed throughout the twentieth century. Back then, registered pharmacists (RPh) across the country worked in hospitals or neighborhood drugstores; they seldom interacted with any health professionals other than physicians. They made sure that prescriptions—the epitome of doctors' orders—were filled exactly as written, that is, dispensed with the right number of the right pills with the right label (a task more likely to be performed now by a pharmacy technician). Pharmacists politely answered customers' over-the-counter questions—being sure not to raise even the slightest doubt about appropriateness of a doctor's prescription. If pharmacists harbored any doubts, they kept them to themselves except in the most egregious circumstances. The registered pharmacist was an important member of the twentieth-century health care delivery team, but in a supporting role that never came close to challenging the physician's role as "captain of the ship."

Much like their counterparts at Schools of Nursing had done in the 1970s and 1980s (as already described in Chapter 3), leaders in pharmacy education began to redefine their profession for the twenty-first century. Training programs were lengthened to encompass remarkable advances in pharmaceutical science and to include clinical rotations at teaching hospitals, ambulatory care clinics, and specialty care settings. The result was today's standard eight-year professional training program for entry into practice with a doctorate in clinical pharmacy (PharmD). This is the same educational benchmark that physicians used for so many years to justify their sole right to independent practice. However, equivalence in years of education doesn't tell the whole story. Pharmacy students take many years to learn about drugs; medical students take only a few courses. Hence, it's one of health care's inexplicable ironies that physicians have full authority over prescribing in so many states. Clinical pharmacists know at least as much about pharmacotherapy as physicians, yet they must still follow doctors' orders in most states. How twentieth century! One more reason why it's time to give consumers direct access to clinical pharmacists and other independent advanced practitioners in all 50 states.

Clinical pharmacists are unquestionably the leading experts in promoting safe and rational use of medication.* Their roles include conducting patient assessments, performing problem-oriented reviews of medication history and patient data, evaluating each medication's safety and effectiveness, identifying side-effects and adverse interactions (not only those involving prescription medication, but also with over-the-counter drugs, herbal and dietary supplements, and food), correcting drug dosage, reconciling different medication, making generic and therapeutic substitutions, managing drug administration, ordering laboratory tests and interpreting results, securing needed drugs from other provider organizations when necessary, and educating patients and their families to manage prescribed medication.† (In Wisconsin, where I now live, customers must talk with a clinical pharmacist when picking up a prescription at a drugstore. I am impressed with how the conversation is patterned to help consumers get the full benefit from their medication.)

PharmDs don't work exclusively in retail pharmacies. Many have moved into primary care and specialty clinics and onto hospital floors where they work directly with patients. For example, as you will soon see in the case study from Colorado (pages 129–131), they have become key caregivers in emergency medicine. Clinical pharmacists are also key caregivers in patient-centered medical homes. Their medication therapy management services are eligible for direct reimbursement under Part D, the Medicare drug benefit program. They are trained to give vaccinations (e.g., shingles, flu, and pneumonia) and prescribe many medications (e.g., dermatological creams, birth control pills‡). They are not your father's drugstore pharmacist. It's therefore no surprise that clinical pharmacists have been found to produce the most cost-effective care§ with positive cost-benefit ratios¶ in their areas of specialization.**

---

* American College of Clinical Pharmacy, "The definition of clinical pharmacy," *Pharmacotherapy*, 2008; 28(6): 816–817; https://www.accp.com/docs/positions/commentaries/Clinpharmdefnfinal.pdf.

† American College of Clinical Pharmacy, "Standards of practice for clinical pharmacists," *Pharmacotherapy*, 2014; 34(8): 794–797; https://www.accp.com/docs/positions/guidelines/StndrsPracClinPharm_Pharmaco8-14.pdf.

‡ C Mollison, "Pharmacists' role in managing contraceptive care continues to evolve," https://www.pharmacytimes.com/conferences/apha-2018/pharmacists-role-in-managing-contraceptive-care-continues-to-evolve.

§ Pacific Research Institute, "Promoting access and lowering costs in health care: The case of empowering pharmacists to increase adult vaccination rates," https://www.pacificresearch.org/wp-content/uploads/2018/04/AdultVaccination_F_web.pdf.

¶ DR Touchette, F Doloresco, KJ Suda, A Perez, S Turner, Y Jalundhwala, MC Tangonan, and JM Hoffman, "Economic evaluations of clinical pharmacy services: 2006–2010," *Pharmacotherapy*, 2014; 34(8): 771–793.

** AE Carroll, "The unsung role of the pharmacist in patient health," *The New York Times*, January 28, 2019; p. B3; https://www.nytimes.com/2019/01/28/upshot/pharmacists-drugs-health-unsung-role.html.

Clinical pharmacists' increasing involvement in health care teams across all these settings exemplifies the remarkable clinical and economic benefits available to consumers and health insurance plans when advanced practitioners have the right to full scope of practice. Unfortunately, only a few states allow clinical pharmacists to do all they are trained and licensed to do.* A majority of states authorize clinical pharmacists to offer one or two of their many advanced practice capabilities, but the overall situation falls far short of the potential across the country. A few states still treat clinical pharmacists like registered pharmacists, denying patients and payers the full benefits of modern pharmacotherapy.

Why do so few states allow clinical pharmacists to practice to full extent of their capabilities? Antiquated reimbursement policies deserve some of the blame, but if you think that responsibility lies largely with organized medicine and the vocal minority of anti-modernist doctors, you get the picture. Protectionism pays; lobbying and other anti-competitive activities are cheap compared to the extra income generated by unjustifiable market dominance. Clinical pharmacists represent a serious economic threat to doctors who want to control all prescribing, to bill consumers for office visits for vaccinations and birth control pills, to dispense medication in their office at non-competitive prices, etc.

In addition, some physicians' egos and reputations are threatened when an equally or more qualified health professional (i.e., a clinical pharmacist) flags errors in their prescribing patterns, even though quality of care is improved in the process. The good news is that many physicians and specialty organizations strongly support clinical pharmacy. They need to be enlisted as allies as states move quickly toward the most important health reform that can be actually be accomplished under current circumstances—granting full scope of practice authority to clinical pharmacists and other advanced practitioners.

Doctors of Physical Therapy (DPTs)

The case to fully empower clinical pharmacists provides a perfect segue to promoting the same positive action for physical therapists and clinical psychologists (next section). The common element is, tragically, the opioid crisis that has killed more than 200,000 Americans. It is strongly associated with scandalous scientific[†] and

---

* A state-by-state summary of pharmacists' scope of practice is published by the Policy Surveillance Program at Temple University Beasley School of Law, http://lawatlas.org/data-sets/pharmacist-scope-of-practice-1509023805. This resource also provides information for other health professions, including advanced practitioners.

† B Meier, *Pain Killer: An Empire of Deceit and The Origin of America's Opioid Epidemic* (New York: Random House, 2018); and PR Keefe, "Empire of pain," *The New Yorker*, October 30, 2017; https://www.newyorker.com/magazine/2017/10/30/the-family-that-built-an-empire-of-pain.

economic* subterfuge perpetrated by a few powerful drug companies, resulting in deadly overprescribing by physicians.† It has caused the federal government's Centers for Disease Control and Prevention (CDC) to issue guidelines for replacing prescription pain medication with exercise therapy and cognitive behavioral therapy whenever possible.‡ Clinical pharmacists are experts in identifying when substitution is appropriate; physical therapists§ and clinical psychologists are experts in providing the recommended non-pharmacologic alternatives. I think it's safe to say that the opioid crisis could have been greatly diminished, maybe even prevented, if all three of these advanced practitioners had been free to practice to the full extent of their training. (How's that for a thinly veiled attack on the medical monopoly?)

In addition to treating pain without drugs, today's physical therapists are the experts in using movement to optimize overall quality of life.¶ They provide hands-on care to manage chronic conditions, to promote recovery from injury, and to prevent recurrent injury. DPTs begin their care for each patient with a physical examination and assessment of complaint(s), and then create a customized treatment plan that reflects individual goals, challenges, and needs. They teach their patients the physical movements and other functional changes that enhance recovery and maintain appropriate types and levels of physical activity. Patient empowerment is a hallmark of their care.

DPTs do not prescribe painkillers and other medication; rather, they collaborate with health professionals who have prescribing privileges whenever a patient's needs cannot be met by physical therapy alone. Fortunately, research consistently shows that their non-pharmaceutical interventions can be at least as effective as surgery for a variety of serious conditions (e.g., meniscal tears and osteoarthritis of the knee, shoulder and spine injuries, degenerative disk disease, lower back pain). DPTs are strongly oriented to collaborative and integrated practice, working closely as members of primary care teams that include physicians, other advanced

---

* SE Hadland, A Rivera-Aguirre, BDL Marshall, and M Cerda, "Association of pharmaceutical industry marketing of opioid products with mortality from opioid-related overdoses," *JAMA Network Open*, 2019; 2(1): e186007.

† F Schulte, "How America got hooked on a deadly drug," *Kaiser Health News*, June 13, 2018; https://khn.org/news/how-america-got-hooked-on-a-deadly-drug/.

‡ "CDC Guideline for Prescribing Opioids for Chronic Pain — United States, 2016," Recommendations and Reports, *Morbidity and Mortality Weekly Report*, March 18, 2016; 65(1): 1–49; https://www.cdc.gov/mmwr/volumes/65/rr/rr6501e1.htm?CDC_AA_refVal=https%3A%2F%2Fwww.cdc.gov%2Fmmwr%2Fvolumes%2F65%2Frr%2Frr6501e1er.htm.

§ For example, see CM Wilson and R Briggs, "Physical therapy's role in opioid use and management during palliative and hospice care," *Physical Therapy*, February, 2018; 98(2): 83–85.

¶ Detailed information about the profession is provided by the American Physical Therapy Association at http://www.apta.org and https://www.moveforwardpt.com/Default.aspx.

practitioners, and allied health professionals.* Physical therapists can obtain additional certification from the American Board of Physical Therapy Specialties in nine areas: cardiovascular/pulmonary, clinical electrophysiology, pediatrics, orthopedics, sports medicine, neurology, geriatrics, women's health, and oncology. These extra qualifications enhance relationships with medical specialists and improve overall patient care.[†]

Becoming a physical therapist now requires the same number of years of university education as becoming a physician (i.e., seven or eight years, with a few six-year accelerated programs starting to appear). Like their physician counterparts, DPTs can also complete residencies and fellowships that add another one to six years to their education. Unlike physicians, DPTs often practice outside traditional health care facilities. They are trained to work in the communities where their patients live, work, learn, and play. DPTs are particularly well-prepared for one of the most important trends in health care, addressing social determinants of health. The profession has a long tradition of leadership in health promotion and disease prevention, especially in the development of worksite wellness programs. Physical therapy has also been a leader in developing pathways for legacy graduates of non-doctoral programs, long known as registered physical therapists (RPTs), to upgrade their qualifications for practice as DPTs.

Like the other advanced practice professions, physical therapy has proven to be a cost-effective alternative to comparable care provided by physicians.[‡] (If the full costs of the opioid crisis were to be taken into account, DPTs' care would be one of the best bargains in the medical marketplace!) As is also the case with the other AP professions, medical monopoly has prevented consumers from having direct access to the full scope of physical therapy services in a majority of states[§]—despite the facts that no physical therapist has ever lost a license due to negligent practice and that no state has withdrawn full scope of DPT practice authority once granted. The medical monopoly's dire warnings about unsupervised DPTs have simply failed to materialize, yet more than half of all Americans must incur the extra costs and inconveniences of getting a physician to make the necessary referral.

---

* Extensive documentation of physical therapists' contributions to primary care in military and civilian health facilities is presented in American Physical Therapy Association, "A perspective: exploring the roles of physical therapists on primary care teams," 2017; http://www.apta.org/PTinMotion/News/2017/6/30/NEXTPrimaryCare/.

† For a detailed example of successful collaboration between physical therapists and physicians in a hospital setting, see WG Boissonault, MB Badke, and JM Powers, "Pursuit and implementation of hospital-based outpatient direct access to physical therapy services: An administrative case report," *Physical Therapy*, January, 2010; 90(1): 1–10.

‡ An excellent summary of comparative economic studies is presented in MB Badke, J Sherry, M Sherry, S Jindrich, K Schick, S Wang, and W Boissonnault, "Physical therapy direct access versus physician patient-referred episodes of care: Comparison of cost, resource utilization, and outcomes," *Physical Therapy Journal of Policy, Administration, and Leadership*, August, 2014; 14(3): 1–13.

§ E Ries, "The state(s) of direct access," October, 2016; PTinMotionmag.org, pp. 32–40.

Having suffered from sporadic lower back pain over many years, I can personally vouch for the waste created by medical monopoly. In pro-competition Colorado, I was able to get the care I needed, when I needed it, directly from a physical therapist. Then, after moving to Chicago, I had to get a physician's referral first. My Illinois health plan paid for several unnecessary visits to an orthopedist, visits that were not required in Colorado. Sure, the orthopedic surgeon who made the referrals would claim he had to rule out the possibility of underlying musculoskeletal problems that a physical therapist might not recognize, but I guarantee you that my DPT would have immediately referred me to an appropriate physician if I had any back-related problems she could not diagnose and treat. My case against the medical monopoly isn't just a result of 50 years studying the health professions; it's based on personal experience, too. From both perspectives, I find physical therapy has advanced to the point that all American consumers now deserve the right to choose a DPT without a doctor's order.

Doctors of Clinical Psychology (PsyDs)

Health insurance has been the main focus of health reform at any given time over the past 75 years, but medical science plays a greater long-run role in defining the strengths and weaknesses of American health care. For example, the discovery of antibiotics in the 1930s transformed hospitals from charitable facilities where poor people went to die (think *hospice)* to factories full of technology to keep anyone alive. At about the same time, the development of radiology and laboratory medicine led to remarkable improvement in diagnostics and enabled the growth of medical specialization. The genetics revolution is now expanding knowledge about human health like nothing before, transforming almost everything in the process.

Yet, all is not well. The health of our population is declining. We waste a lot of money through overspecialization while underinvesting in primary care and mental/behavioral services. For efficient and effective health care, ultimately producing a healthier population, we must reallocate resources to these two areas. We've already seen how unleashing advanced practitioners is generally the most cost-effective way to meet our needs for primary care. We will now see why every state must specially ensure direct consumer access to doctorally trained clinical psychologists who are able to practice at the full scope of their professional licenses. Clinical psychologists are not only trained to meet Americans' behavioral and mental health needs; they are also central pillars of primary care.*

---

* For an in-depth overview of mental health's powerful links to primary care, including citations of over 60 supportive publications, see BF Miller and SH Hubley, "The history of fragmentation and the promise of integration: A primer on behavioral health and primary care," Chapter 2 in ME Maruish (editor) Handbook of Psychological Assessment in Primary Care Settings (New York: Routledge, 2017).

I feel a bit guilty for failing to include clinical psychologists in the first two editions of this book, but they weren't really on the health policy radar back in the 1990s. Further, their physician counterparts, psychiatrists, were low in the hierarchy of physicians. Psychiatrists' average salaries were at or near the bottom for doctors, which suggests they didn't have much power within the medical monopoly. They were also marginalized by their peers. A common in-joke was that only crazy medical students went into psychiatry … so they could understand themselves. (One of my aunts was a Yale-trained psychiatrist; she complained throughout her long career that the specialty didn't get any respect from other doctors.) Psychiatry's traditional hallmark, psychoanalysis, was generally seen as a medical curiosity because it was not based on scientific research. It was the subject of irreverent *New Yorker* cartoons over many decades. I can't remember any cartoon image featured more often than the psychiatrist's couch, and I've read just about every issue since the mid-1950s.

However, the main reason for psychiatry's second-class status was that physicians hadn't yet recognized the powerful links between mental/behavioral problems and physical illness. Professional acceptance within the medical community improved when psychiatry's clinical focus shifted from psychoanalysis to pharmacology in the 1980s and 1990s with the development of psychotropic medication (e.g., drugs for anxiety, depression, personality disorders, addictive behavior). The Mental Health Parity and Addiction Equity Act wasn't even passed until 2008. Clinical psychology was coming into its own at about the same time. Doctoral graduates from academic psychology programs began to treat more patients whose health care needs were not being met by psychiatry's evolving clinical model with its focus on pharmacological therapy.

The two professions have a lot in common, but there's an important point behind the fact that psychiatrists and psychologists use some different approaches to treat many patients with the same mental and behavioral health issues. I do not see this as a problem—remember, *vive la différence* in scientifically based clinical models— and certainly not as a problem that requires clinical psychologists to work under a psychiatrist's supervision. The differences in professional paradigms must not be cast as a battle to decide which approach is the "right" one. Both professions are actively engaged in scientific research to improve patient care within their respective clinical models. In addition, clinical psychologists have developed highly detailed training requirements that licensed practitioners must meet before prescribing medications for their patients. These criteria are specified and enforced by government boards in states that authorize prescriptive authority for clinical psychologists.*

Further, my research for this book discovered that psychiatrists and clinical psychologists are working very well together in a variety of clinical settings across the country. (An excellent example of synergy is presented in the next chapter's case

---

* Information about clinical psychologists' training requirements for prescribing medications is available at https://www.apa.org/search?query=prescriptive%20authority.

study on the Cherokee Health System in Tennessee, pages 131–134.) They refer to each other and learn from each other. I found that psychiatrists who are practicing side-by-side with clinical psychologists felt no need to supervise them. The small but vocal group of medical doctors who want to control advanced practitioners are motivated by something other than ensuring clinical competence—once again, a sign of monopoly behavior. Clinical psychologists are as qualified as psychiatrists to be captains of their own ship.

Clinical psychology's practice model is firmly based on an understanding of psychopathology. Its advanced practitioners are trained in human behavior and the assessment and diagnosis of cognitive and behavioral disorders, including dementia, depression, suicidal tendencies, pain, sleep problems, and social pathologies and other dysfunctional relationships.* (They generally have far more training in these areas than physicians who are legally "qualified" to supervise them in medical monopoly states!) Specialty areas include neuropsychology, psychoanalysis, school psychology, industrial–organizational psychology, behavioral and cognitive management, and meeting the needs of specific populations (e.g., children, adolescents, senior citizens, couples and families, and victims of psychological trauma). Clinical psychologists are trained for diagnosis and intervention across the lifespan and range of patients' specific environments. They have a strong orientation toward primary and outpatient care, and are trained to think as members of multi-professional care delivery teams.

Clinical psychologists are at least as well prepared as any other health professionals for addressing our nation's growing and complex problems with opioid abuse, worksite and school violence, suicide, dementia, depression, drug and alcohol abuse, sleep disorders, and related dysfunctions—yet most states still have laws and regulations that prevent these doctorally trained experts from practicing to the full extent of their education and licensure. Health plans' outdated supervisory requirements also deprive patients of necessary care.† Anti-competitive restrictions will inevitably lead to further declines in population health, given the strong relationship between mental and physical well-being, and the overall situation will get even worse due to the looming shortage of psychiatrists.‡ Psychiatrists are going to be so busy treating their own patients that they won't have time to supervise clinical psychologists. Imagine how this bottleneck will reduce the supply of mental health

---

* For detailed current information about the educational requirements for a doctorate in clinical psychology, visit https://www.apa.org/about/policy/approved-guidelines.

† For first-hand accounts of these problems, see American Psychological Association, "Psychologists' stories of the need for Medicare independent practice authority," 2019; https://www.apaservices.org/practice/advocacy/state/leadership/medicare-independent-practice.pdf?_ga=2.139507319.535816246.1550589026-956160867.1548968856. Although the report focuses on Medicare, the same problems are created across the country by private health plans regulated by state insurance commissions.

‡ SR Johnson, "Seeking solutions for behavioral health shortage," *Modern Healthcare*, January 9, 2017, pp. 18–19.

services in states that require supervision. Clinical psychologists will go to states that do not.

Supervision requirements also affect the mental health of nurses, physicians, and other caregivers. Clinical psychologists are among the few professionals adequately trained to help colleagues deal with the mounting stress of being a health professional.* Finally, Medicare's declining reimbursement for psychological services (down around 20% over the past decade) and monopoly-driven restrictions on reimbursement combine to remove clinical psychologists' economic incentives to practice in many areas, reducing the availability and quality of care.[†] States can't change Medicare, but they change insurance laws and regulations that hinder fair private payment for clinical psychologists. There is no longer any scientifically or economically defensible justification for states to restrict consumer choice between psychiatrists and clinical psychologists. We need every one of them, and then some, to meet our nation's growing demand for mental and behavioral health services.

Advanced Practitioners and Workforce Planning

Federal and state governments are seriously challenged by a shortage of physicians, nurses, and other health professionals. An inadequate supply of caregivers in any health profession creates significant economic and political problems, so government leaders need to anticipate shortages and to appropriate money for expanding education programs accordingly.[‡] Their task is complicated by an aging workforce and early retirement (due to stress and job dissatisfaction) that are creating shortages in virtually every health profession. Ironically, these trends help explain why health care is considered such as good career choice for college students. Demand for caregivers is almost certain to exceed supply.

Workforce studies raise serious concerns about solving the problem.[§] The baby boom generation is already creating an unprecedented demand for health care, and

---

* For a related discussion of this threat to health care delivery, see ML Mealer, A Shelton, B Berg, B Rothbaum, and M Moss, "Increased prevalence of post-traumatic stress disorder in critical care nurses," *American Journal of Respiratory and Critical Care Medicine*, 2006; 175: 693–697; and M Mealer, D Conrad, J Evans, K Jooste, J Solyntjes, B Rothbaum, and M Moss, "Feasibility and acceptability of a resilience training program for intensive care unite nurses," *American Journal of Critical Care*, 2014; 23(6): e97–e105.

[†] For related discussions, see https://www.apaservices.org/practice/advocacy/state/leadership/psychologists-medicare.pdf.

[‡] The national agency responsible for leadership in this area is the Health Resources and Services Administration (HRSA) of the Department of Health and Human Services. For detailed information on its mission and work, visit https://bhw.hrsa.gov/shortage-designation. Most states have organizations that study the health care workforce within their borders and make related policy recommendations. To locate these workforce organizations and their reports, contact the health policy division at the state health department.

[§] For details, see https://bhw.hrsa.gov/health-workforce-analysis/research.

Americans of all ages with chronic diseases have even greater needs. Rationing is inevitable unless something changes.* We must therefore increase our supply of health professionals, which includes creating incentives to retain those who are planning early retirement. Policy analysts propose expanding existing programs and opening new schools, but we cannot do either fast enough to solve the problem. Besides, the cost of adding educational capacity is staggering. Given today's political climate, it's hard to imagine governments dedicating more money to health training.

The good news is that we already have a quick and inexpensive solution: ending the medical monopoly. State legislatures and regulators simply need to give consumers direct access to advanced practitioners with full scope of practice authority. Creating fair competition won't solve all our problems, but it can do more good within the next few years than any other health reform. Perhaps best of all, it won't cost states any additional money. All it requires is bipartisan courage to resist special interests' outdated and unsupported claims that physicians should control advanced practitioners.

We saw in Chapter 2 how enabling input substitution (i.e., removing barriers that hinder using advanced practitioners for services they provide at least as well as physicians) could reduce total medical spending by nearly 5%. The money saved can be reallocated to provide more care. Other sections of this book have exposed the waste created by reimbursement procedures that require advanced practitioners to bill for their services through physicians' practices—procedures that allow "collaborating" physicians to pocket the difference between doctors' fees and the lower costs of APs. Additional care could be provided with this unearned income that physicians are currently retaining. We've also seen how unnecessary physician supervision creates inconvenience and expense for patients who choose an advanced practitioner for their care. And I haven't even addressed the costs that advanced practitioners incur fighting the medical monopoly. APs' pro-competition efforts demand a lot of time, money, and mental energy that should be spent treating patients instead.

Finally, we've seen that monopoly's harms are not exclusively monetary. The adverse effects of suppressing innovation cannot be directly measured in dollars. A serious disservice is done by physicians fighting to control other health professionals who are now qualified to be captains of their own ships, regardless of the costs involved. Unless the protectionists can provide valid proof to the support their sensationalist claims about the inferiority of potential competitors, all the existing evidence shows they are denying consumer access to scientifically supported models of care that deserve to stand on their own.

Even if advanced practitioners did not cost less than physicians, their practice models respond to differences in consumer preferences. They are constantly

---

* H Bauchner, "Rationing of health care in the United States: An inevitable consequence of increasing health care costs," *JAMA*, published online February 13, 2019; https://jamanetwork-com.proxy.hsl.ucdenver.edu/journals/jama/fullarticle/2725150.

evolving along with the realm of possibilities generated in competitive markets where all sellers play by the same rules. APs illustrate the benefits of the creative destruction that threatens monopolists to their core. Hence, it is with considerable excitement that I conclude this book with seven in-depth case studies of world-class health services developed by advanced practitioners. Special recognition goes to community leaders and public servants who helped make progress possible by removing barriers to direct access and full scope of practice authority. Their counterparts in every state should now do the same as part of workforce planning.

Chapter 6

Case Studies

CHI St. Alexius Minot Medical Plaza, Minot, North Dakota

From the outside, Minot Medical Plaza (MMP) looks like any other three-year-old, two-story medical office building. The sign out front displays the colorful logo of a large national health system, Catholic Health Initiative (CHI), next to the name of one of North Dakota's largest hospitals, St. Alexius Medical Center (located 110 miles to the south in Bismarck). Signage in MMP's front lobby points to familiar service areas: clinics, laboratory, radiology, physical therapy, pharmacy, etc. There's the normal flurry of activity as patients and employees move about the building.

A first-time observer would reasonably assume MMP is the outpatient center for doctors affiliated with a nearby CHI hospital. Well, it's not. Patients come there instead to see nurse practitioners, certified nurse midwives, and other advanced practice caregivers who take care of a wide range of health care needs and refer patients to medical doctors whenever a problem is outside their scope of independent practice. Physicians from several specialties rent space in the facility on a weekly or monthly basis, but MMP is built and operated to support the work of advanced practitioners . The clinic's AP staff works with—not for—physicians.

This uncommon arrangement has worked well for all concerned for nearly three years now. The APCs at Minot Medical Plaza see approximately 15,000 patients per year, and patient volume is steadily growing. Patients who require more advanced care are referred to medical specialists or admitted to a hospital. MMP works just like the medical group practice it resembles, but patients walk into the facility knowing it is a nursing group practice. Patients made a personal choice to see an AP at MMP instead of one of the many doctors elsewhere in the community.

A large medical office building operated by and for APs would be totally unexpected just about anywhere else, but Minot is not just anywhere else. It's a city with several special attributes that allowed one of the country's largest health systems to do something truly innovative. It all started with "Mother Nature." A cataclysmic flood destroyed half of Minot in 2011, including the downtown area where CHI/ St. Alexius maintained a clinic for its Bismarck-based specialists who came to see patients in Minot. The devastation compelled a "greenfield" replacement (one not encumbered by historical constraints, in the language of architects and developers) in an area outside the floodplain.

However, the flood wasn't the only major force of change. Minot's population (now 60,000) was in the process of doubling at the time due to an oil boom and expansion of the military base on the edge of town. CHI realized that it not only had a compelling need for a replacement facility but also a rare opportunity to meet the health care needs of thousands and thousands of new residents. Establishing the replacement clinic with APs was a perfect solution because the new residents were predominantly millennials (the generation focused on new products and new ways of buying things, not old sellers' credentials) and soldiers (comfortable with the military health system, which has used APs extensively for decades).

Three other factors simultaneously supported CHI's ability to innovate: (1) the supply of physicians was not growing anywhere near fast enough to meet the rising population's medical care needs; (2) North Dakota, a predominantly rural state, has long been a national leader in extending the full scope of independent practice authority to qualified health professionals; and (3) the leading health insurer, Blue Cross Blue Shield of North Dakota, has a progressive history of reimbursing qualified non-physicians because its data consistently validate the quality of their care. CHI was well-positioned to harness these forces because it was already an innovator in using clinical and marketing studies to create consumer-focused care models that optimize efficiency and effectiveness.

Given CHI's regional approach to innovation, market coverage has grown beyond Minot. Its AP care model is fully implemented at several rural clinics and critical access hospitals in outlying areas. I spent an afternoon interviewing staff and observing patient care at one of them, the Washburn (population 1,200) Family Clinic, and I didn't note any significant differences from dozens of rural doctors' offices I have visited over many decades. The nurse practitioners and aides in Washburn were intently focused on meeting the health needs of the local population, as evidenced by their ongoing continuing education choices. They had direct 24-hour communication links with medical specialists in urban hospitals and a paramedic-staffed ambulance to transport critical patients to a full-service hospital when necessary.

CHI's regional managers in Fargo closely monitor advanced practitioners' performance in the rural practices, which has been exemplary since the beginning. The AP concept has proven itself in Washburn as well as in Minot; locals no longer see it as a stopgap measure until "real doctors" can be recruited. Some resistance from the medical community still exists, but it is steadily declining as the non-physician caregivers meet or exceed expectations and as the community expresses satisfaction with APs. Further, physicians have discovered that the value of referrals received from APs is greater than routine visit income lost to the competition. Medical specialists have even indicated they have more time to deal with complicated patients when APs deal with primary care.

On all the bottom lines, clinical as well as economic, the Minot Medical Plaza and its affiliated delivery sites offer proof that local medical care is enhanced when consumers have a choice between traditional doctors and equally qualified non-physicians. The flood of 2011 confirmed the old adage that "a rising tide lifts all boats." CHI's success in Minot shows that APs can add value to local markets. Competition doesn't need to be a zero-sum game between physicians and advanced practitioners, and consumers can benefit from the synergy.

Allcare Health, Grants Pass, Oregon

Reimbursement became a growing concern for doctors in 1994 after the Clintons failed at health reform and the Republicans recaptured control of Congress. Americans were still pressing politicians on both sides to do something about the "skyrocketing" costs of health care. Governments and insurers consequently started experimenting with several new approaches to paying doctors, with no consensus on how to restructure the process. Like their counterparts all across the country, a group of physicians in southwest Oregon decided to prepare for the resulting uncertainties by organizing as an independent practice association (IPA), one of the alternatives being tested nationwide.

The IPA model provided an independent alternative to increasingly common arrangements where physicians sold their practices and became employees of a health system or medical group. IPAs allowed doctors to continue owning their private practices while forming a corporation of private practices to negotiate payment contracts with health plans and hospitals. The IPA model preserved at least the illusion of private practice in a marketplace that was making self-employment difficult for physicians. Most IPAs were formed to preserve doctors' independent economic power—that's what monopolists generally do—rather than improve health care in the United States.

IPA results varied widely over time and by region. Failures have outnumbered successes, but some of the successes are impressive. They have transformed health care for the better by reinventing the way services are delivered—something monopolists generally don't do. One of the nation's best examples of successful creative destruction (as already shown, a good thing in economic theory and antitrust law) via an IPA originally formed in Grants Pass, Oregon, in 1994. True to its name, Allcare Health, it is an all-encompassing (i.e., not physician-centric) integrated organization.

Allcare Health's original slogan was "Physicians Working Together," but it quickly evolved to "Working Together," as the physician leaders realized their member practices could not, by themselves, respond successfully to the increasing threats and changes impacting local health care. Those changes included rapid decline in the area's lumber-based economy, which hindered physician recruitment. The resulting unemployment and geographic isolation made it nearly impossible to compete with Portland's thriving medical community. The state of Oregon, under the leadership of a physician (Governor John Kitzhaber), was implementing a unique plan to freeze and ration spending under Medicaid. The changes to Medicaid ultimately allowed Allcare to transform local health services through integration that addressed the root causes of poor health (e.g., homelessness, food insecurity, low income). Other health-related changes, including legalization of physician-assisted suicide and the use of marijuana, were also evolving in the state at the same time.

Oregon was deeply committed to health reform back in the 1990s, but on its own terms. Fortunately, Oregon's own terms included some of the country's most progressive state health care practice acts. The state was already a national leader in giving consumers direct access to independent non-physician practitioners, allowing Allcare's physician leaders to proceed in an environment that respected independence and ingenuity. They decided to build a health system to meet local needs with local resources. There was never any thought of copying what had already been done somewhere else, much less waiting for direction from Washington, DC (pretty much a "never event" in Oregon), or begging for subsidies to save rural health.

Having concluded that doctors could not meet all the local market's health needs on their own, the founding physicians created a 15-member holding company board with 5 community (i.e., non-physician) representatives. Some 25 years later, 6 members of the board are physicians, 3 are advanced practice caregivers, and 6 are community business and government leaders. Also, 10 out of 21 members of the organization's Community Coordinated Care Organization (Medicaid CCO) board are community stakeholders, and a consumer advisory committee reports to the holding CCO company board from each of the 3 counties in the service area.

A significant number of non-physician health professionals are shareholders in Allcare Health's subsidiary insurance company corporations—100% locally owned—established to meet state requirements for participation in Medicare and Medicaid programs and commercial insurance product lines. Allcare Health is also registered with the State of Oregon as a Certified B Corporation (http://www.bcorporation.net), "using business as a force for good" by consistently and closely assessing its human, business, and environmental impacts on the communities it serves. The corporation publicly reports data on cultural competency and responsiveness, social determinants of health, patient satisfaction, and environmental impact. Allcare Health is also recognized as one of Oregon's Top Workplaces in all industries, not just health care.

However, Allcare Health's exemplary success as a community-centered business enterprise must not overshadow the equally impressive evolution of its clinical services. Allcare Health has grown from an IPA of a few dozen physicians to an integrated system of 1,300 health professionals providing comprehensive care to more than 50,000 members in three counties (total population of approximately 300,000) that include two retirement and tourism centers, Medford and Ashland. Residents in this marketplace arguably have more health care choices—a key gauge of competition—than Americans in any other part of the country. Southwest Oregon is a national model of the benefits of locally driven health reform, thanks in large part to Allcare Health.

In addition to a fairly traditional complement of physicians, the organization's clinical staff includes advanced practice nurses, physical and respiratory therapists, clinical pharmacists, dentists and dental hygienists, mental and behavioral health professionals, and community and public health officers. Nearly 30 nurse practitioners maintain private practice offices dispersed across the network's geographic area, providing primary care services without physician oversight. Selected alternative and complementary caregivers, including acupuncturists and homeopaths, are also available to patients in accord with local concepts of health care. Direct consumer access to an array of qualified caregivers is an accepted fact in Allcare Health's service area.

Given that medical monopoly elsewhere in the country reflects doctors' century-old claim they alone are qualified to control medical care, Allcare Health does an exemplary job of measuring and *publicly* reporting clinical performance measures to show that its competitive model "works for patients," the organization's formal brand promise. It is one of three competing Community Care Organizations serving southwest Oregon under the Oregon Health Authority (OHA) Medicaid incentive model, with income bonuses awarded to caregivers based on annual assessments of Triple Aim performance tied to patient experience, health of the populations served, and reduced per capita costs of care.

Published data show targeted improvement in health measures, including increased adolescent well-care, childhood immunizations, colorectal cancer screening, emergency department utilization, depression screening and follow-up, and reduced hospital readmissions and inappropriate emergency room visits. When consumer surveys showed that existing transportation was a major roadblock to care for many people in the communities, Allcare created an innovative transportation system. Its drivers are trained as members of the health care team, not only helping patients get to their appointments, but also collecting their medication for caregivers to review with them and stopping to fill prescriptions and buy appropriate foods on the way home. Drivers also make sure that Allcare's patients have adequate heat during the cold Oregon winters.

If only all medical enterprises would be so openly responsive and accountable to the communities they serve! Allcare Health offers absolute proof that collaboration between physicians and advanced practitioners, public health officers, and behavioral and social service providers can dramatically improve local health care in ways that non-collaborating groups cannot accomplish on their own. I offer sincere compliments to the Grants Pass doctors who made it all possible by refusing to act like monopolists when confronted with new economic challenges 25 years ago. They are heroes in my book.

CHI Franciscan Birth Center at St. Joseph, Tacoma, Washington

Stellar examples of collaboration between advanced practitioners and physicians, like Minot Medical Plaza and Allcare Health, tend to be community (i.e., non-hospital) primary care (i.e., non-specialized) clinics providing basic health services. The concentration of APs in general practice is understandable, given the historical development of non-physician caregivers. It is also desirable because many studies demonstrate the benefits of shifting more resources to primary care from specialty care. Indeed, health policy analysts of all political persuasions generally support spending more on primary care—not only because it costs less, but because it yields greater marginal returns in terms of the overall health of the population. Health reform proposals should therefore promote an optimal balance. Primary care can't solve all our health problems; specialists have valuable roles to play as well. Fortunately, APs are not limited to primary care; the CHI Franciscan Midwifery Birth Center at St. Joseph Hospital in Tacoma shows how they also prove their value in providing specialty care.

As measured by hospital admissions over many decades, the top specialty service in American medicine has been delivering babies—care mostly provided by physicians who have completed extensive, hospital-based training in obstetrics. (Obstetricians are not the only doctors who deliver babies. Family practice physicians, generally classified as primary care practitioners, can qualify to manage births in hospitals by completing a specialty fellowship in obstetrics after completing their family medicine residencies.) Doctors with specialty training in obstetrics are unquestionably the only caregivers qualified to perform surgical procedures, such as Cesarean sections, to save a compromised baby and provide critical care for a mother with complications.

However, approximately half of all pregnancies proceed to term without complications. These normal pregnancies can be professionally and competently managed from start to finish by a certified nurse midwife, a bachelor-trained nurse with a master's or doctoral degree in midwifery from an accredited school of nursing. Wouldn't it make perfect sense, then, for health systems to provide birthing services with collaborating groups of certified nurse midwives *and* obstetricians, each specializing in the care they provide most cost-effectively? And doesn't it also make perfect sense to give patients a choice of practitioners, based on personal preferences, economic resources, and medical needs? Of course, this choice makes sense and shows why all Americans should have direct access to APs working within their full scope of practice! However, due to medical monopoly, this choice is not available to most American women with normal pregnancies—even though it has been proven to work at least as well and cost less than the traditional system of doctor-managed birthing.

Franciscan's Midwifery Birth Center (MBC) clearly shows why consumers should have the right to choose specialized advanced practitioners in every state. Its top-quality, competitively priced birthing option is evident the moment a pregnant woman walks into the door for an introductory consultation. A nurse sits down with her to review materials that explain the differences between physician-managed care at Franciscan's Family Birth Center in the hospital and prenatal-to-postpartum care at the Midwifery Birth Center in an office building across the street. Plenty of time is set aside for the mom-to-be to ask questions, visit the facility, talk to the staff, and read the contract she would sign to enter the birthing program under the care of a certified nurse midwife. The agreement clearly states that the pregnant woman will be transferred to the physician-managed service in the adjacent hospital if her pregnancy develops any signs or symptoms that are outside the definition of low (normal) risk.

Because the midwife and physician birthing centers are owned and operated by the same health system, there's no pressure to manipulate the woman's choice for non-medical (e.g., economic) reasons. The consumer clearly has the right to choose the physician-managed program, even if she is qualified for midwifery care. Any low-risk woman who wants a natural birth experience can choose the Midwifery Birth Center. About half of all pregnant women in the general population would be medically eligible to choose the midwifery option; about half of those eligible for the Midwifery Birth Center—approximately 25% of all pregnant women—do so at St. Joseph in Tacoma. Of those who deliver at the midwifery center, consumer surveys consistently show that 100% would recommend it to a friend.

Hence, St. Joseph's Midwifery Birth Center is a very appealing option for a significant portion of pregnant women. For starters, it costs less than the traditional medical program at the hospital as long as the pregnancy proceeds normally—giving the mother a strong incentive to follow the healthy prenatal behaviors that are the foundations of the midwife model! Although the final cost for any given woman cannot be known until she and her baby are safely at home postpartum, the average cost at the Midwifery Birth Center is about half the average cost of birth at the hospital. MBC effectively charges a package price for prenatal care and delivery, unlike hospitals that bill for each day in a hospital bed, anesthesia, surgical interventions, medications, and doctors' visits in accord with traditional insurance policies. The dramatically lower cost is sufficient reason for states to pass laws that guarantee women with normal pregnancies the right to choose care in a clinic operated by Certified Nurse Midwives.

In the introductory session, the mom-to-be also learns about the coaching and support she will receive from professional nurse midwives and their practice partners (including nutritionists, health educators, and doulas) throughout the course of the pregnancy. The choices of birth methods (e.g., water, nitrous oxide, hammock, different body positions) are also explained during a visit to one of the home-like birthing rooms—each including a deluxe queen-size bed, large soaking tub, and rocking chair. The center's up-to-date security is also highlighted, with controlled and locked access, as well as the quick transfer route to state-of-the-art medical care in the adjacent hospital if any problems occur during delivery in the midwife clinic. Finally, the midwifery center's early postpartum discharge policy is covered; going home with the baby 6 to 8 hours after a normal birth turns out to be one of the MBC's most appealing benefits.

On the day I visited Franciscan's birthing services, I had a leisurely lunch with the doctors who run the traditional birthing program in the hospital. They could not have been more supportive of the Midwifery Birth Center and the certified nurse midwives who run it. The doctors even recommend MBC to low-risk women so that they can concentrate on providing the best possible care to women who need specialty services, including patients who the midwives refer to the doctors for necessary surgical interventions and other treatment of serious gynecological problems. They noted that the MBC was actually started by an obstetrician in 1980 and the clinical and corporate cultures of St. Joseph Hospital are ingrained in the center. The physicians and the CNMs are part of the same medical staff; they share call (i.e., backup coverage) together, which reinforces the professions' mutual respect for each other. They all participate in the same compensation plan with incentives for productivity and quality, and they follow shared clinical guidelines that they developed together.

The St. Joseph birthing model has expanded successfully to Franciscan's rural facilities as well. I personally observed it at St. Elizabeth Hospital in Enumclaw, a 25-bed critical access hospital about an hour's drive from Tacoma. Collaboration between certified nurse midwives and local physicians allows the hospital to deliver about 30 babies a month—a remarkable accomplishment, especially when compared with the fact that many rural facilities of comparable size have discontinued birthing services due to a shortage of rural doctors. The certified nurse midwives at St. Elizabeth do about one-third of the deliveries, following the same protocols in the same state-of-the-art birthing rooms found at St. Joseph in Tacoma. They also have the same successful collaborative relationship with the doctors. Three local physicians with obstetrics training told me the model works so well in Enumclaw because the midwives and doctors have a clear and shared understanding of circumstances that require transferring a patient from one to the other, which goes both ways. (Ironically, resistance came from the hospital's regular nursing staff as the model was being implemented in Enumclaw because some nurses did not initially understand the nurse midwives' full scope of expertise in maternity care.)

If imitation is the sincerest form of flattery, Franciscan's Midwifery Birth Center is getting a true compliment in the local marketplace; Tacoma's other major health system is also opening a midwifery birth center. This imitation is a sign of successful competition. Therefore, the growth of midwifery in Washington state is proof that consumers deserve this choice in every state. Legislators and regulators elsewhere should turn a deaf ear on any doctors who try to prevent direct consumer access to birth clinics operated by certified nurse midwives. Trying to preserve physicians' control over all births is monopoly behavior, pure and simple. Franciscan's Midwifery Birth Center proves that many pregnant women can save money and get top-quality care from advanced practitioners —care made possible by collaboration between certified nurse midwives and medical specialists who respect each other's skills and work together in the best interest of their patients.

Emergency Department, Ellenville Regional Hospital, Ellenville, New York

If advanced practice clinicians were second-best substitutes for doctors—a premise completely contradicted by the evidence in this book—the number of visits to a rural hospital's emergency department would surely decline as emergency physicians were replaced with nurse practitioners and physician assistants. Consumers would only go to the facility for emergency services when they did not have time to get to a physician-staffed ER, right? And wouldn't the hospital's financial viability suffer because a significant number of inpatient admissions come from the emergency department?

Recent experience at Ellenville Regional Hospital, a 25-bed critical access facility halfway between Albany and New York City, shows the exact opposite to be true. The hospital proved that staffing ERs with advanced practice clinicians is not a step backward—clinically or economically. It was part of a turnaround instead. Ellenville Regional was a typical rural hospital in the early 2000s, fighting for its own survival. Patient visits to the ER had fallen to 7,600 per annum—a volume that is not financially viable and a sure sign that consumers were going elsewhere for urgent and emergency care. Physician recruitment became more difficult as the financial situation worsened, to the point that the doctor in charge of the hospital's emergency services had to hire a nurse practitioner in 2004 just to keep the ER open.

The nurse practitioner, Bob Donaldson, had solid experience in emergency care at big hospitals in New York City and other small hospitals upstate. He quickly gained respect from Ellenville hospital's medical staff, overcoming resistance to hiring more APs when other emergency physicians needed to be replaced. Within a few years, all the caregivers in Ellenville Regional's emergency department were nurse practitioners and physician assistants. And by 2017, the number of patient visits had nearly doubled, to 14,500! Patients clearly accepted ER care provided by the non-physician staff. If New York State's professional practice acts had not provided full practice authority to qualified non-physicians, thousands of residents and tourists obviously would not have had access to emergency services at a local hospital. Indeed, the hospital might have been forced to close. Direct consumer access to APs—competition at work—is a major reason why Ellenville Regional Hospital has not only survived but thrived.

Bob Donaldson is obviously a skilled clinician, given how well the hospital's doctors and patients accepted him, despite their initial hesitancy about using a nurse practitioner in a position traditionally filled by an emergency physician. But "the rest of the story" (to borrow journalist Paul Harvey's famous storyline) shows that APs can contribute a lot more than top-level clinical skills to an organization. Like many health professionals, Bob had done well in a different career first. He had risen through the ranks of a national company to become general manager of its largest distribution center, where he managed a multimillion-dollar budget. But he did not find corporate success personally rewarding. In his early 40s, Bob decided to follow in his mother's footsteps and become a nurse. He methodically went through every stage of training—from nursing assistant to licensed practical nurse to registered nurse to nurse practitioner—with a focus on emergency care along the way.

Once accepted as a fully credentialed practitioner in the hospital's emergency room, Bob began to use his business skills for improving overall operations, including customer service and quality of care. Community response was so positive that two remarkable things happened. First, Bob was selected as the hospital's Clinical Director of Emergency Medicine (a position that had always been held by a physician). Then, lest anyone think that the hospital's physicians were feeling defeated or resentful, they elected Bob as president of the Hospital Medical Staff (another position that had always been held by a physician). Widely recognized as the first nurse practitioner to be elected president of a hospital medical staff anywhere in the country, he served three two-year terms in the position. The hospital won several awards and grants during this period, including top state recognition for its opioid reduction program. Bob's success as president of the hospital medical staff also established a precedent; he is no longer the only nurse practitioner to serve in that role.

The point of this exemplary case study is absolutely not that nurse practitioners should take over hospitals, nor that APs are better than doctors. Rather, it proves that impressive synergy is possible when different health professionals respect each other's unique skill sets and collaborate to build a better delivery system. Health care consumers in Ellenville are much better off today because the State of New York promotes competition by ensuring full practice authority for qualified caregivers … and because local leaders approached the future of the hospital as innovators drawing on a new realm of opportunities, not as monopolists fighting to protect outdated ways of doing things. By accepting nurse practitioners and other APs as fully qualified members of the care delivery team, Ellenville Regional Hospital established a model for dealing successfully with challenges that cause many comparable facilities to fail. Other small and rural hospitals throughout the country should take note!

Partnership for Removing Barriers to Full Practice, West Virginia

Like their counterparts in other states with antiquated restrictions on practicing to the full extent of their training and license, West Virginia's nurse practitioners found themselves in limbo a few years ago. On the one hand, NPs were allowed to apply their clinical skills in independent practices, but they could only prescribe medication under collaborative practice agreements with a physician. (As shown elsewhere in this book, NPs are well-trained to write prescriptions and adequately regulated by their state board of nursing. Physician oversight is unnecessary in today's practice environment.) On the other hand, negotiating and managing the collaborative agreements took a lot of time and money—reducing consumer access and adding unnecessary costs in the process.

To make matters worse, NPs had no prescriptive authority at all whenever the collaborative practice agreements lapsed. And what patient would want to see an otherwise qualified caregiver who didn't have the right to prescribe medication? This Catch-22 caused some NPs to leave the state, or even to quit practicing altogether. The result was a reduced supply of health care because nurse practitioners are so important in a predominantly rural and economically disadvantaged state like West Virginia. West Virginians weren't getting medical services that should have been available to them locally but were available in neighboring states. The problem had to be solved.

Fortunately, key local leaders in several domains knew that being in limbo isn't necessarily hopeless. It is a state of constraints, but it can be transitional. They also knew that a new alliance was needed to transition from the old constraints to a new and better arrangement. Letting nurses and doctors fight their old battles wouldn't bring any better outcomes this time than it had in the past. The problem was community-wide and multi-dimensional, requiring a diverse coalition of interests to solve it. Its leaders developed a plan to remove unnecessary practice barriers during the 2016 legislative session.

The American Association of Retired Persons (AARP) was ideally positioned to lead the new multi-stakeholder coalition for updating competition in the medical marketplace. AARP has played a respected role in health reform nationally for several decades, with a staff of policy experts noted for looking at the "big picture." Significantly, AARP's state director in West Virginia was an experienced lobbyist with necessary skills in the political art of getting things done. She was not a health professional; neither the doctors nor the nurses could charge her with favoritism for the other side. Importantly, she had good contacts on both sides of the political divide.

In addition, the West Virginia Nurse's Association hired a consultant who was also able to help bridge the political divide due to prior experience working in the Governor's office. (Given a recent shift in political power, different voices were needed to gain the support of the political party that had just taken control.) The consultant collected research aligned with the party's policies and brought in a Fellow from a Washington think tank. The Fellow, a faculty member at a nationally respected school of nursing, had authored a report demonstrating how APs could solve many of the nation's health care problems. Acting as a third-party validator, the Fellow focused the effort on solving problems rather than battling over professional turf. The Fellow delivered the message to prominent party leaders, testified in committee hearings, and wrote "one-pagers" tying the new legislation to economic modernization, including deregulation and consumer choice.

The coalition's strictly non-partisan focus on common goals allowed opposing forces to align in West Virginia. State chapters of both Americans for Prosperity (the conservative advocacy group founded by the Koch brothers) and Citizens Action (a liberal activist group around since the 1960s) joined AARP to get a full practice authority bill through the legislature. The West Virginia Funeral Directors and Crematory Operators Association helped because their members needed NPs to have the power to sign death certificates. The local media were also helpful with news coverage and editorials. The Federal Trade Commission wrote a supportive report that attracted national attention.* Groups representing a few key health care constituencies (e.g., hospitals, insurance companies) maintained strict neutrality to avoid politicizing the issue.

The alliance of conservative and liberal groups agreed on four goals embodied in the bill for full practice authority: reducing regulatory red tape, eliminating artificial barriers to competition, letting the marketplace work, and enhancing access to care in underserved areas. (By design, these goals resonated with the state's political mood during the national elections taking place at the same time.) These goals were supported with local data showing that doctors would not lose business under the new law because demand for medical care greatly exceeded their capacity to supply it and also that the medical care would be more affordable for consumers in some of the lowest income areas of the state. The coalition's leaders kept the entire effort focused on consumer and rural issues, not differences between doctors and nurses.

Contrary to how previous legislative battles would have been waged, advanced practice nurses were not brought to the statehouse to lobby on behalf of the bill. Talking to legislators is not something they are usually trained to do. However, NPs are very well trained to talk to patients, so they were extensively used in local communities to prepare voters to lobby elected officials about solving cost and access problems by eliminating the requirement for collaborative agreements. Consumers were also given information to show legislators how changing the law would promote primary and chronic care in West Virginia—clinical areas where evidence shows better outcomes and lower costs when consumers have direct access to APCs with full practice authority.

The coordinated, constructive campaign succeeded. Mandatory collaborative practice agreements were eliminated and cannot be required for insurance reimbursement, with one exception. APs covered by the bill must still have a collaborative practice agreement with a physician to write a prescription for Schedule II (i.e.,

---

* Federal Trade Commission Staff Comment to the Senate of West Virginia Concerning the Competitive Impact of WV Senate Bill 516 on the Regulation of Certain Advanced Practice Registered Nurses (APRNs). (February, 2016); https://www.ftc.gov/policy/policy-actions/advocacy-filings/2016/02/ftc-staff-comment-senate-west-virginia-concerning.

addictive) medication, a compromise effectively compelled by the opioid problem in West Virginia.

West Virginia's remarkable lesson for the rest of the country is how to use a positively focused, consumer-driven, multi-stakeholder partnership when the medical monopoly must be challenged and changed. AARP led the way, but the organization's state director is the first to emphasize that it succeeded as a team effort to achieve common goals. Conservatives and liberals worked together, using competition to achieve a social goal. As a result, West Virginians can now use physicians *and* advanced practitioners to provide more health care at lower overall costs. Hopefully, health professionals will follow the example of the non-medical leaders who made the improvement possible, respecting each other's differences while working as a team for the health of the population.

Emergency Department, UC Health Hospital, Aurora, Colorado

If asked to identify the health professionals you would want in an emergency department about to treat you for a serious medical problem, a clinical pharmacist probably wouldn't be on the list. Advanced practice pharmacists simply aren't part of our TV-show image of caregivers who save lives in the emergency room ("ER"). However, after several hours of observing emergency care on the Anschutz Campus of the University of Colorado (as I did in researching this case study), you would want one on the team. The clinical pharmacists who work there 24/7 are one of the reasons this emergency department (ED) is considered to be among the best in the nation.

Because of respect gained for the work they do, in addition to the doctoral degree they have earned, these clinical pharmacists are increasingly addressed as "Doctor." Not only do they provide many diagnostic and therapeutic services traditionally reserved for physicians, they also do many things that ED doctors do not have time to do well, if at all. It's no surprise that a growing number of articles in peer-reviewed clinical journals show EDs with clinical pharmacists are more efficient and effective than those without them.* Therefore, because these specialized

---

* For a general description of the valuable roles played by clinical pharmacists in emergency departments around the country, see G Jacknin, T Nakamura, AJ Smalley, and RM Ratzan, "Using pharmacists to optimize patient outcomes and costs in the ED," *American Journal of Emergency Medicine*, 2014; 32(: 673–677. This article, with three physician authors and published in a medical journal, illustrates the excellent interprofessional relationships that have developed in states where advanced practitioners are fully recognized. For a report on how clinical pharmacists help solve a specific problem in emergency departments, filling prescriptions upon discharge, see B Farris, C Shakowski, SW Muller, S Phong, TH Kiser, and G Jacknin, "Patient nonadherence to filling discharge medication prescriptions from the emergency department: Barriers and clinical implications," *American Journal of Health-System Pharmacists*, 2018; 75(5):316–320.

pharmacists improve quality and reduce costs, consumers all across the country should have access to an ED with a PharmD in the house. Any state medical practice act that prevents this choice is protecting an outdated medical monopoly and needs to be amended.

Stroke care at UC Health Hospital, a Certified Comprehensive Stroke Center, demonstrates the excellence of carefully structured teamwork between emergency physicians, specialized nurses, paramedics and emergency medical technicians, and clinical pharmacists. (Note that collaboration is the key to success; no member of the team possesses all the skills or has the time to do everything that needs to be done for treating stroke.) Under the UC Health model, a clinical pharmacist is called to the patient's bedside along with the other health professionals. After reviewing clinical parameters with the doctor and participating in a protocol-driven discussion of pharmacotherapy (best drug, dose, route of administration, etc.), the clinical pharmacist conducts a second check, mixes the medication, and sets up the administration mechanism (e.g., prepares an infusion pump and primes tubing) so that the principal caregiver only needs to hit the start button.

If I were the patient, I wouldn't want it any other way; medication is more important than ever in emergency care. Outcomes are better when a clinical pharmacist is regularly at the bedside, making sure all pharmaceutical care is done correctly for patients with stroke, heart attack, serious burns, pre-birth complications, trauma, and many other life-threatening conditions covered in a clinical pharmacist's training. Yet, in states that prevent full scope of practice for APs or in delivery systems controlled by old-school physicians, the doctor would make all the decisions and then issue orders for nurses, technicians, and therapists. Given clinical pharmacy's areas of special expertise—such as pharmacokinetic monitoring and therapeutic exchange—best practices simply don't occur in the ED if a clinical pharmacist is not involved in hands-on patient care.

Clinical pharmacists in the ED on the Anschutz campus also perform many of their quality-enhancing, cost-reducing services away from the bedside. They oversee the preparation of condition-specific protocols to be followed by all caregivers, ensuring consistent quality for all patients at all times. They monitor all documentation of pharmaceutical care in the institution's electronic health record (EHR), oversee changes in entries when required, and work with the vendor (Epic) to build best-practice pathways into the EHR. They follow up with other caregivers when lab results indicate changes in a patient's condition that may require a change in medication. If an appropriate medication is not available in the ED pharmacy, they find and procure it from elsewhere in the hospital, or the rest of the University of Colorado system (five hospitals from Colorado Springs to Fort Collins and growing).

The clinical pharmacists provide ongoing education to update the entire ED staff when a new drug appears on the formulary or new research suggests changes in the use of old drugs. They oversee the institution's extensive research into the efficiency and effectiveness of ED care, and write many articles that are published in respected journals. And they engage very visibly in "management by walking around." (On the day I shadowed a clinical pharmacist, she was stopped numerous times by attending physicians, residents, nurses, and an emergency medical technician to discuss pharmacy care for individual patients. She also answered many phone calls, emails, and text messages.) Last, and definitely not least, clinical pharmacists at UC Health Hospital discuss prescribed medication with patients upon discharge. This involves helping the department's social workers secure prescription medication for patients who do not have the financial resources or mobility to fulfill prescriptions on their own. Making sure that discharged patients have and take prescribed medication is one of the ED's most important contributions to preventing unnecessary return visits and hospital admissions.

Many of the essential tasks will not be performed optimally, if at all, in an ED without an empowered clinical pharmacist on the patient care team. Yet, given the scope and magnitude of clinical pharmacists' contributions to excellence in care, using them might seem unaffordable outside the special economic environment of academic health centers. Fortunately, cost-benefit analysis suggests otherwise. The annual salary of a clinical pharmacist is approximately one-third of an emergency physician's income, yet research shows they are at least as good as physicians in performing a wide range of tasks that define top-quality care.

When working collaboratively with a clinical pharmacist, a physician is able to concentrate on doing the best possible work in his or her unique areas of expertise—one more compelling reason that all states should eliminate any legal or regulatory barriers that prevent clinical pharmacists from working within their full scope of practice. The team approach at UC Health Hospital in Denver is a worthy model for emergency departments everywhere in the US. Letting medical monopoly get in the way can no longer be justified with the argument that doctor alone knows best.

Cherokee Health Systems, Knoxville, Tennessee

It's tempting to start the final case study with "Last, but not least," or even "Saving the best for last," but these common end-of-list introductions would be unfair to the other exemplars of real health reform. All are worthy of top recognition for their innovative uses of advanced practitioners to reduce consumer expenditures and advance quality while improving population health. My temptation to give a little extra nod to Cherokee Health Systems probably reflects regret for not including mental and behavioral health professionals in the first two editions of *Not What the Doctor Ordered*. Like most health policy commentators, I openly supported parity for mental health care back in the 1990s, but advanced practitioners in mental health had not yet attained professional recognition comparable to nurse practitioners, certified nurse midwives, CRNAs, clinical pharmacists, and physical and respiratory therapists, who were all featured in the earlier versions. I simply didn't have enough information back then to write a chapter in defense of direct consumer access to psychologists, clinical social workers, and other behavioral therapists with the proven skills to practice independently of physicians.

Cherokee Health has more than made up for the lost time. The system demonstrates not only the remarkable progress mental health professionals have made over the past 25 years, but also what can be accomplished by removing barriers to competition in the medical marketplace. The organization was chartered as a Community Mental Health Center (CMHC) in 1960. When Dr. Dennis Freeman arrived as CEO in 1978, the organization began reaching out to primary care clinics. Having worked as a clinical psychologist in mental health and primary care settings, he knew that many patients with mental health problems shunned mental health centers. However, these patients would go to Federally Qualified Health Centers (FQHC), primary care clinics that did not have the stigma associated with mental health centers. As he started developing an obvious solution—surreptitiously providing mental health care in primary care clinics—local health officials needed someone to take over a failing FQHC that served the same population. It would have merged with another FQHC under normal circumstances, but Dr. Freeman proposed merging the CMHC and FQHC into a single primary care clinic. His innovative proposal was ultimately accepted.

Offering physical, mental, and social services in a single clinic has become a fairly common arrangement called integrated care. Mental health and medical professionals in integrated care models are said to be in collaborative practice. They work closely together, following shared protocols and referring to one another but generally staying in their traditional roles when treating patients. Not surprisingly, Dr. Freeman and his team have recently taken integrated care and collaborative practice one step further, setting a new benchmark for progress by replacing old-but-familiar ways of doing things with a new approach. Cherokee's transformational model is called *blended practice*. I had not heard of blended practice before doing the research for this case study, but I believe it will quickly gain traction in states where advanced practitioners are not only allowed, but encouraged, to use the full scope of their professional skills. In other words, higher prices and compromised overall quality are more likely in states that continue allowing doctors to control independently qualified APs.

The difference between collaborative practice and blended practice is akin to the difference between a sundae and a fruit smoothie. Each topping's flavor is discernable in a sundae, whereas a single taste emerges in a smoothie made of the same ingredients. The analogy works in health care. A collaborative practice (i.e., a sundae) consists of physicians, nurses, therapists, pharmacists, and other ancillary caregivers, where each provides the services associated with his or her profession. Turf battles may be eliminated, but professional silos are not. Members of collaborative teams agree on best practices and are evaluated for how well they follow common guidelines, but they work within the traditional roles defined by training and degrees.

Conversely, team members at Cherokee Health do not believe one size fits all. They believe patients are different in ways that require individual blends of care for best results. In consultation with each patient, clinicians coordinate their different professional perspectives to customize a treatment plan and then deliver it seamlessly. For example, a pharmacist might help a senior citizen with chronic diseases make appropriate behavioral modifications while ascertaining that the patient has all the prescribed medications and knows how to take them (e.g., how to use an inhaler). An OB-GYN physician could include exercise and nutrition education in prenatal visits for a diabetic mom-to-be. A dentist would explain necessary changes in diet and treat oral manifestations of systemic disease while restoring teeth and gums. Individualized interventions to manage drug or alcohol abuse would be reinforced in a social worker's services or a home health nurse's visits to evaluate environmental factors that affect outcomes.

Patients get a consistent "blend" (i.e., a smoothie) of their individualized treatment plan from every member of the Cherokee team, which often means receiving services from caregivers who would not normally be expected to provide them. The team can also include specialists in meeting needs of the homeless, the disabled, migrants, and refugees. Indeed, the right blend often involves professionals from outside health care, because individual health is clearly determined by non-health factors—the social determinants of health. In addition, any member of the team could be the captain, depending on who has the best overall set of skills that mesh with the patient's overall needs and expectations. Finally, consistent with a key economic point of this book, no health professional at Cherokee controls practitioners from other professions based on the traditional hierarchy of academic degrees. All recognize that competence in specific tasks, not length of training, creates the special synergy of blended care. Caregivers are expected to learn many skills through continuing education because the knowledge base of every health profession is constantly changing.

Blended practice is supported by a unique, carefully crafted operational structure. It starts with Cherokee's hiring process. Potential employees are screened for their openness to the blended approach to care (i.e., ability to work closely and enthusiastically with others), in addition to their professional qualifications. It is reinforced in the compensation system. All clinicians are paid straight salaries. There are no financial incentives to promote specific types of care or use certain personnel, and this allows the staff to focus on what needs to be done for each patient without regard to productivity (e.g., more pay for seeing more patients) or meeting performance quotas. Because caregivers are personally committed to seamless team practice all the time, they have very few meetings. Blended care is also built into Cherokee's customized information technology infrastructure. The scheduling system includes special routines to handle the intricacies of matching patients' needs with caregivers who are commonly working outside traditional roles. The customized electronic health record enhances nontraditional workflows by merging physical, mental, and behavioral information. Last, and definitely not least, leadership is focused on guarding the mission, hiring committed and energetic professionals, and staying out of their way while these professionals do the work.

Although I did not foresee the emergence of independent mental health professionals when I wrote the earlier editions of *Not What the Doctor Ordered*, since then I have not been alone in recognizing the need for direct consumer access to their services. Nor am I alone in recognizing Cherokee Health Services for proving that top-quality care does not require physician leadership or oversight. (To be clear, Cherokee's CEO and Chief Clinical Officer are psychologists, while physicians and non-clinical professionals fill out the ranks of the executive team. Physician involvement in patient care is an essential element in Cherokee's success. Staff psychiatrists have been very supportive of the Cherokee model, recognizing from the beginning that they could not meet the population's psychiatric needs on their own.) The Agency for Healthcare Research and Quality (AHRQ) has published studies that position blended care as a model for widespread implementation.* Health professionals from all 50 states have visited Cherokee, and numerous stories about the system have appeared in professional and popular publications. Perhaps the best proof of Cherokee's success is its statewide growth; Cherokee Health now has clinics in 24 communities in east Tennessee and recently opened a clinic in Memphis. Similar organizations should be proliferating across the entire country. There's no longer any justification for anti-competitive barriers to stand in the way.

Conclusions

These case studies are excellent examples of recent progress in American health care. They illustrate the benefits of focusing health reform on changing the way health care is delivered rather than expanding insurance access to a broken system. These innovative programs have achieved efficiency and effectiveness through input substitution, producing a healthier population at lower cost. They were only possible in states that ended the medical monopoly and gave consumers direct access to independently qualified advanced practitioners. Therefore, the book concludes with a few general observations drawn from the case studies.

First, there's no one-size-fits-all solution for the persistent problems of health care in the United States. The problems tend to be consistent across the country, but resources available to solve them are not. Solutions need to be tailored to the specific circumstances of different geographic markets—a point reinforced by the diversity of approaches taken in the case studies. The common commitment to innovation, not the specific details of any single case study, should inspire local leaders responsible for improving health care in their communities. The takeaway is the fundamental importance of creativity and the willingness to do things

---

* For more detail on Cherokee's patient care protocols and procedures, see https://integratio-nacademy.ahrq.gov/expert-insight/success-stories/health-it-case-studies

differently in the context of local resources. Simply replicating a case study from another market misses the point because each one was customized to a different set of problems, possibilities, and resources.

Second, it's not necessary to build new local solutions around federal programs. Leaders behind these case studies did not feel constrained by HITECH, ACA, MACRA, or the government's other unpredictable attempts to redefine reimbursement policy. The case studies' innovative leaders did not abandon their efforts just because the government wouldn't pay for them—a response that I find all too often in my interactions with health system leaders. Instead, they sought creative (and legal!) ways to make each new system financially viable. Finding the least-expensive way to do something that needed to be done was a common denominator across all the case studies, which often included identifying alternative sites of care, using transportation and telemedicine to eliminate unnecessary face-to-face encounters, and involving patients and their families directly in care delivery through education and social support services. In other words, problem-solving was driven by the belief that success required doing new things instead of finding different ways to do old things.

Third, the case studies show that advanced practitioners can provide excellent care to all patients, insured or uninsured, in any marketplace, large or small. It's therefore demeaning and unfair to position APs as a "second-best" solution for disadvantaged populations or rural areas that do not have sufficient resources to support traditional physician practices and full-service health systems. There's simply no geographic or demographic dimension of the case for ensuring direct consumer access to advanced practitioners who provide services at the full scope of their practice authority. Advanced practitioners' capabilities are population-agnostic and location-neutral. The case study programs use APs to care for all patients who walk in the door, and they have made care more affordable by using the least-cost qualified practitioner for specific services. Regarding rural health, they have successfully scaled their urban operations to the smaller communities they also serve. Therefore, legislative action to eliminate the medical monopoly must be seen as something for the benefit of everyone in the state—not as a concession to the disadvantaged or underserved.

Fourth, the innovators behind these successful programs realized that everyone with a stake in their community's health had to be at the table. Collectively, they developed multi-stakeholder partnerships that involved providers, purchasers (public and private employers), payers, and patients. They worked with public health departments, educational institutions, transportation systems, police and fire departments, employers, churches, social services, political organizations, service clubs, retirees, volunteer groups, individual community leaders, and any other concerned citizens who wanted to help. They proved the enduring wisdom of Margaret Mead's observation about change: "Never doubt that a small group of thoughtful, committed citizens can change the world. Indeed, it's the only thing that ever has."

Last, and definitely not least, all the featured programs used independent advanced practitioners to the maximum extent of their scope of practice—but in integrated systems with team-based care models that include physicians as partners. (Hopefully, it's clear by now that I'm not playing favorites. My view of exemplary health care puts physicians and advanced practitioners on equal footing; I just want a level playing field to make sure that it happens.) The case studies prove that full practice authority should not be the end in itself. Rather, it is an absolutely essential foundation for locally focused health care that draws out the best from all professionals, working together with mutual respect toward the healthiest community that available resources can produce. And it happens in states that have fully recognized the skills of today's advanced practitioners.

The lesson of history is clear for the many states that have not yet taken this essential step. End the medical monopoly. Remove outdated laws that allow physicians to control comparably qualified competitors, and good things will happen. Unlike expanding health insurance access to an inefficient and ineffective health care delivery system, enabling fair competition and consumer choice will create a healthier population without increasing costs.

Additional Reading

Aguiar PM, Brito GdC, Lima TdM, Santos APAL, Lyra Jr. DP, Storpirtis S. Investigating sources of heterogeneity in randomized controlled trials of the effects of pharmacist interventions on glycemic control in type 2 diabetic patients: A systematic review and meta-analysis. *PLOS ONE.* 2016;11(3):1–23.

Allen JK, Dennison Himmelfarb CR, Szanton SL, Frick KD. Cost-effectiveness of nurse practitioner/community health worker care to reduce cardiovascular health disparities. *Journal of Cardiovascular Nursing.* 2014;29(4):308–314.

Altavela JL, Jones MK, Ritter M. A prospective trial of a clinical pharmacy intervention in a primary care practice in a capitated payment system. *Journal of Managed Care Pharmacy.* 2008;14(9):831–843.

Anderson, A. "The Impact of the Affordable Care Act on the Health Care Workforce" Heritage Foundation, March 18, 2014; https://www.heritage.org/health-care-reform/report/the-impact-the-affordable-care-act-the-health-care-workforce

Arts EE, Landewe-Cleuren SA, Schaper NC, Vrijhoef HJ. The cost-effectiveness of substituting physicians with diabetes nurse specialists: A randomized controlled trial with 2-year follow-up. *Journal of Advanced Nursing.* 2012;68(6):1224–1234.

Athey EK, Leslie MS, Briggs LA, Park J, Falk NL, Pericak A, El-Banna MM, Greene J. How important are autonomy and work setting to nurse practitioners' job satisfaction? *Journal of the American Association of Nurse Practitioners.* 2016;28(6):320–326.

Ball L. Interventional radiology: New roles for nurse practitioners. *Nephrology Nursing Journal.* 2006;33(5):565–569, 592.

Benkert R, Peters R, Tate N, Dinardo E. Trust of nurse practitioners and physicians among African Americans with hypertension. *Journal of the American Academy of Nurse Practitioners.* 2008;20(5):273–280.

Bergman AA, Jaynes HA, Gonzalvo JD, Hudmon KS, Frankel RM, Kobylinski AL, Zillich AJ. Pharmaceutical role expansion and developments in pharmacist-physician communication. *Health Communication.* 2016;31(2):161–170.

Bhatt, K. "Modernizing Health Care Regulations to Lower the Costs of Medical Services" Hoover Institution, 2017; https://www.hoover.org/sites/default/files/pages/docs/hispbc-_directorsawardbhatt.pdf

Blackmore CC, Edwards JW, Searles C, Wechter D, Mecklenburg R, Kaplan GS. Nurse practitioner-staffed clinic at Virginia mason improves care and lowers costs for women with benign breast conditions. *Health Affairs.* 2013;32(1):20–26.

Booth JW. An update on vicarious liability for certified nurse-midwives/certified midwives. *Journal of Midwifery & Women's Health.* 2007;52(2):153–157.

Boucher NA, McMillen MA, Gould JS. Agents for change: Nonphysician medical providers and health care quality. *Permanente Journal.* 2015;19(1):90–93.

Braithwaite RS. Expanding the role of advanced nurse practitioners. *New England Journal of Medicine.* 2013;369(10):981–982.

Brock DM, Nicholson JG, Hooker RS. Physician assistant and nurse practitioner malpractice trends. *Medical Care Research & Review.* 2017;74(5):613–624.

Brooten D, Youngblut JM, Donahue D, Hamilton M, Hannan J, Felber Neff D. Women with high-risk pregnancies, problems, and APN interventions. *Journal of Nursing Scholarship.* 2007;39(4):349–357.

Brown DJ. Consumer perspectives on nurse practitioners and independent practice. *Journal of the American Academy of Nurse Practitioners.* 2007;19(10):523–529.

Budzi D, Lurie S, Singh K, Hooker R. Veterans' perceptions of care by nurse practitioners, physician assistants, and physicians: A comparison from satisfaction surveys. [Erratum appears in J Am Acad Nurse Pract. 2010 Jun;22(6):330; PMID: 20536632]. *Journal of the American Academy of Nurse Practitioners.* 2010;22(3):170–176.

Buerhaus, P. "Nurse Practitioners: A Solution to American's Primary Care Crisis" American Enterprise Institute, September 2018; http://www.aei.org/wp-content/uploads/2018/09/Nurse-practitioners.pdf

Buerhaus PI, DesRoches CM, Dittus R, Donelan K. Practice characteristics of primary care nurse practitioners and physicians. *Nursing Outlook.* 2015;63(2):144–153.

Burman ME, Hart AM, Conley V, Brown J, Sherard P, Clarke PN. Reconceptualizing the core of nurse practitioner education and practice. *Journal of the American Academy of Nurse Practitioners.* 2009;21(1):11–17.

Carr KC, Jevitt C. Working with certified nurse-midwives does not increase obstetrical liability. *American Journal of Obstetrics & Gynecology.* 2006;195(5):1495–1496; author reply 1496.

Chaney AJ, Harnois DM, Musto KR, Nguyen JH. Role development of nurse practitioners and physician assistants in liver transplantation. *Progress in Transplantation.* 2016;26(1):75–81.

Chapman SA, Wides CD, Spetz J. Payment regulations for advanced practice nurses: Implications for primary care. *Policy, Politics & Nursing Practice.* 2010;11(2):89–98.

Chen C, McNeese-Smith D, Cowan M, Upenieks V, Afifi A. Evaluation of a nurse practitioner-led care management model in reducing inpatient drug utilization and cost. *Nursing Economics.* 2009;27(3):160–168.

Choe HM, Farris KB, Stevenson JG, Townsend K, Diez HL, Remington TL, Rockafellow S, Shimp LA, Sy A, Wells T, Standiford CJ. Patient-centered medical home: Developing, expanding, and sustaining a role for pharmacists. *American Journal of Health-System Pharmacy.* 2012;69(12):1063–1071.

Choi M, De Gagne JC. Autonomy of nurse practitioners in primary care: An integrative review. *Journal of the American Association of Nurse Practitioners.* 2016;28(3):170–174.

Cipher DJ, Hooker RS, Guerra P. Prescribing trends by nurse practitioners and physician assistants in the United States. *Journal of the American Academy of Nurse Practitioners.* 2006;18(6):291–296.

Cody JT, Adamson KA, Parker RL, Morrey SL, Maxwell EE. Performance of military-trained physician assistants on the physician assistant national certification examination. *Military Medicine.* 2004;169(1):34–37.

Colvin L, Cartwright A, Collop N, Freedman N, McLeod D, Weaver TE, Rogers AE. Advanced practice registered nurses and physician assistants in sleep centers and clinics: A survey of current roles and educational background. *Journal of Clinical Sleep Medicine.* 2014;10(5):581–587.

Conover C, Richards R. Economic benefits of less restrictive regulation of advanced practice nurses in North Carolina. *Nursing Outlook.* 2015;63(5):585–592.

Cooper RA. New directions for nurse practitioners and physician assistants in the era of physician shortages. *Academic Medicine.* 2007;82(9):827–828.

Davis C, Carr D. State legal innovations to encourage naloxone dispensing. *Journal of the American Pharmacists Association.* 2017;57(2S):S180–S184.

Day LW, Siao D, Inadomi JM, Somsouk M. Non-physician performance of lower and upper endoscopy: A systematic review and meta-analysis. *Endoscopy.* 2014;46(5):401–410.

de Gruchy A, Granger C, Gorelik A. Physical therapists as primary practitioners in the emergency department: Six-month prospective practice analysis. *Physical Therapy.* 2015;95(9):1207–1216.

DeKoninck B, Christenbery T. Skin cancer screening in the medically underserved population: A unique opportunity for APNs to make a difference. *Journal of the American Association of Nurse Practitioners.* 2015;27(9):501–506.

Deshefy-Longhi T, Swartz MK, Grey M. Characterizing nurse practitioner practice by sampling patient encounters: An APRNet study. *Journal of the American Academy of Nurse Practitioners.* 2008;20(5):281–287.

DesRoches CM, Clarke S, Perloff J, O'Reilly-Jacob M, Buerhaus P. The quality of primary care provided by nurse practitioners to vulnerable medicare beneficiaries. *Nursing Outlook.* 2017;65(6):679–688.

DesRoches CM, Gaudet J, Perloff J, Donelan K, Iezzoni LI, Buerhaus P. Using medicare data to assess nurse practitioner-provided care. *Nursing Outlook.* 2013;61(6):400–407.

Devine EB, Hoang S, Fisk AW, Wilson-Norton JL, Lawless NM, Louie C. Strategies to optimize medication use in the physician group practice: The role of the clinical pharmacist. *Journal of the American Pharmacists Association.* 2009;49(2):181–191.

DiCicco-Bloom B, Cunningham RS. Complex patients and interprofessional relationships: Perceptions of primary care nurse practitioners and primary care physicians. *Journal of the American Association of Nurse Practitioners.* 2015;27(11):646–652.

Dillon D, Gary F. Full practice authority for nurse practitioners. *Nursing Administration Quarterly.* 2017;41(1):86–93.

Doescher MP, Andrilla CH, Skillman SM, Morgan P, Kaplan L. The contribution of physicians, physician assistants, and nurse practitioners toward rural primary care: Findings from a 13-state survey. *Medical Care.* 2014;52(6):549–556.

Donelan K, DesRoches CM, Dittus RS, Buerhaus P. Perspectives of physicians and nurse practitioners on primary care practice. *New England Journal of Medicine.* 2013;368(20):1898–1906.

Donker JM, de Vries J, de Lepper CC, Wielders D, Ho GH, Mulder PG, van der Laan L. A novel finding: The effect of nurse practitioners on the relation to quality of life, anxiety, and depressive symptoms in vascular surgery. *Annals of Vascular Surgery.* 2014;28(3):644–650.

Dunn SP, Birtcher KK, Beavers CJ, Baker WL, Brouse SD, Page RL, Bittner V, Walsh MN. The role of the clinical pharmacist in the care of patients with cardiovascular disease. *Journal of the American College of Cardiology.* 2015;66(19):2129–2139.

Evangelista JA, Connor JA, Pintz C, Saia T, O'Connell C, Fulton DR, Hickey P. Paediatric nurse practitioner managed cardiology clinics: Patient satisfaction and appointment access. *Journal of Advanced Nursing.* 2012;68(10):2165–2174.

Evans SW. Convenient care clinics: Making a positive change in health care. *Journal of the American Academy of Nurse Practitioners.* 2010;22(1):23–26.

Everett C, Thorpe C, Palta M, Carayon P, Bartels C, Smith MA. Physician assistants and nurse practitioners perform effective roles on teams caring for medicare patients with diabetes. *Health Affairs*. 2013;32(11):1942–1948.

Everett CM, Morgan P, Jackson GL. Primary care physician assistant and advance practice nurses roles: Patient healthcare utilization, unmet need, and satisfaction. *Healthcare*. 2016;4(4):327–333.

Ference EH, Min JY, Chandra RK, Schroeder Jr. JW, Ciolino JD, Yang A, Holl J, Shintani Smith S. Antibiotic prescribing by physicians versus nurse practitioners for pediatric upper respiratory infections. *Annals of Otology, Rhinology, & Laryngology*. 2016;125(12):982–991.

Fletcher CE, Copeland LA, Lowery JC, Reeves PJ. Nurse practitioners as primary care providers within the VA. *Military Medicine*. 2011;176(7):791–797.

Fox K. The role of the acute care nurse practitioner in the implementation of the commission on cancer's standards on palliative care. *Clinical Journal of Oncology Nursing*. 2014;18(S1):39–44.

Foreman DM, Morton S. Nurse-delivered and doctor-delivered care in an attention deficit hyperactivity disorder follow-up clinic: A comparative study using propensity score matching. *Journal of Advanced Nursing*. 2011;67(6):1341–1348.

Freed GL, Dunham KM, Loveland-Cherry C, Martyn KK, Moote MJ, American Board of Pediatrics Research Advisory Committee. Nurse practitioners and physician assistants employed by general and subspecialty pediatricians. *Pediatrics*. 2011;128(4):665–672.

Furlow B. Nurse practitioners outscore physicians in patent satisfaction survey. *Clinical Adviser*. June 24, 2011, www.clinicaladvisor.com/nurse-practitioners-outscore-physicians-in-patient-satisfaction-survey/article/206090.

Garson A, Jr. New systems of care can leverage the health care workforce: How many doctors do we really need? [Erratum appears in Acad Med. 2014 Jan;89(1):181]. *Academic Medicine*. 2013;88(12):1817–1821.

Geiss DM, Cavaliere TA. Neonatal nurse practitioners provide quality, cost-effective care. *Pediatric Annals*. 2003;32(9):577–583.

Ghosh AK, Lipkin M, Jr. Expanding the role of advanced nurse practitioners. *New England Journal of Medicine*. 2013;369(10):981–982.

Giberson S, Yoder S, Lee MP. *Improving Patient and Health System Outcomes through Advanced Pharmacy Practice. A Report to the U.S. Surgeon General*. Office of the Chief Pharmacist. U.S. Public Health Service, December 2011.

Gielen SC, Dekker J, Francke AL, Mistiaen P, Kroezen M. The effects of nurse prescribing: A systematic review. *International Journal of Nursing Studies*. 2014;51(7):1048–1061.

Gillard JN, Szoke A, Hoff WS, Wainwright GA, Stehly CD, Toedter LJ. Utilization of PAs and NPs at a level I trauma center: Effects on outcomes. *JAAPA*. 2011;24(7):34, 40–33.

Goldgar C. Expanding the role of advanced nurse practitioners. *New England Journal of Medicine*. 2013;369(10):982.

Graves JA, Mishra P, Dittus RS, Parikh R, Perloff J, Buerhaus PI. Role of geography and nurse practitioner scope-of-practice in efforts to expand primary care system capacity: Health reform and the primary care workforce. *Medical Care*. 2016;54(1):81–89.

Green T, Newcommon N. Advancing nursing practice: The role of the nurse practitioner in an acute stroke program. *Journal of Neuroscience Nursing*. 2006;38(4):328–330.

Grimes DE, Thomas EJ, Padhye NS, Ottosen MJ, Grimes RM. Do state restrictions on advanced practice registered nurses impact patient care outcomes for hypertension and diabetes control? *Journal for Nurse Practitioners*. 2018;14(8):620–625.

Grumbach K, Hart LG, Mertz E, Coffman J, Palazzo L. Who is caring for the underserved? A comparison of primary care physicians and nonphysician clinicians in California and Washington. *Annals of Family Medicine*. 2003;1(2):97–104.

Hallas D, Shelley D. Role of pediatric nurse practitioners in oral health care. *Academic Pediatrics*. 2009;9(6):462–466.

Hansen-Turton T, Ware J, Bond L, Doria N, Cunningham P. Are managed care organizations in the United States impeding the delivery of primary care by nurse practitioners? A 2012 update on managed care organization credentialing and reimbursement practices. *Population Health Management*. 2013;16(5):306–309.

Hanson RL, Habibi M, Khamo N, Abdou S, Stubbings J. Integrated clinical and specialty pharmacy practice model for management of patients with multiple sclerosis. *American Journal of Health-System Pharmacy*. 2014;71(6):463–469.

Harris BR, Yu J. Attitudes, perceptions and practice of alcohol and drug screening, brief intervention and referral to treatment: A case study of New York state primary care physicians and non-physician providers. *Public Health*. 2016;139:70–78.

Hatch J. The role of the neonatal nurse practitioner in the community hospital level I nursery. *Neonatal Network*. 2012;31(3):141–147.

Hawkins CM, Bowen MA, Gilliland CA, Walls DG, Duszak R, Jr. The impact of non-physician providers on diagnostic and interventional radiology practices: Operational and educational implications. *Journal of the American College of Radiology*. 2015;12(9):898–904.

Heiby EM. Concerns about substandard training for prescription privileges for psychologists. *Journal of Clinical Psychology*. 2010;66(1):104–111.

Hemphill, T. "Affordable Care act and Doctor Shortages: A Bad Situation Worsens" Insight, American Action Forum, February 27, 2013; https://www.americanactionforum.org/insight/affordable-care-act-and-doctor-shortages-a-bad-situation-worsens/

Henrichs BM, Avidan MS, Murray DJ, Boulet JR, Kras J, Krause B, Snider R, Evers AS. Performance of certified registered nurse anesthetists and anesthesiologists in a simulation-based skills assessment. *Anesthesia & Analgesia*. 2009;108(1):255–262.

Hicho MD, Rybarczyk A, Boros M. Interventions unrelated to anticoagulation in a pharmacist-managed anticoagulation clinic. *American Journal of Health-System Pharmacy*. 2016;73(11 S3):S80–S87.

Hing E, Hooker RS, Ashman JJ. Primary health care in community health centers and comparison with office-based practice. *Journal of Community Health*. 2011;36(3):406–413.

Hooker RS, Cipher DJ. Physician assistant and nurse practitioner prescribing: 1997–2002. *Journal of Rural Health*. 2005;21(4):355–360.

Horstmann E, Trapskin K, Wegner MV. The Wisconsin pharmacy quality collaborative – A team-based approach to optimizing medication therapy outcomes. *WMJ*. 2014;113(3):95–98.

Hoth AB, Carter BL, Ness J, Bhattacharyya A, Shorr RI, Rosenthal GE, Kaboli PJ. Development and reliability testing of the clinical pharmacist recommendation taxonomy. *Pharmacotherapy*. 2007;27(5):639–646.

Hoyt KS. Why the terms "mid-level provider" and "physician extender" are inappropriate. *Advanced Emergency Nursing Journal*. 2012;34(2):93–94.

Huang PY, Yano EM, Lee ML, Chang BL, Rubenstein LV. Variations in nurse practitioner use in Veterans Affairs primary care practices. *Health Services Research*. 2004;39(4 Pt 1): 887–904.

Hughes, C. "Medical Licensing in the States: Some Room for Agreement—and Reform" Cato Institute, July 1, 2014; https://www.cato.org/blog/medical-licensing-states-some-room-agreement-reform

Iglehart JK. Expanding the role of advanced nurse practitioners – Risks and rewards. *New England Journal of Medicine*. 2013;368(20):1935–1941.

Ignoffo R, Knapp K, Barnett M, Barbour SY, D'Amato S, Iacovelli L, Knudsen J, Koontz SE, Mancini R, McBride A, McCauley D. Board-certified oncology pharmacists: Their potential contribution to reducing a shortfall in oncology patient visits. *Journal of Oncology Practice*. 2016;12(4):e359–e368.

Institute for Alternative Futures. *Primary Care 2025: A scenario exploration*. Alexandria, VA, 2012. http://www.altfutures.org/wp-content/uploads/2016/04/2012_Report_Primary-Care-2025-Scenarios.pdf.

Institute of Medicine, National Academy of Sciences. *The Future of Nursing: Leading Change, Advancing Health*. Washington DC: The National Academies Press, 2011.

Ip EJ, Shah BM, Yu J, Chan J, Nguyen LT, Bhatt DC. Enhancing diabetes care by adding a pharmacist to the primary care team. *American Journal of Health-System Pharmacy*. 2013;70(10):877–886.

Isasi F, Krofah E. *The Expanding Role of Pharmacists in a Transformed Health Care System*. Washington, DC: National Governors Association Center for Best Practices, 2015.

Johnson MP, Abrams SL. Historical perspectives of autonomy within the medical profession: Considerations for 21st century physical therapy practice. *Journal of Orthopaedic & Sports Physical Therapy*. 2005;35(10):628–636.

Jones J, Kotthoff-Burrell E, Kass-Wolff J, Brownrigg V. Nurse practitioner graduates "speak out" about the adequacy of their educational preparation to care for older adults: A qualitative study. *Journal of the American Association of Nurse Practitioners*. 2015;27(12):698–706.

Jordan L. Studies support removing crna supervision rule to maximize anesthesia workforce and ensure patient access to care. *AANA Journal*. 2011;79(2):101–104.

Kaasalainen S, Martin-Misener R, Carter N, Dicenso A, Donald F, Baxter P. The nurse practitioner role in pain management in long-term care. *Journal of Advanced Nursing*. 2010;66(3):542–551.

Kaasalainen S, Ploeg J, McAiney C, Martin LS, Donald F, Martin-Misener R, Brazil K, Taniguchi A, Wickson-Griffiths A, Carter N, Sangster-Gormley E. Role of the nurse practitioner in providing palliative care in long-term care homes. *International Journal of Palliative Nursing*. 2013;19(10):477–485.

Kaldy J. Carving out the pharmacist's role in the elusive aco. *Consultant Pharmacist*. 2012;27(3):165–170.

Kalist DE, Molinari NA, Spurr SJ. Cooperation and conflict between very similar occupations: The case of anesthesia. *Health Economics, Policy, & Law*. 2011;6(2):237–264.

Kalowes P. Improving end-of-life care prognostic discussions: Role of advanced practice nurses. *AACN Advanced Critical Care*. 2015;26(2):151–166.

Kemp AE. Mass-gathering events: The role of advanced nurse practitioners in reducing referrals to local health care agencies. *Prehospital & Disaster Medicine*. 2016;31(1):58–63.

Kenison TC, Silverman P, Sustin M, Thompson CL. Differences between nurse practitioner and physician care providers on rates of secondary cancer screening and discussion of lifestyle changes among breast cancer survivors. *Journal of Cancer Survivorship*. 2015;9(2):223–229.

Kennedy J. Demystifying the role of nurse practitioners in hospice: Nurse practitioners as an integral part of the hospice plan of care. *Home Healthcare Nurse*. 2012;30(1):48–51.

Kidik PJ, Holbrook KF. The nurse practitioner role in evidence-based medication strategies. *Journal of Perianesthesia Nursing*. 2008;23(2):87–93.

Kiel PJ, McCord AD. Pharmacist impact on clinical outcomes in a diabetes disease management program via collaborative practice. *Annals of Pharmacotherapy*. 2005;39(11):1828–1832.

Kildow DC, Sisson EM, Carl DE, Baldwin DR. Addressing access to care for the uninsured: Clinical pharmacists as physician extenders. *Journal of the American Pharmacists Association*. 2010;50(4):448–449.

Kleinpell RM, Ely EW, Grabenkort R. Nurse practitioners and physician assistants in the intensive care unit: An evidence-based review. *Critical Care Medicine*. 2008a;36(10):2888–2897.

Kleinpell RM, Hanson NA, Buchner BR, Winters R, Wilson MJ, Keck AC. Hospitalist services: An evolving opportunity. *Nurse Practitioner*. 2008b;33(5):9–10.

Klemenc-Ketis Z, Terbovc A, Gomiscek B, Kersnik J. Role of nurse practitioners in reducing cardiovascular risk factors: A retrospective cohort study. *Journal of Clinical Nursing*. 2015;24(21–22):3077–3083.

Kosevich G, Leinfelder A, Sandin KJ, Swift E, Taber S, Weber R, Finkelstein M. Nurse practitioners in medical rehabilitation settings: A description of practice roles and patterns. *Journal of the American Association of Nurse Practitioners*. 2014;26(4):194–201.

Kotzer AM. Characteristics and role functions of advanced practice nurses in a tertiary pediatric setting. *Journal for Specialists in Pediatric Nursing*. 2005;10(1):20–28.

Kozhimannil KB, Avery MD, Terrell CA. Recent trends in clinicians providing care to pregnant women in the United States. *Journal of Midwifery & Women's Health*. 2012;57(5):433–438.

Kozhimannil KB, Henning-Smith C, Hung P. The practice of midwifery in rural US hospitals. *Journal of Midwifery & Women's Health*. 2016;61(4):411–418.

Kralewski J, Dowd B, Curoe A, Savage M, Tong J. The role of nurse practitioners in primary healthcare. *American Journal of Managed Care*. 2015;21(6):e366–e371.

Kuethe MC, Vaessen-Verberne AA, Elbers RG, Van Aalderen WM. Nurse versus physician-led care for the management of asthma. *Cochrane Database of Systematic Reviews*. 2013;2(2):CD009296.

Kuo YF, Chen NW, Baillargeon J, Raji MA, Goodwin JS. Potentially preventable hospitalizations in medicare patients with diabetes: A comparison of primary care provided by nurse practitioners versus physicians. *Medical Care*. 2015a;53(9):776–783.

Kuo YF, Goodwin JS, Chen NW, Lwin KK, Baillargeon J, Raji MA. Diabetes mellitus care provided by nurse practitioners vs primary care physicians. *Journal of the American Geriatrics Society*. 2015b;63(10):1980–1988.

Kurtzman ET, Barnow BS, Johnson JE, Simmens SJ, Infeld DL, Mullan F. Does the regulatory environment affect nurse practitioners' patterns of practice or quality of care in health centers? *Health Services Research*. 2017;52(S1):437–458.

Lambing AY, Adams DL, Fox DH, Divine G. Nurse practitioners' and physicians' care activities and clinical outcomes with an inpatient geriatric population. *Journal of the American Academy of Nurse Practitioners.* 2004;16(8):343–352.

Lee LA, Jones LR. Developing a strategic plan for a neonatal nurse practitioner service. *Advances in Neonatal Care.* 2004;4(5):292–305.

Levin PJ, Bateman R. Organizing and investing to expand primary care availability with nurse practitioners. *Journal of Community Health.* 2012;37(2):265–269.

Lewis SR, Nicholson A, Smith AF, Alderson P. Physician anaesthetists versus non-physician providers of anaesthesia for surgical patients. *Cochrane Database of Systematic Reviews.* 2014;7(7):CD010357.

Lowery B, Scott E, Swanson M. Nurse practitioner perceptions of the impact of physician oversight on quality and safety of nurse practitioner practice. *Journal of the American Association of Nurse Practitioners.* 2016;28(8):436–445.

Lowery B, Varnam D. Physician supervision and insurance reimbursement: Policy implications for nurse practitioner practice in North Carolina. *North Carolina Medical Journal.* 2011;72(4):310–313.

Manolakis PG, Skelton JB. Pharmacists' contributions to primary care in the United States collaborating to address unmet patient care needs: The emerging role for pharmacists to address the shortage of primary care providers. *American Journal of Pharmaceutical Education.* 2010;74(10):S7.

Markowitz S, Adams EK, Lewitt MJ, Dunlop AL. Competitive effects of scope of practice restrictions: Public health or public harm? *Journal of Health Economics.* 2017;55:201–218.

Maylone MM, Ranieri L, Quinn Griffin MT, McNulty R, Fitzpatrick JJ. Collaboration and autonomy: Perceptions among nurse practitioners. *Journal of the American Academy of Nurse Practitioners.* 2011;23(1):51–57.

McBane SE, Dopp AL, Abe A, Benavides S, Chester EA, Dixon DL, Dunn M, Johnson MD, Nigro SJ, Rothrock-Christian T, Schwartz AH, Thrasher K, Walker S. Collaborative drug therapy management and comprehensive medication management—2015. *Pharmacotherapy.* 2015;35(4):e39–e50.

McLachlan A, Sutton T, Ding P, Kerr A. A nurse practitioner clinic: A novel approach to supporting patients following heart valve surgery. *Heart, Lung & Circulation.* 2015;24(11):1126–1133.

McNally GA, Florence KJ, Logue AC. The evolution of a malignant hematology nurse practitioner service. *Clinical Journal of Oncology Nursing.* 2015;19(3):367–369.

Mitchell P, Wynia M, Golden R, McNellis B, Okun S, Webb CE, Rohrbach V, Von Kohorn I. *Core Principles & Values of Effective Team-Based Health Care.* Washington, DC: Institute of Medicine, 2012.

Morgan PA, Shah ND, Kaufman JS, Albanese MA. Impact of physician assistant care on office visit resource use in the United States. *Health Services Research.* 2008;43(5 Pt 2): 1906–1922.

Mossialos E, Courtin E, Naci H, Benrimoj S, Bouvy M, Farris K, Noyce P, Sketris I. From "retailers" to health care providers: Transforming the role of community pharmacists in chronic disease management. *Health Policy.* 2015;119(5):628–639.

Mower-Wade D, Pirrung JM. Advanced practice nurses making a difference: Implementation of a formal rounding process. *Journal of Trauma Nursing.* 2010;17(2):69–71; quiz 72–73.

Murawski M, Villa KR, Dole EJ, Ives TJ, Tinker D, Colucci VJ, Perdiew J. Advanced-practice pharmacists: Practice characteristics and reimbursement of pharmacists certified for collaborative clinical practice in New Mexico and North Carolina. *American Journal of Health-System Pharmacy.* 2011;68(24):2341–2350.

Nandwana SB, Walls DG, Ibraheem O, Murphy F, Tridandapani S, Cox K. Image-guided nontargeted renal biopsies performed by radiology-trained nurse practitioners: A safe practice model. *Journal of the American College of Radiology.* 2016;13(7):819–821.

Negrusa B, Hogan PF, Warner JT, Schroeder CH, Pang B. Scope of practice laws and anesthesia complications: No measurable impact of certified registered nurse anesthetist expanded scope of practice on anesthesia-related complications. *Medical Care.* 2016;54(10):913–920.

Niezen MG, Mathijssen JJ. Reframing professional boundaries in healthcare: A systematic review of facilitators and barriers to task reallocation from the domain of medicine to the nursing domain. *Health Policy.* 2014;117(2):151–169.

Nguyen M, Zare M. Impact of a clinical pharmacist-managed medication refill clinic. *Journal of Primary Care & Community Health.* 2015;6(3):187–192.

Norton L, Tsiperfal A, Cook K, Bagdasarian A, Varady J, Shah M, Wang P. Effectiveness and safety of an independently run nurse practitioner outpatient cardioversion program (2009 to 2014). *American Journal of Cardiology.* 2016;118(12):1842–1846.

O'Brien JL, Martin DR, Heyworth JA, Meyer NR. A phenomenological perspective on advanced practice nurse-physician collaboration within an interdisciplinary healthcare team. *Journal of the American Academy of Nurse Practitioners.* 2009;21(8):444–453.

O'Brien JM. How nurse practitioners obtained provider status: Lessons for pharmacists. *American Journal of Health-System Pharmacy.* 2003;60(22):2301–2307.

O'Brien P. The role of the nurse practitioner in congenital heart surgery. *Pediatric Cardiology.* 2007;28(2):88–95.

Otsuka SH, Sen S, Melody KT, Ganetsky VS. A practical guide for pharmacists to establish a transitions of care program in an outpatient setting. *Journal of the American Pharmacists Association.* 2015;55(5):527–533.

Packard K, Herink M, Kuhlman P. Pharmacist's role in an interdisciplinary cardiac rehabilitation team. *Journal of Allied Health.* 2012;41(3):113–117, 117a, 117b.

Palmer E, Hart S, Freeman PR. Development and delivery of a pharmacist training program to increase naloxone access in Kentucky. *Journal of the American Pharmacists Association.* 2017;57(2S):S118–S122.

Patwardhan A, Duncan I, Murphy P, Pegus C. The value of pharmacists in health care. *Population Health Management.* 2012;15(3):157–162.

Pericak A. Increased autonomy for nurse practitioners as a solution to the physician shortage. *Journal of the New York State Nurses Association.* 2011;42(1–2):4–7; quiz 24, 27–28.

Petersen PA, Keller T, Way SM, Borges WJ. Autonomy and empowerment in advanced practice registered nurses: Lessons from New Mexico. *Journal of the American Association of Nurse Practitioners.* 2015;27(7):363–370.

Peterson M, Potter RL. A proposal for a code of ethics for nurse practitioners. *Journal of the American Academy of Nurse Practitioners.* 2004;16(3):116–124.

Phillips SJ. 25th annual legislative update: Evidence-based practice reforms improve access to APRN care. *Nurse Practitioner.* 2013;38(1):18–42.

Pilon BA, Ketel C, Davidson HA, Gentry CK, Crutcher TD, Scott AW, Moore RM, Rosenbloom ST. Evidence-guided integration of interprofessional collaborative practice into nurse managed health centers. *Journal of Professional Nursing.* 2015;31(4):340–350.

Poghosyan L, Liu J. Nurse practitioner autonomy and relationships with leadership affect teamwork in primary care practices: A cross-sectional survey. *Journal of General Internal Medicine.* 2016;31(7):771–777.

Poghosyan L, Lucero R, Rauch L, Berkowitz B. Nurse practitioner workforce: A substantial supply of primary care providers. *Nursing Economics.* 2012;30(5):268–274, 294.

Poghosyan L, Nannini A, Smaldone A, Clarke S, O'Rourke NC, Rosato BG, Berkowitz B. Revisiting scope of practice facilitators and barriers for primary care nurse practitioners: A qualitative investigation. *Policy, Politics & Nursing Practice.* 2013;14(1):6–15.

Potera C. Advanced practice nurses and physicians provide comparable care. *American Journal of Nursing.* 2011;111(11):15.

Potera C. NPs continue to break down practice barriers. *American Journal of Nursing.* 2013;113(9):14.

Randolph TC. Expansion of pharmacists' responsibilities in an emergency department. *American Journal of Health-System Pharmacy.* 2009;66(16):1484–1487.

Rapp MP. Opportunities for advance practice nurses in the nursing facility. *Journal of the American Medical Directors Association.* 2003;4(6):337–343.

Reagan PB, Salsberry PJ. The effects of state-level scope-of-practice regulations on the number and growth of nurse practitioners. *Nursing Outlook.* 2013;61(6):392–399.

Reilly BK, Brandon G, Shah R, Preciado D, Zalzal G. The role of advanced practice providers in pediatric otolaryngology academic practices. *International Journal of Pediatric Otorhinolaryngology.* 2013;77(1):36–40.

Rhoads J, Ferguson LA, Langford CA. Measuring nurse practitioner productivity. *Dermatology Nursing.* 2006;18(1):32–34, 37–38.

Richard JL, Liu BP, Casalino DD, Russell EJ, Horowitz JM. Radiology education of physician extenders: What role should radiologists play? *Academic Radiology.* 2017;24(5):633–638.

Riley L, Harris C, McKay M, Gondran SE, DeCola P, Soonasra A. The role of nurse practitioners in delivering rheumatology care and services: Results of a U.S. Survey. *Journal of the American Association of Nurse Practitioners.* 2017;29(11):673–681.

Roblin DW, Becker ER, Adams EK, Howard DH, Roberts MH. Patient satisfaction with primary care: Does type of practitioner matter? *Medical Care.* 2004a;42(6):579–590.

Roblin DW, Howard DH, Becker ER, Kathleen Adams E, Roberts MH. Use of midlevel practitioners to achieve labor cost savings in the primary care practice of an MCO. *Health Services Research.* 2004b;39(3):607–626.

Rohrer JE, Angstman KB, Garrison GM, Pecina JL, Maxson JA. Nurse practitioners and physician assistants are complements to family medicine physicians. *Population Health Management.* 2013;16(4):242–245.

Rosenfeld P, Kobayashi M, Barber P, Mezey M. Utilization of nurse practitioners in long-term care: Findings and implications of a national survey. *Journal of the American Medical Directors Association.* 2004;5(1):9–15.

Rubio-Valera M, Chen TF, O'Reilly CL. New roles for pharmacists in community mental health care: A narrative review. *International Journal of Environmental Research & Public Health.* 2014;11(10):10967–10990.

Rudner Lugo N, O'Grady ET, Hodnicki D, Hanson C. Are regulations more consumer-friendly when boards of nursing are the sole regulators of nurse practitioners? *Journal of Professional Nursing*. 2010;26(1):29–34.

Ruegg TA. A nurse practitioner-led urgent care center: Meeting the needs of the patient with cancer. *Clinical Journal of Oncology Nursing*. 2013;17(4):E52–E57.

Running A, Kipp C, Mercer V. Prescriptive patterns of nurse practitioners and physicians. *Journal of the American Academy of Nurse Practitioners*. 2006;18(5):228–233.

Ryan R, Santesso N, Lowe D, Hill S, Grimshaw JM, Prictor M, Kaufman C, Cowie G, Taylor M. Interventions to improve safe and effective medicines use by consumers: An overview of systematic reviews. *Cochrane Database of Systematic Reviews*. 2014;4(4):CD007768.

Sampson DA. Alliances of cooperation: Negotiating New Hampshire nurse practitioners' prescribing practice. *Nursing History Review*. 2009;17:153–178.

Samsson KS, Bernhardsson S, Larsson ME. Perceived quality of physiotherapist-led orthopaedic triage compared with standard practice in primary care: A randomised controlled trial. *BMC Musculoskeletal Disorders*. 2016;17:257.

Santschi V, Chiolero A, Colosimo AL, Platt RW, Taffé P, Burnier M, Burnand B, Paradis G. Improving blood pressure control through pharmacist interventions: A meta-analysis of randomized controlled trials. *Journal of the American Heart Association*. 2014;3(2):e000718.

Sarro A, Rampersaud YR, Lewis S. Nurse practitioner-led surgical spine consultation clinic. *Journal of Advanced Nursing*. 2010;66(12):2671–2676.

Saseen JJ, Ripley TL, Bondi D, Burke JM, Cohen LJ, McBane S, McConnell KJ, Sackey B, Sanoski C, Simonyan A, Taylor J, Vande Griend JP. ACCP clinical pharmacist competencies. *Pharmacotherapy*. 2017;37(5):630–636.

Schirle L, McCabe BE. State variation in opioid and benzodiazepine prescriptions between independent and nonindependent advanced practice registered nurse prescribing states. *Nursing Outlook*. 2016;64(1):86–93.

Schlessman AM, Martin K, Ritzline PD, Petrosino CL. The role of physical therapists in pediatric health promotion and obesity prevention: Comparison of attitudes. *Pediatric Physical Therapy*. 2011;23(1):79–86.

Schnipper JL, Kirwin JL, Cotugno MC, Wahlstrom SA, Brown BA, Tarvin E, Kachalia A, Horng M, Roy CL, McKean SC, Bates DW. Role of pharmacist counseling in preventing adverse drug events after hospitalization. *Archives of Internal Medicine*. 2006;166(5):565–571.

Schorn MN, Dietrich MS, Donaghey B, Minnick AF. US physician and midwife adherence to active management of the third stage of labor international recommendations. *Journal of Midwifery & Women's Health*. 2017;62(1):58–67.

Schorn MN, Minnick A, Donaghey B. An exploration of how midwives and physicians manage the third stage of labor in the United States. *Journal of Midwifery & Women's Health*. 2015;60(2):187–198.

Schramp LC, Holtcamp M, Phillips SA, Johnson TP, Hoff J. Advanced practice nurses facilitating clinical translational research. *Clinical Medicine & Research*. 2010;8(3–4):131–134.

Sears JM, Wickizer TM, Franklin GM, Cheadle AD, Berkowitz B. Expanding the role of nurse practitioners: Effects on rural access to care for injured workers. *Journal of Rural Health*. 2008;24(2):171–178.

Sears JM, Wickizer TM, Franklin GM, Cheadle AD, Berkowitz B. Nurse practitioners as attending providers for injured workers: Evaluating the effect of role expansion on disability and costs. *Medical Care.* 2007;45(12):1154–1161.

Seden K, Bradley M, Miller AR, Beadsworth MB, Khoo SH. The clinical utility of HIV outpatient pharmacist prescreening to reduce medication error and assess adherence. *International Journal of STD & AIDS.* 2013;24(3):237–241.

Sewell MJ, Riche DM, Fleming JW, Malinowski SS, Jackson RT. Comparison of pharmacist and physician managed annual medicare wellness services. *Journal of Managed Care & Specialty Pharmacy.* 2016;22(12):1412–1416.

Shane-McWhorter L, Oderda GM. Providing diabetes education and care to underserved patients in a collaborative practice at a Utah community health center. *Pharmacotherapy.* 2005;25(1):96–109.

Solomon DH, Bitton A, Fraenkel L, Brown E, Tsao P, Katz JN. Roles of nurse practitioners and physician assistants in rheumatology practices in the US. *Arthritis Care & Research.* 2014;66(7):1108–1113.

Sookaneknun P, Richards RM, Sanguansermsri J, Teerasut C. Pharmacist involvement in primary care improves hypertensive patient clinical outcomes. *Annals of Pharmacotherapy.* 2004;38(12):2023–2028.

Stahlke Wall S, Rawson K. The nurse practitioner role in oncology: Advancing patient care. *Oncology Nursing Forum.* 2016;43(4):489–496.

Stange K. How does provider supply and regulation influence health care markets? Evidence from nurse practitioners and physician assistants. *Journal of Health Economics.* 2014;33(1):1–27.

Stenner K, Carey N, Courtenay M. Implementing nurse prescribing: A case study in diabetes. *Journal of Advanced Nursing.* 2010;66(3):522–531.

Stowers RE. Expanding the role of advanced nurse practitioners. *New England Journal of Medicine.* 2013;369(10):982.

Street D, Cossman JS. Does familiarity breed respect? Physician attitudes toward nurse practitioners in a medically underserved state. *Journal of the American Academy of Nurse Practitioners.* 2010;22(8):431–439.

Streeter RA, Zangaro GA, Chattopadhyay A. Perspectives: Using results from HRSA's health workforce simulation model to examine the geography of primary care. *Health Services Research.* 2017;52;(S1):481–507.

Swain LD. A pharmacist's contribution to an ambulatory neurology clinic. *Consultant Pharmacist.* 2012;27(1):49–57.

Swart E, Vasudeva E, Makhni EC, Macaulay W, Bozic KJ. Dedicated perioperative hip fracture comanagement programs are cost-effective in high-volume centers: An economic analysis. *Clinical Orthopaedics & Related Research.* 2016;474(1):222–233.

Tan EC, Stewart K, Elliott RA, George J. Pharmacist services provided in general practice clinics: A systematic review and meta-analysis. *Research in Social & Administrative Pharmacy.* 2014;10(4):608–622.

Thompson S, Moorley C, Barratt J. A comparative study on the clinical decision-making processes of nurse practitioners vs. medical doctors using scenarios in a secondary care environment. *Journal of Advanced Nursing.* 2017;73(5):1097–1110.

Timmons EJ. The effects of expanded nurse practitioner and physician assistant scope of practice on the cost of medicaid patient care. *Health Policy.* 2017;121(2):189–196.

Tinelli M, Bond C, Blenkinsopp A, Jaffray M, Watson M, Hannaford P. Patient evaluation of a community pharmacy medications management service. *Annals of Pharmacotherapy.* 2007;41(12):1962–1970.

Tobler L. A primary problem: More patients under federal health reform with fewer primary care doctors spell trouble. *State Legislatures.* 2010;36(10):20–24.

Touchette DR, Doloresco F, Suda KJ, Perez A, Turner S, Jalundhwala Y, Tangonan MC, Hoffman JM. Economic evaluations of clinical pharmacy services: 2006–2010. *Pharmacotherapy.* 2014;34(8):771–793.

Trautmann J, Epstein E, Rovnyak V, Snyder A. Relationships among moral distress, level of practice independence, and intent to leave of nurse practitioners in emergency departments: Results from a national survey. *Advanced Emergency Nursing Journal.* 2015;37(2):134–145.

Van Hoover C, Holt L. Midwifing the end of life: Expanding the scope of modern midwifery practice to reclaim palliative care. *Journal of Midwifery & Women's Health.* 2016;61(3):306–314.

Viktil KK, Blix HS. The impact of clinical pharmacists on drug-related problems and clinical outcomes. *Basic & Clinical Pharmacology & Toxicology.* 2008;102(3):275–280.

Weeks G, George J, Maclure K, Stewart D. Non-medical prescribing versus medical prescribing for acute and chronic disease management in primary and secondary care. *Cochrane Database of Systematic Reviews.* 2016;11:CD011227.

Wright WL. New Hampshire nurse practitioners take the lead in forming an accountable care organization. *Nursing Administration Quarterly.* 2017;41(1):39–47.

Yang YT, Attanasio LB, Kozhimannil KB. State scope of practice laws, nurse-midwifery workforce, and childbirth procedures and outcomes. *Women's Health Issues.* 2016;26(3):262–267.

Yao NA, Rose K, LeBaron V, Camacho F, Boling P. Increasing role of nurse practitioners in house call programs. *Journal of the American Geriatrics Society.* 2017;65(4):847–852.

Zhang C, Zhang L, Huang L, Luo R, Wen J. Clinical pharmacists on medical care of pediatric inpatients: A single-center randomized controlled trial. *PloS One.* 2012;7(1):e30856.

Zhu Z, Islam S, Bergmann SR. Effectiveness and outcomes of a nurse practitioner-run chest pain evaluation unit. *Journal of the American Association of Nurse Practitioners.* 2016;28(11):591–595.

Zillich AJ, Jaynes HA, Bex SD, Boldt AS, Walston CM, Ramsey DC, Sutherland JM, Bravata DM. Evaluation of pharmacist care for hypertension in the Veterans Affairs patient-centered medical home: A retrospective case-control study. *American Journal of Medicine.* 2015;128(5):539.e1–539.e6.

Index